the Accepted Whispers

"Munājāt-e-Maqbūl"

the Accepted Whispers

"Munājāt-e-Maqbūl"

ٱدْعُوا۟ رَبَّكُمْ تَضَرُّعًا وَخُفْيَةً ۚ

Call on your Lord humbly and secretly...
(Al-Aʿrāf, 7:55)

مناجاتِ مقبول

Compiled by
MAWLĀNĀ ASHRAF ʿALĪ THĀNAWĪ

Translation and Commentary
KHALID BAIG

OVER 200 DUʿĀ'S FROM THE QUR'ĀN AND
ḤADĪTH FOR DAILY READING

openmind press
GARDEN GROVE • CALIFORNIA

First Edition Shaʿbān 1426/September 2005
Second Printing Rabīʿ al-Awwal 1427/April 2006
Third Printing Ramaḍān 1429/September 2008

PUBLISHED BY
Open Mind Press
PO Box 1338
Garden Grove, CA 92842
www.openmindpress.com

Printed in the United States of America

Library of Congress Control Number: 2005932684

ISBN 0-9755157-1-3

This book is printed on acid-free paper.

Cover: Hassan II Mosque, Morocco. Courtesy S. Desmond/Paintdrying.com

To

محمد صلى الله عليه وسلم

Muḥammad, son of Abdullah
The Seal of the prophets,
The Mercy to the worlds.
His prayers are another gift of mercy and compassion to us.
What would be life without them!
What would be life without him!

May Allah سبحانه وتعالى *shower His Blessings and Peace upon him,*
his family, his Companions, and his followers

صلى الله عليه وسلم

Transliteration Key

ء (ئ ؤ إ أ)	’ (a slight catch in the breath)	غ	gh (similar to French r)
ا	a	ف	f
ب	b	ق	q (heavy k, from the throat)
ة and ت	t (ة has an “h” sound at the end of a sentence)	ك	k
ث	th (as in “thorn”)	ل	l
ج	j	م	m
ح	ḥ (heavy h, from deep within the throat)	ن	n
خ	kh (“ch” in Scottish loch)	ه	h (as in “help”)
د	d (the hard “th” in “the”)	و	w
ذ	dh (the soft “th” in “the”)	ي	y (as in “yellow”)
ر	r		**Vowels**
ز	z	ـَ ـً	a (slightly softer than the “u” in “but”); an
س	s	ـِ ـٍ	i (as in “in”); in
ش	sh	ـُ ـٌ	u (“oo” in “book”); un
ص	ṣ (heavy s, from the upper mouth)	ـٰ ا آ	ā (elongated a, as when you would stretch the “a” in “plastic”)
ض	ḍ (heavy d, from the upper mouth)	آ	ā at the start of a word, ’ā in the middle (pronounced like ءَا)
ط	ṭ (heavy t, from the upper mouth)	ـُ and و	ū (“u” in “glue”)
ظ	ẓ (heavy z, from the upper mouth)	ـِ and ي	ī (“ee” in “feet”)
ع	‘ (like two a’s from deep within the throat)	ـّ	stress symbol, indicated by repetition of letter

Honorifics

﷾	Glorified and Most High	ﷺ	May Allah’s blessings and peace be upon him
﵇	May peace be upon him	﵁ , ﵂	May Allah be pleased with him/her

Contents

بسم الله الرحمن الرحيم

Introduction

Once Prophet Muḥammad ﷺ passed by a people who were suffering from some affliction. "Why don't they make *duʿā'* (supplication) to Allah for protection," he said. With all the suffering and disasters Muslims are facing in various parts of the world, the question can be directed to all of us today.

It is not that we have forgotten duʿā' completely; we refer to it regularly. But our ideas and practice regarding duʿā' have become distorted. Often it is reduced to the level of a ritual. Generally it is considered when all our efforts have failed—an act of last resort. It is belittled through actions and sometimes even with words. Is it any wonder that today mostly a mention of duʿā' is meant to indicate the hopelessness of a situation.

What a tragedy, for duʿā' is the most potent weapon of a believer. It can change fate, while no action of ours ever can. It is the essence of *ʿibādah* (worship). With it we can never fail; without it we can never succeed. In the proper scheme of things, duʿā' should be the first and the last resort of the believer, with all his plans and actions coming in between. In every difficulty we ask Allah سبحانه وتعالى to show us the way to handle that difficulty; we seek His help in following the path He shows to us; we seek His aid in making our efforts successful. When we fall sick, we know that we cannot find the right doctor without His Will; that the best doctor may not be able to diagnose our condition without His Command; that the best treatment plan will not succeed without His Permission. We make duʿā' for all of these. We make duʿā' before we seek medical help, while we are receiving it and after it has been delivered. The same is true of all other difficulties we may encounter.

Duʿā' is conversation with Allah ﷿, our Creator, our Lord and Master, the All Knowing, the All Powerful. This act in itself is of extraordinary significance. It is the most uplifting, liberating, empowering, and transforming conversation a person can ever have. We turn to Him because we know that He alone can lift our sufferings and solve our problems. We feel relieved after describing our difficulties to our Creator. We feel empowered after having communicated with the All Mighty. We sense His mercy all around us after talking to the Most Merciful.

Allah ﷿ gave us life and everything that we possess, without our having any right to it. It is His design and it is with a purpose. Our conditions of health and sickness, our affluence and poverty, our joys and sorrows, our apparent successes and failures, our gains and losses—all of them are just a test. "He created death and life that He may test you which of you is best in deed" (*Al-Mulk*, 67:2).

Our ultimate success or failure—in the Hereafter—will depend solely on how we acted in the different circumstances that He chose for us. Did we seek His help when we needed help or were we too arrogant to ask? Did we accept His Will when things did not turn out our way? Did we show gratitude for His favors or were we proud of our own achievements?

We pray to Him because only He can give. He is not answerable to any authority and everyone is answerable to Him. He has power over everything and none can overpower Him. His knowledge is infinite while ours is infinitesimal compared to His. He is the Lord; we are His slaves. He may grant our duʿā's here; or He may reward us for them in the Hereafter; or He may give us something better than what we asked for.

We should make duʿā' for all things big and small. It is the beginning of wisdom to realize that "big" and "small" are arbitrary labels that are totally irrelevant in this context. Nothing is too big for the One we are asking from; nothing is too small for the one who is asking. That is why we have been taught to ask Allah ﷿ even when we need something as small as shoelaces. We should ask as a beggar, as a destitute person, for that is what we in reality are in relationship to Allah ﷿. At the same time we should ask with great hope and conviction that we shall be granted our duʿā's, for a duʿā' lacking concentration and conviction is no duʿā' at all.

A praying person can never lose, for duʿā' is the highest form of submission to Him. "Prophet Muḥammad ﷺ was the best of mankind because he was the best in submission to Allah," says Mawlānā Manẓūr Nuʿmānī. "Anyone who studies his supplications cannot but be awestruck by the perfect understanding of our relationship to the Creator reflected by them." For this ummah, his duʿā's are one of his greatest spiritual gifts.

Quite naturally many scholars have collected them into separate books. Among these was *Al-Ḥiṣn al-Ḥaṣīn* (The Impregnable Fortress) by Muḥammad ibn Muḥammad al-Jazrī (751- 833 AH), a well-known authority on Qur'ānic recitation, Ḥadīth, and Fiqh. The book was written in Dhul-Ḥijjah 791 AH when an invading army had sieged Damascus. After a few days of reciting these duʿā's by the compiler, the army suddenly left the helpless and frightened city. The event gave the book its popularity as a collection of duʿā's to be read for protection against calamities. It was divided into seven parts, one for each day of the week, to facilitate that reading.

Subsequently, *Al-Ḥizb al-Aʿẓam* (The Great Prayer Book) was organized for a daily reading by its compiler Mullā ʿAlī al-Qārī (d. 1014 AH). This has the advantage that these duʿā's can become a part of our daily schedule. One may find that the best part of his day is the one dedicated to these duʿā's. Additionally after some time one may find that he has memorized a large number of these duʿā's without any special effort. He may then find himself saying these duʿā's at other occasions also, for which they are particularly suited.

The Accepted Whispers is a translation of *Munājāt-e-Maqbūl*, which was patterned after and drew from *Al-Ḥizb*. It was compiled by Mawlānā Ashraf ʿAlī Thānawī as *Qurubāt ʿIndAllāhi wa Ṣalawāt ar-Rasūl* (Prayers that Bring One Close to Allah and the Invocations of the Messenger) and translated into Urdu poetry and prose by his associates. The translation was given the title "Munājāt-e-Maqbūl." Like his *Bihishtī Zewar* (Heavenly Ornaments), *Munājāt-e-Maqbūl* has been very popular in the countries of the Indian subcontinent, where it has become a household name.

This book provides the Arabic text with references, transliteration, translation, and commentary. The commentary aims at providing explanation as well as special merits or historic background of the duʿā'. This should help enhance our understanding of the meaning and significance of the duʿā's thereby helping us derive much greater benefit from them.

In preparing this book, the Arabic text of published editions of *Munājāt* was compared with the books of Ḥadīth and changes were made wherever deemed necessary. Also, existing editions of *Munājāt* contained many typographical errors. These have been fixed. Detailed references to the source texts have also been provided. The transliteration was produced directly from the Arabic text using proprietary software.

My children have played a major role in producing this book. My daughters Areeba and Sumayya typed the Arabic text. Sohaib helped with its proofreading. Muneeb checked the original Arabic sources and produced copious notes with attention to detail. He also wrote the transliteration software. He was also responsible for the page layout and production of the camera-ready copy. And as always my wife provided the inspiration, encouragement, and support without which this work would not have been possible. I request the readers to kindly remember me, my family, and everyone who helped in the publication of this book in their duʿā's.

We need duʿā's in all circumstances and all times. But in the dark ages that we are living in today, we need them even more. Every day brings fresh news about atrocities committed against our brothers and sisters around the world. What can we do? We can continue to just feel frustrated and depressed. We can just forget all this and move on to some other subject. Or we can stand up before Allah ﷻ and pray for His help, Who alone can help.

The duʿā' can change our life, our outlook, and our fate. It is the most potent weapon of a believer. May Allah ﷻ make this book an instrument of delivering that power to us.

Khalid Baig

16 Rajab 1426/21 August 2005

Prayer (دعاء) and its Etiquettes

THE QUR'ĀN AND ḤADĪTH LITERATURE tell us about the extraordinary importance of praying to Allah سبحانه وتعالى for all our needs. They also teaches us its proper etiquettes. This is a brief selection.

Significance

وَقَالَ رَبُّكُمُ ٱدْعُونِىٓ أَسْتَجِبْ لَكُمْ ۚ إِنَّ ٱلَّذِينَ يَسْتَكْبِرُونَ عَنْ
عِبَادَتِى سَيَدْخُلُونَ جَهَنَّمَ دَاخِرِينَ ﴿٦٠﴾

And your Lord says: Call on Me; I will answer your (Prayer): but those who are too arrogant to serve Me shall soon enter Hell—in humiliation. (*Ghāfir*, 40:60)

This verse uses the words du'ā' and 'ibādah interchangeably, thereby affirming that du'ā' (supplication) is an act of worship.

وَإِذَا سَأَلَكَ عِبَادِى عَنِّى فَإِنِّى قَرِيبٌ ۖ أُجِيبُ دَعْوَةَ ٱلدَّاعِ إِذَا دَعَانِ ۖ
فَلْيَسْتَجِيبُوا۟ لِى وَلْيُؤْمِنُوا۟ بِى لَعَلَّهُمْ يَرْشُدُونَ ﴿١٨٦﴾

And when My servants ask you concerning Me, surely I am very near; I answer the prayer of the suppliant when he calls on Me, so they should answer My call and believe in Me in order that they may be led aright. (*Al-Baqarah*, 2:186)

أَمَّن يُجِيبُ ٱلْمُضْطَرَّ إِذَا دَعَاهُ وَيَكْشِفُ ٱلسُّوٓءَ وَيَجْعَلُكُمْ خُلَفَآءَ ٱلْأَرْضِ ۗ أَءِلَٰهٌ مَّعَ ٱللَّهِ ۚ قَلِيلًا مَّا تَذَكَّرُونَ ﴿٦٢﴾

Or, Who answers the distressed one when he calls upon Him and removes the evil, and makes you successors in the earth. Is there a god with Allah? Little do they reflect! (*An-Naml*, 27:62)

عَنْ ابْنِ عُمَرَ قَالَ قَالَ رَسُوْلُ اللهِ صَلَّى اللهُ عَلَيْهِ وَسَلَّمَ مَنْ فُتِحَ لَهُ مِنْكُمْ بَابُ الدُّعَاءِ فُتِحَتْ لَهُ أَبْوَابُ الرَّحْمَةِ وَمَا سُئِلَ اللهُ شَيْئًا يَعْنِي أَحَبَّ إِلَيْهِ مِنْ أَنْ يُّسْأَلَ الْعَافِيَةَ. (رواه الترمذي و ابن ماجة)

ʿAbdullāh ibn ʿUmar ﷺ narrates that the Prophet ﷺ said: "Anyone of you for whom the door to duʿā' has been opened, the doors to mercy have been opened for him. And the thing that Allah likes most to be asked for is *ʿāfiyah* (health, security, protection)." (*Sunan at-Tirmidhī* and *Ibn Mājah*)

عَنْ أَبِيْ هُرَيْرَةَ قَالَ قَالَ رَسُوْلُ اللهِ صَلَّى اللهُ عَلَيْهِ وَسَلَّمَ مَنْ لَّمْ يَسْأَلِ اللهَ يَغْضَبْ عَلَيْهِ. (رواه الترمذي)

Abū Hurayrah ﷺ narrates that the Prophet ﷺ said: "Allah is angry with those who do not make supplications to Him." (*Sunan at-Tirmidhī*)

عَنْ ابْنِ عُمَرَ قَالَ قَالَ رَسُوْلُ اللهِ صَلَّى اللهُ عَلَيْهِ وَسَلَّمَ إِنَّ الْدُّعَاءَ يَنْفَعُ مِمَّا نَزَلَ وَمِمَّا لَمْ يَنْزِلْ فَعَلَيْكُمْ عِبَادَ اللهِ بِالدُّعَاءِ. (رواه الترمذي و رواه أحمد عن معاذ بن جبل)

ʿAbdullāh ibn ʿUmar ﷺ narrates that the Prophet ﷺ said: "Duʿā' is beneficial regarding calamities that have fallen and calamities that have not fallen. So, servants of Allah, devote yourselves to duʿā'." (*Sunan at-Tirmidhī* and *Musnad Aḥmad*)

It means that duʿā' can prevent a disaster that was going to happen as well as lift the one that has already happened.

Attitude

ٱدۡعُواْ رَبَّكُمۡ تَضَرُّعٗا وَخُفۡيَةًۚ إِنَّهُۥ لَا يُحِبُّ ٱلۡمُعۡتَدِينَ ﴿٥٥﴾

Call on your Lord humbly and secretly; surely He does not love those who exceed the limits. (*Al-Aʿrāf*, 7:55)

عَنْ أَبِيْ هُرَيْرَةَ قَالَ قَالَ رَسُوْلُ اللهِ صَلَّى اللهُ عَلَيْهِ وَسَلَّمَ أُدْعُوْ اللهَ وَأَنْتُمْ مُّوْقِنُوْنَ بِالْإِجَابَةِ وَاعْلَمُوْا أَنَّ اللهَ لَا يَسْتَجِيْبُ دُعَاءً مِّنْ قَلْبٍ غَافِلٍ لَّاهٍ. (رواه الترمذي)

Abū Hurayrah ﵁ narrates that the Prophet ﷺ said: "Pray to Allah with the conviction that you will be answered and know that Allah does not answer a supplication that comes from a careless and inattentive heart." (*Sunan at-Tirmidhī*)

عَنْ أَبِيْ هُرَيْرَةَ قَالَ قَالَ رَسُوْلُ اللهِ صَلَّى اللهُ عَلَيْهِ وَسَلَّمَ مَنْ سَرَّهُ أَنْ يَّسْتَجِيْبَ اللهُ لَهُ عِنْدَ الشَّدَائِدِ وَالْكُرَبِ فَلْيُكْثِرِ الدُّعَاءَ فِي الرَّخَاءِ. (رواه الترمذي)

Abū Hurayrah ﵁ narrates that the Prophet ﷺ said: "Whoever likes that Allah answer his duʿā's in hard times and periods of worry, he should abundantly make duʿā's in good times." (*Sunan at-Tirmidhī*)

Practice

1. Ḥalāl earnings and consumption are necessary for duʿā's to be answered

عَنْ أَبِيْ هُرَيْرَةَ قَالَ قَالَ رَسُوْلُ اللهِ صَلَّى اللهُ عَلَيْهِ وَسَلَّمَ يَا أَيُّهَا النَّاسُ إِنَّ اللهَ طَيِّبٌ لَّا يَقْبَلُ إِلَّا طَيِّبًا وَإِنَّ اللهَ أَمَرَ الْمُؤْمِنِيْنَ بِمَا أَمَرَ بِهِ الْمُرْسَلِيْنَ فَقَالَ «يَا أَيُّهَا الرُّسُلُ كُلُوْا مِنَ الطَّيِّبَاتِ وَاعْمَلُوْا صَالِحًا إِنِّيْ بِمَا تَعْمَلُوْنَ عَلِيْمٌ» وَ قَالَ «يَا أَيُّهَا الَّذِيْنَ آمَنُوْا كُلُوْا مِنْ طَيِّبَاتِ مَا رَزَقْنَاكُمْ» ثُمَّ ذَكَرَ الرَّجُلَ يُطِيْلُ السَّفَرَ أَشْعَثَ أَغْبَرَ يَمُدَّ يَدَيْهِ إِلَى السَّمَاءِ يَا رَبِّ يَا رَبِّ وَمَطْعَمُهُ حَرَامٌ وَمَشْرَبُهُ حَرَامٌ وَمَلْبَسُهُ حَرَامٌ وَغُذِّيَ بِالْحَرَامِ فَأَنَّى يُسْتَجَابُ لِذَالِكَ. (رواه مسلم عن ابي هريرة)

Abū Hurayrah ﵁ narrates that the Prophet ﷺ said: "O People, Allah is pure and accepts only the pure offerings. He commanded the believers as He commanded the prophets. He said to the prophets: 'O Prophets, eat the pure things and perform righteous deeds. I am well aware of what you do.' And He said: 'O believers, eat from the pure things that We have provided to you.'" Then the Prophet ﷺ mentioned a man who has come from a long journey and as a result he is disheveled and is covered with dust. "He prays: 'O Lord, O Lord.' But his food is ḥarām (impermissible in Islamic Law), his drink is ḥarām, his clothing is ḥarām, and his body has been nurtured on ḥarām. So how can his duʿā's be accepted?" (*Ṣaḥīḥ Muslim*)

2. PRAY FOR YOURSELF BEFORE PRAYING FOR OTHERS

عَنْ أُبَيِّ بِنْ كَعْبٍ قَالَ كَانَ رَسُوْلُ اللهِ صَلَّى اللهُ عَلَيْهِ وَسَلَّمَ إِذَا ذَكَرَ أَحَدًا فَدَعَا لَهُ بَدَأَ بِنَفْسِهِ. (رواه الترمذي)

Ubayy ibn Kaʿb رضي الله عنه narrates that when Allah's Messenger ﷺ mentioned anyone and prayed for him, he began with himself (*Sunan at-Tirmidhī*).

There is great wisdom in this Prophetic teaching. We are all in need of Allah's mercy all the time. This practice will, inshā Allah, ensure that our duʿā's to Allah for others do not lead us to think that we are superior to them.

3. BEGIN WITH ḤAMD AND ṢALĀT ʿALAN NABĪ

عَنْ فُضَالَةَ بْنِ عُبَيْدٍ قَالَ قَالَ سَمِعَ رَسُوْلُ اللهِ صَلَّى اللهُ عَلَيْهِ وَسَلَّمَ رَجُلًا يَّدْعُوْ فِيْ صَلٰوتِهِ لَمْ يَحْمَدِ اللهَ وَ لَمْ يُصَلِّ عَلَى النَّبِيِّ صَلَّى اللهُ عَلَيْهِ وَسَلَّمَ فَقَالَ رَسُوْلُ اللهِ صَلَّى اللهُ عَلَيْهِ وَسَلَّمَ عَجَّلَ هٰذَا ثُمَّ دَعَاهُ فَقَالَ لَهُ أَوْ لِغَيْرِهِ إِذَا صَلّٰى أَحَدُكُمْ فَلْيَبْدَأْ بِتَحْمِيْدِ رَبِّهِ وَالثَّنَاءِ عَلَيْهِ ثُمَّ يُصَلِّيْ عَلَى النَّبِيِّ صَلَّى اللهُ عَلَيْهِ وَسَلَّمَ ثُمَّ يَدْعُوْ بَعْدَ بِمَا شَاءَ. (رواه الترمذي وأبو داود)

Fuḍālah ibn ʿUbayd رضي الله عنه narrates that the Prophet ﷺ heard a person make duʿā' in his ṣalāt without saying *ḥamd* (praise of Allah) and without saying *ṣalāt ʿalan-Nabī* (sending salutations on the Prophet ﷺ). So he said, "He made haste." Then he called him and said to him or to someone else, "Whenever any of you offers ṣalāt, then (before making duʿā') he should begin with *ḥamd* and *thanā'* for his Lord, then say *ṣalāt ʿalan*

Nabī, then he should make his duʿā'." (*Sunan at-Tirmidhī* and *Sunan Abī Dāwūd*)

While this ḥadith refers to the duʿā' with the ṣalāt, there is consensus of ʿulamā' that *ḥamd* and *ṣalāt ʿalan Nabī* should be said in the beginning and end of every duʿā' session, whether in the ṣalāt or outside it.

4. End with Āmīn

عَنْ أَبِيْ زُهَيرٍ النُّمَيْرِيِّ قَالَ خَرَجْنَا مَعَ رَسُوْلِ اللهِ صَلَّى اللهُ عَلَيْهِ وَسَلَّمَ لَيْلَةً فَأَتَيْنَا عَلٰى رَجُلٍ قَدْ أَلَّحَ فِي الْمَسْئَلَةِ فَوَقَفَ صَلَّى اللهُ عَلَيْهِ وَسَلَّمَ يَسْتَمِعُ مِنْهُ فَقَالَ صَلَّى اللهُ عَلَيْهِ وَسَلَّمَ أَوْجَبَ إِنْ خَتَمَ فَقَالَ رَجُلٌ مِّنَ الْقَوْمِ بِأَيِّ شَيْءٍ يَخْتِمُ يَا رَسُوْلَ اللهِ قَالَ بِآمِيْنَ فَإِنَّهُ إِنْ خَتَمَ بِآمِيْنَ فَقَدْ أَوْجَبَ (رواه أبو داود)

Abū Zuhayr an-Numayrī ﷺ narrates: "One night we were out with the Prophet ﷺ, when we passed by a man who was supplicating with great devotion and humility. The Prophet ﷺ stopped and listened to him. Then he said, 'It will become incumbent if he seals it.' A person asked, 'With what can he seal it?' He said, 'By saying Āmīn. If he ends the duʿā' with Āmīn, then it will become incumbent.'" (*Sunan Abī Dāwūd*)

5. Request others to pray for you

عَنْ عُمَرَ بْنِ الْخَطَّابِ قَالَ إِسْتَأْذَنْتُ النَّبِيَّ صَلَّى اللهُ عَلَيْهِ وَسَلَّمَ فِي الْعُمْرَةِ فَأَذِنَ وَقَالَ أَشْرِكْنَا يَا أُخَيَّ فِي دُعَائِكَ وَلَا تَنْسَنَا فَقَالَ كَلِمَةً مَّا يَسُرُّنِيْ أَنَّ لِيْ بِهَا الدُّنْيَا. (رواه أبو داود والترمذي)

ʿUmar ibn al-Khaṭṭāb ﷺ narrates: "I asked the Prophet ﷺ for permission to perform an ʿUmrah and he gave me permission saying, 'Dear brother, include us in your supplication and do not forget us.' This expression ('dear brother') that he said, I would not be willing to exchange it for the world." (*Sunan Abī Dāwūd* and *Sunan at-Tirmidhī*)

Ukhayy is the diminutive form of *akh*. It means little brother and is used to express love. That is why Sayyidnā ʿUmar ﷺ considered this expression from the Prophet's mouth more valuable than the whole world. This ḥadīth shows that we should request those visiting the holy places to make duʿā' for us. It also shows that we can request our juniors for duʿā's.

Most Likely Accepted Duʿā's

عَنْ أَبِيْ هُرَيْرَةَ قَالَ قَالَ رَسُوْلُ اللهِ صَلَّى اللهُ عَلَيْهِ وَسَلَّمَ ثَلٰثُ دَعَوَاتٍ مُّسْتَجَابَاتٌ لَّا شَكَّ فِيْهِنَّ: دَعْوَةُ الْوَالِدِ وَدَعْوَةُ الْمُسَافِرِ وَدَعْوَةُ الْمَظْلُومِ. (رواه الترمذي وأبو داود وابن ماجه)

Abū Hurayrah ﵁ narrates that the Prophet ﷺ said: "Three duʿā's are answered, there is no doubt about them: the duʿā' of a parent, the duʿā' of a traveler, and the duʿā' of the one who has been wronged." (*Sunan at-Tirmidhī*, *Sunan Abī Dāwūd*, and *Ibn Mājah*)

This has several implications. We should pray for our children. If we are fortunate that our parents are alive, we should request them for duʿā's and try to earn it by winning their hearts through our good treatment. We should take care of travelers so we can earn their duʿā's. (It goes without saying that the traveler meant here is one traveling for a good cause. It does not apply to those engaged in sin.) And we must be very alert never to wrong any person, for Allah ﷻ accepts the duʿā' of the wronged. On the other hand we should help a person who has been wronged so he or she prays for us.

عَنْ ابْنِ عَبَّاسٍ عَنِ النَّبِيِّ صَلَّى اللهُ عَلَيْهِ وَسَلَّمَ قَالَ خَمْسُ دَعَوَاتٍ يُّسْتَجَابُ لَهُنَّ: دَعْوَةُ الْمَظْلُومِ حَتّٰى يَنْتَصِرَ وَدَعْوَةُ الْحَاجِّ حَتّٰى يَصْدِرَ وَدَعْوَةُ الْمُجَاهِدِ حَتّٰى يُفْقَدَ وَدَعْوَةُ الْمَرِيْضِ حَتّٰى يَبْرَأَ وَدَعْوَةُ الْأَخِ لِأَخِيْهِ بِظَهْرِ الْغَيْبِ ثُمَّ قَالَ وَأَسْرَعُ هٰذِهِ الدَّعَوَاتِ إِجَابَةً دَعْوَةُ الْأَخِ بِظَهْرِ الْغَيْبِ (رواه البيهقي قي الدعوات الكبير)

ʿAbdullāh ibn ʿAbbās ﵄ narrates that the Prophet ﷺ said: "Five duʿā's are answered: the duʿā' of the one who has been wronged till help comes, the duʿā' of a pilgrim until he comes home, the duʿā' of one engaged in jihād until he stops, the duʿā' of a sick person until he recovers, and the duʿā' of someone for a brother in his absence. Then he added, 'Of these the one that gets the quickest answer is that for a brother in his absence.'" (*Ad-Daʿawāt al-Kabīr*)

عَنْ الْعِرْبَاضِ بْنِ سَارِيَةَ قَالَ قَالَ رَسُوْلُ اللهِ صَلَّى اللهُ عَلَيْهِ وَسَلَّمَ مَنْ صَلَّى فَرِيْضَةً فَلَهُ دَعْوَةٌ مُّسْتَجَابَةٌ وَمَنْ خَتَمَ الْقُرْاٰنَ فَلَهُ دَعْوَةٌ مُّسْتَجَابَةٌ (رواه الطبراني في الكبير)

Al-ʿIrbāḍ ibn Sāriyah ﵁ narrates that the Prophet ﷺ said: "Whoever finished his obligatory ṣalāt, his duʿā' will be accepted. Whoever finished a reading of the Qur'ān, his duʿā' will be accepted." (*Ṭabarānī*)

عَنْ جَابِرٍ قَالَ سَمِعْتُ النَّبِيَّ صَلَّى اللهُ عَلَيْهِ وَسَلَّمَ إِنَّ فِي اللَّيْلِ لَسَاعَةً لَّا يُوَافِقُهَا رَجُلٌ مُّسْلِمٌ يَسْأَلُ اللهَ فِيْهَا خَيْرًا مِّنْ أَمْرِ الدُّنْيَا وَالْاٰخِرَةِ إِلَّا أَعْطَاهُ إِيَّاهُ وَذٰلِكَ كُلَّ لَيْلَةٍ (رواه مسلم)

Jābir ibn ʿAbdillāh ﵁ says: "I heard the Prophet ﷺ say: 'During the night there is a moment such that if a Muslim man begs Allah for any good of this world or the Hereafter at that moment, Allah grants that to him. And that happens every night.'" (*Ṣaḥīḥ Muslim*)

عَنْ أَبِيْ سَعِيْدِ الْخُدْرِيِّ أَنَّ النَّبِيَّ صَلَّى اللهُ عَلَيْهِ وَسَلَّمَ قَالَ مَا مِنْ مُسْلِمٍ يَّدْعُو بِدَعْوَةٍ لَّيْسَ فِيْهَا إِثْمٌ وَلَا قَطِيْعَةُ رَحْمٍ إِلَّا أَعْطَاهُ اللهُ بِهَا إِحْدٰى ثَلٰثٍ إِمَّا أَنْ يُّعَجِّلَ لَهُ دَعْوَتَهُ وَإِمَّا أَنْ يَّدَّخِرَهَا لَهُ فِي الْاٰخِرَةِ وَإِمَّا أَنْ يَّصْرِفَ عَنْهُ مِنَ السُّوْءِ مِثْلَهَا قَالُوْا إِذًا نُّكْثِرُ قَالَ اللهُ أَكْثَرُ (رواه أحمد)

Abū Saʿīd al-Khudrī ﵁ narrates that the Prophet ﷺ said: "To any Muslim who makes a duʿā', provided the duʿā' contains nothing which is sinful or which involves breaking family ties, Allah will give one of three things: He will quickly grant him what he asked for, or save the reward for him for the Hereafter, or turn away from him a similar hardship (that would have hit him in the absence of that duʿā')." Those who heard it said they would greatly increase their duʿā's. He replied, "Allah has even more." (*Musnad Aḥmad*)

How to Use this Book

This book is for daily reading. It is best to set aside a fixed time for this purpose.

It is recommended that one reads the translation and commentary at least once in the beginning to understand the meaning and significance of the duʿā'. This is essential if we want to really make a duʿā' instead of merely reciting it. Afterwards the translation and commentary may be browsed from time to time as needed.

The daily reading should be of the Arabic duʿā's, which have been displayed in a separate box so they can be read without interruption from the translation and commentary. The duʿā' on the following page can be read everyday or occasionally, at the preference of the reader, before the duʿā's for that day.

Transliteration has been provided for those who cannot read Arabic. However, it is strongly recommended that they do make it a goal to learn to read Arabic and use the transliteration only as an interim measure. The transliteration is provided below the corresponding Arabic text so the process of learning to read Arabic will be facilitated.

A Duʿāʾ

composed by Mawlānā Ashraf ʿAlī Thānawī

نَحْمَدُكَ يَا خَيْرَ مَأْمُولٍ، وَأَكْرَمَ مَسْئُوْلٍ، عَلٰى مَا عَلَّمْتَنَا مِنَ الْمُنَاجَاتِ الْمَقْبُولِ، مِنْ قُرُبَاتٍ عِنْدَ اللهِ وَصَلَوَاتِ الرَّسُوْلِ. فَصَلِّ عَلَيْهِ مَا اخْتَلَفَ الدَّبُوْرُ وَالْقَبُوْلُ، وَانْشَعَبَتِ الْفُرُوْعُ مِنَ الْأُصُوْلِ. ثُمَّ نَسْأَلُكَ بِمَا سَنَقُوْلُ. وَمِنَّا السُّؤَالُ وَمِنْكَ الْقُبُوْلُ.

Naḥmaduka yā Khayra maʾmūl(in), wa Akrama masʾūl(in), ʿalā mā ʿallamtanā minal-munājātil-maqbūl(i), min qurubātin ʿindAllāhi wa ṣalawātir-Rasūl(i). Fa ṣalli ʿalayhi makh-talafad-dabūru wal-qabūl(u), wan-shaʿabatil-furūʿu minal-ʾuṣūl(i). Thumma nasʾaluka bimā sanaqūl(u). Wa minnas-suʾālu wa minkal-qubūl(u).

We praise You, O the Best of those in Whom hopes can be placed and the Most Generous of those who can be beseeched, for teaching us the Accepted Whispers. Taken from the book Qurubāt ʿIndAllāhi wa Ṣalawāt ar-Rasūl (Prayers that Bring One Close to Allah and the Invocations of the Messenger). Bless him (the Messenger ﷺ) as long as the westerly and easterly winds blow and branches continue to grow from the roots (i.e. until the Day of Judgment). We beg You in the words that follow (in the rest of the book). Asking is from us and acceptance is from you.

SATURDAY

In the Name of Allah, the Most Compassionate, the Most Merciful

(1) Our Lord, give unto us in this world that which is good and in the Hereafter that which is good, and protect us from the punishment of the Fire.

(2) Our Lord, pour out patience on us, plant firmly our feet, and give us victory over the disbelieving people.

---

(1) [*Al-Baqarah*, 2:201]

This is a very well-known duʿāʾ. If a Muslim knows any duʿāʾs in Arabic, it is very probable that this is one of them. However, its message and significance escape many.

It is a unique feature of Islam that it strikes a perfect balance everywhere, including between this world and the Hereafter. This world is important as is the Hereafter; we will reap there what we sow here. We pray for both, and mention them in their natural chronological order. But what we are seeking—and here is the crucial difference—are not the goods of this world, but the good. Here and in the Hereafter. *Ḥasanah* denotes every conceivable form of good: health, livelihood, fulfillment of genuine needs (not wants), good morals, virtuous deeds, beneficial knowledge, honor and prestige, strength of faith, and sincerity in worship. Actually, everything in this world is good that will lead, directly or indirectly, to the good in the Hereafter. A Muslim informed by this duʿāʾ will neither focus entirely on this world, seeking exclusively the comforts here, nor will he declare that he has nothing to do with it.

Prophet Muḥammad ﷺ once visited a man who had been debilitated by sickness and asked him whether he had been making any supplication. He had. It was, "O Allah, whatever punishment you are going to give me in the Hereafter, give it to me here." Prophet Muḥammad ﷺ asked him why he had not made this duʿāʾ instead. He did and was cured.

The Prophet ﷺ used to make this duʿāʾ very often (*Ṣaḥīḥ al-Bukhārī*). He used to recite this duʿāʾ between the Rukn-e-Yamāni and the Black Stone while making ṭawāf (circumambulation of the →

يوم السبت

بِسْمِ اللّٰهِ الرَّحْمٰنِ الرَّحِيْمِ

﴿١﴾ رَبَّنَآ اٰتِنَا فِي الدُّنْيَا حَسَنَةً وَّفِي الْاٰخِرَةِ حَسَنَةً وَّقِنَا عَذَابَ النَّارِ ۝

﴿٢﴾ رَبَّنَآ أَفْرِغْ عَلَيْنَا صَبْرًا وَّثَبِّتْ أَقْدَامَنَا وَانْصُرْنَا عَلَى الْقَوْمِ الْكٰفِرِيْنَ ۝

1. Rabbanā ātinā fid-dunyā ḥasanatan wa fil-ākhirati ḥasanatan wa qinā ʿadhāban-nār.

2. Rabbanā afrigh ʿalaynā ṣabran wa thabbit aqdāmanā wan-ṣurnā ʿalal-qawmil-kāfirīn.

Kaʿbah) (*Sunan Abī Dāwūd*). Whenever he shook hands with a person he did not leave his hand without making this duʿā' (*Ibn as-Sunnī*). Imām Nawawī recommends this duʿā' at the time of great difficulties or when facing major issues. It is also recommended after praying Ṣalāt-ul-Ḥājah (a special ṣalāt at the time of need).

(2) [*Al-Baqarah,* 2:250]
This was the duʿā' of the Children of Israel fighting under the leadership of King Ṭalūt (Saul) against the Philistines who were fighting under Jalūt (Goliath). The Children of Israel were the Muslims of the time. Allah ﷻ accepted this duʿā' and gave them victory over Goliath as Prophet Dāwūd (David) عليه السلام slew him.

The trials and tribulations of this life constantly require *ṣabr*, which implies more than just patience. It implies patience in the face of hardships, steadfastness to refrain from evil in the face of temptations, and determination in overcoming obstacles to doing good. Thus overcoming laziness in offering daily ṣalāts is part of *ṣabr*, as is remaining firm in the face of peer pressure. Of course perseverance in the face of oppression is a big part of it.

This duʿā' reminds us that *ṣabr* is the key to victory. *Ṣabr* that

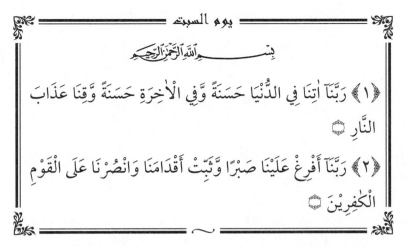

(3) Our Lord, do not take us to task if we forget or make a mistake. Our Lord, do not place such a burden on us as You had placed on those before us. Our Lord, burden us not with that which we have not the strength to bear. Pardon us, grant us forgiveness, and have mercy on us. You are our Protector so help us to victory over the disbelieving people.

(4) Our Lord, do not let our hearts falter after You have guided us, and grant us mercy from Your presence. Surely You are the most generous Grantor.

(5) Our Lord, surely we have believed, so forgive us our sins and shield us from the punishment of the Fire.

---

emanates from a strong heart and trust in Allah سبحانه وتعالى leads to firmness of the feet which in turn leads to victory. But for each step on this path to victory, we need Allah's help. Hence the duʿāʾ.

(3) [*Al-Baqarah,* 2:286]
There are several aḥādith in *Musnad Aḥmad*, *Sunan ad-Dārimī*, and *Mustadrak Ḥākim* that inform us about the extraordinary importance of the last two verses of Sūrah *Al-Baqarah*, which contain this duʿāʾ. They were given to Prophet Muḥammad ﷺ out of His grace, during *miʿrāj* (Ascension) out of the special treasure underneath the *ʿArsh* (Divine Throne) and they were not given to any previous Prophet.

We say this duʿāʾ out of deep gratitude for this ummah was relieved of the stringent burdens placed on the Israelites, as is obvious to anyone who compares Islamic Sharīʿah with Jewish Laws.

Sayyidnā ʿUmar رضي الله عنه and Sayyidnā ʿAlī رضي الله عنه said they thought that anybody who had any sense would never go to bed without having recited these verses.

(4) [*Āl-i-ʿImrān,* 3:8]
As the previous verse of this sūrah states, this is the duʿāʾ of those who are firmly grounded in knowledge. They never become complacent with their *īman* (faith), being fully aware that one's īman is one's most precious treasure and needs to be carefully guarded. →

﴿٣﴾ رَبَّنَا لَا تُؤَاخِذْنَآ إِنْ نَّسِيْنَآ أَوْ أَخْطَأْنَا ۚ رَبَّنَا وَلَا تَحْمِلْ عَلَيْنَآ

إِصْرًا كَمَا حَمَلْتَهُ عَلَى الَّذِيْنَ مِنْ قَبْلِنَا ۚ رَبَّنَا وَلَا تُحَمِّلْنَا مَا لَا طَاقَةَ

لَنَا بِهِ ۖ وَاعْفُ عَنَّا وَاغْفِرْ لَنَا وَارْحَمْنَا ۚ أَنْتَ مَوْلَانَا فَانْصُرْنَا عَلَى

الْقَوْمِ الْكَافِرِيْنَ ۞

﴿٤﴾ رَبَّنَا لَا تُزِغْ قُلُوْبَنَا بَعْدَ إِذْ هَدَيْتَنَا وَهَبْ لَنَا مِنْ لَّدُنْكَ رَحْمَةً ۚ

إِنَّكَ أَنْتَ الْوَهَّابُ ۞

﴿٥﴾ رَبَّنَآ إِنَّنَآ اٰمَنَّا فَاغْفِرْ لَنَا ذُنُوْبَنَا وَقِنَا عَذَابَ النَّارِ ۞

3. Rabbanā lā tu'ākhidhnā in nasīnā aw akhṭa'nā. Rabbanā wa lā taḥmil ʿalaynā iṣran kamā ḥamaltahū ʿalal-ladhīna min qablinā. Rabbanā wa lā tuḥammilnā mā lā ṭāqata lanā bih(ī), wa-ʿ-fu ʿannā wagh-fir lanā war-ḥamnā. Anta Mawlānā fan-ṣurnā ʿalal-qawmil-kāfirīn.

4. Rabbanā lā tuzigh qulūbanā baʿda idh hadaytanā wa hab lanā min ladunka raḥma(tan). Innaka Antal-Wahhāb.

5. Rabbanā innanā āmannā fagh-fir lanā dhunūbanā wa qinā ʿadhāban-nār.

Further, we cannot guarantee its protection; we must turn to Allah to seek His help in doing so.

Needless to say, it is unimaginable that anyone consciously making this duʿā' will knowingly engage in such enterprises as may pose danger to his īmān.

(5) [Āl-i-ʿImrān, 3:16]

The verses before and after the one containing this duʿā' character-ize the people making this duʿā' as the ones who fear Allah; are patient, truthful, devout, and charitable; and who seek forgiveness in the pre-dawn hours. Yet by invoking solely their īmān here as

(6) Our Lord, You have not created all this in vain! Glory be to You; shield us then from the punishment of the Fire.

(7) Our Lord, surely whomsoever You sentence to the Fire, You have disgraced him indeed. And for wrongdoers there will be no supporters.

(8) Our Lord, surely we heard a caller calling to the faith, saying: believe in your Lord. And we believed. Our Lord, forgive us therefore our sins, and blot out from us our evil deeds, and in death join us with the righteous.

(9) Our Lord, grant us what You have promised to us through Your messengers, and do not disgrace us on the Day of Judgment; surely You never break Your promise.

(10) Our Lord, we have wronged our souls. And if You do not forgive us and grant us mercy, we shall certainly be among the losers.

(11) Our Lord, pour out patience over us and make us die as Muslims.

---

the basis of forgiveness they affirm that this is the most valuable treasure of a believer.

(6-9) [*Āl-i-ʿImrān,* 3:191-94]
These beautiful duʿā's are of the really wise persons, as described by the Qur'ān. They are the ones who reflect on the creation of the heavens and the earth and in the alternation of the day and night, and this reflection leads them to the belief in the Creator and a deep concern for their accountability before Him. The Prophet ﷺ said: "Ruined is the person who recited these verses but failed to reflect therein."

The reference to Allah سبحانه وتعالى never breaking His promise is not meant to reassure themselves of this fact. Rather it implies the plea that Allah سبحانه وتعالى enable them to become deserving of that promise.

(10) [*Al-Aʿrāf,* 7:23]
This duʿā' was taught by Allah سبحانه وتعالى to Sayyidnā Ādam (Adam) عليه السلام.

﴿٦﴾ رَبَّنَا مَا خَلَقْتَ هٰذَا بٰطِلًا سُبْحٰنَكَ فَقِنَا عَذَابَ النَّارِ ۝

﴿٧﴾ رَبَّنَآ إِنَّكَ مَنْ تُدْخِلِ النَّارَ فَقَدْ أَخْزَيْتَهٗ ۖ وَمَا لِلظّٰلِمِيْنَ مِنْ أَنْصَارٍ ۝

﴿٨﴾ رَبَّنَآ إِنَّنَا سَمِعْنَا مُنَادِيًا يُّنَادِيْ لِلْإِيْمَانِ أَنْ اٰمِنُوْا بِرَبِّكُمْ فَاٰمَنَّا ۚ رَبَّنَا فَاغْفِرْ لَنَا ذُنُوْبَنَا وَكَفِّرْ عَنَّا سَيِّاٰتِنَا وَتَوَفَّنَا مَعَ الْأَبْرَارِ ۝

﴿٩﴾ رَبَّنَا وَاٰتِنَا مَا وَعَدْتَّنَا عَلٰى رُسُلِكَ وَلَا تُخْزِنَا يَوْمَ الْقِيٰمَةِ ۗ إِنَّكَ لَا تُخْلِفُ الْمِيْعَادَ ۝

﴿١٠﴾ رَبَّنَا ظَلَمْنَآ أَنْفُسَنَا وَإِنْ لَّمْ تَغْفِرْ لَنَا وَتَرْحَمْنَا لَنَكُوْنَنَّ مِنَ الْخٰسِرِيْنَ ۝

﴿١١﴾ رَبَّنَآ أَفْرِغْ عَلَيْنَا صَبْرًا وَّتَوَفَّنَا مُسْلِمِيْنَ ۝

6. Rabbanā mā khalaqta hādhā bāṭilan subḥānaka fa qinā ʿadhāban-nār.

7. Rabbanā innaka man tudkhilin-nāra fa qad akhzaytah(ū), wa mā liẓ-ẓālimīna min anṣār.

8. Rabbanā innanā samiʿnā munādiyan yunādī lil-īmāni an āminū birabbikum fa āmannā. Rabbanā fagh-fir lanā dhunūbanā wa kaffir ʿannā sayyi'ātinā wa tawaffanā maʿal-'abrār.

9. Rabbanā wa ātinā mā waʿadttanā ʿalā rusulika wa lā tukhzinā yawmal-qiyāma(ti). Innaka lā tukhliful-mīʿād.

10. Rabbanā ẓalamnā anfusanā wa in lam taghfir lanā wa tarḥamnā lanakūnanna minal-khāsirīn.

11. Rabbanā afrigh ʿalaynā ṣabran wa tawaffanā Muslimīn.

(12) You are our Protector. So forgive us and show us mercy, for You are the best of those who forgive.

(13) Our Lord, do not turn us into a victim of the unjust people and save us through Your mercy from the disbelieving people.

(14) O the Creator of the heavens and the earth, You are my Protector in this world and in the Hereafter. Make me die a Muslim and unite me with the righteous.

(15) My Lord, make me and my offspring establish ṣalāt. Our Lord, accept my supplication.

(16) Our Lord, forgive me and my parents and all believers on the day when the Reckoning will be set up.

The Qur'ān says: "Then Ādam learned certain words (of duʿā') from his Lord; so Allah accepted his repentance" (*Al-Baqarah*, 2:37).

(11) [*Al-Aʿrāf*, 7:126]
This was the duʿā' of the magicians in the court of the Pharaoh after they declared faith and were threatened by a furious Pharaoh with severe torture over this defiance. This is the response of the believers to the threats of dire consequences by worldly powers over their faith.

(12) [*Al-Aʿrāf*, 7:155]
This was the duʿā' of Sayyidnā Musa (Moses) عليه السلام, when seventy Jewish leaders who accompanied him to Mount Sinai were punished because of their iniquity.

(13) [*Yūnus*, 10:85-86]
This was the duʿā' of the Israelites against persecution by the Pharaoh.

(14) [*Yūsuf*, 12:101]
This was the duʿā' of Sayyidnā Yūsuf (Joseph) عليه السلام after he had been united with his parents and brothers. At the height of his worldly power his concern was still with dying as a Muslim and getting the company of the pious. →

﴿١٢﴾ أَنْتَ وَلِيُّنَا فَاغْفِرْ لَنَا وَارْحَمْنَا وَأَنْتَ خَيْرُ الْغٰفِرِيْنَ ۝

﴿١٣﴾ رَبَّنَا لَا تَجْعَلْنَا فِتْنَةً لِّلْقَوْمِ الظّٰلِمِيْنَ ۝ وَنَجِّنَا بِرَحْمَتِكَ مِنَ الْقَوْمِ الْكٰفِرِيْنَ ۝

﴿١٤﴾ فَاطِرَ السَّمٰوٰتِ وَالْأَرْضِ أَنْتَ وَلِيِّيْ فِي الدُّنْيَا وَالْاٰخِرَةِ تَوَفَّنِيْ مُسْلِمًا وَّأَلْحِقْنِيْ بِالصّٰلِحِيْنَ ۝

﴿١٥﴾ رَبِّ اجْعَلْنِيْ مُقِيْمَ الصَّلٰوةِ وَمِنْ ذُرِّيَّتِيْ رَبَّنَا وَتَقَبَّلْ دُعَاءِ ۝

﴿١٦﴾ رَبَّنَا اغْفِرْ لِيْ وَلِوٰلِدَيَّ وَلِلْمُؤْمِنِيْنَ يَوْمَ يَقُوْمُ الْحِسَابُ ۝

12. Anta waliyyunā fagh-fir lanā war-ḥamnā, wa anta Khayrul-ghāfirīn.

13. Rabbanā lā tajʿalnā fitnatan lil-qawmiẓ-ẓālimīn(a). Wa najjinā biraḥmatika minal-qawmil-kāfirīn.

14. Fāṭiras-samāwāti wal-'arḍi anta Waliyyī fid-dunyā wal-ākhira(ti), tawaffanī musliman wa alḥiqnī biṣ-ṣāliḥīn.

15. Rabbij-ʿalnī muqīmaṣ-ṣalāti wa min dhurriyyatī. Rabbanā wa taqabbal duʿā'.

16. Rabbanagh-fir lī wa liwālidayya wa lil-mu'minīna yawma yaqūmul-ḥisāb.

---

(15) [*Ibrāhīm*, 14:40]
This was the duʿā' of Sayyidnā Ibrāhīm (Abraham) عليه السلام. His concern for the ṣalāt of his children should set an example for us. We should provide proper Islamic education and training to our children. At the same time we should be praying for their steadfastness in Islamic practices.

(17) My Lord, show them (my parents) mercy just as they cared for me when I was a little child.

(18) My Lord, make me enter through a rightful entrance and leave by a rightful exit and grant me supporting authority from Your presence.

(19) Our Lord, grant us mercy from Your presence and provide us with guidance in our affair.

(20) My Lord, open up my heart for me, make my task easy for me, and loose a knot from my tongue so they may understand my speech.

---

(16) [*Ibrāhīm*, 14:41]
Sayyidnā Ibrāhīm عليه السلام initially made this duʿā' for his father, but later stopped it. The Qur'ān says: "And the duʿā' of Ibrāhīm for the forgiveness of his father was but due to a promise he had made to him. Later when it became clear to him that he was an enemy of Allah, he withdrew himself from him" (*At-Tawbah*, 9:114).

A Muslim should pray for his non-Muslim parents in their life for their guidance. But it is not permissible to pray for the *maghfirah* (forgiveness) of anyone who dies in a state of unbelief.

(17) [*Al-Isrā'*, 17:24]
This duʿā' comes in the Qur'ān immediately after the verse that tells us that deference to parents is the second most important obligation of a believer after the obligation to worship Allah سبحانه وتعالى alone. That placement in addition to the fact that Allah سبحانه وتعالى Himself is teaching us how to supplicate for our parents should tell us the value of this duʿā'. That also raises our hopes regarding the acceptance of this duʿā' when made sincerely.

Needless to say, it is an important parenting goal for Muslim parents to raise such children who will make this duʿā' for them in their life and after their death.

(18) [*Al-Isrā'*, 17:80]
Prophet Muḥammad ﷺ was taught this duʿā' when he was commanded to migrate from Makkah to Madīnah. He had been sur- →

﴿١٧﴾ رَبِّ ارْحَمْهُمَا كَمَا رَبَّيٰنِيْ صَغِيْرًا ۝

﴿١٨﴾ رَبِّ أَدْخِلْنِيْ مُدْخَلَ صِدْقٍ وَّأَخْرِجْنِيْ مُخْرَجَ صِدْقٍ
وَّاجْعَلْ لِّيْ مِنْ لَّدُنْكَ سُلْطٰنًا نَّصِيْرًا ۝

﴿١٩﴾ رَبَّنَآ اٰتِنَا مِنْ لَّدُنْكَ رَحْمَةً وَّهَيِّئْ لَنَا مِنْ أَمْرِنَا رَشَدًا ۝

﴿٢٠﴾ رَبِّ اشْرَحْ لِيْ صَدْرِيْ ۝ وَيَسِّرْ لِيْ أَمْرِيْ ۝ وَاحْلُلْ
عُقْدَةً مِّنْ لِّسَانِيْ ۝ يَفْقَهُوْا قَوْلِيْ ۝

17. Rabbir-ḥamhumā kamā rabbayānī ṣaghīra.

18. Rabbi adkhilnī mudkhala ṣidqin wa akhrijnī mukhraja ṣidqin waj-ʿal lī min ladunka sulṭānan naṣīra.

19. Rabbanā ātinā min ladunka raḥmatan wa hayyi' lanā min amrinā rashada.

20. Rabbish-raḥ lī ṣadrī. Wa yassir lī amrī. Waḥ-lul ʿuqdatam min lisānī. Yafqahū qawlī.

---

rounded by the Makkan pagan leaders intent to kill him and he had no visible means of defense, yet Allah سُبْحَانَهُ وَتَعَالَىٰ shielded him and provided for him a safe exit. Similarly, Madīnah was a difficult city to live in because of its weather. Yet, Allah سُبْحَانَهُ وَتَعَالَىٰ changed it into a very pleasant city, which it has been ever since. Some ʿulamā' have stated that this duʿā' is beneficial for all objectives and purposes.

(19) [*Al-Kahf*, 18:10]
When there seems to be no way out we turn to Allah سُبْحَانَهُ وَتَعَالَىٰ for both mercy and guidance.

This duʿā' was made by the young men who sought refuge from persecution in a cave. Their story is related in Sūrah *Al-Kahf*. Reports differ on whether these men were the followers of Sayyidnā

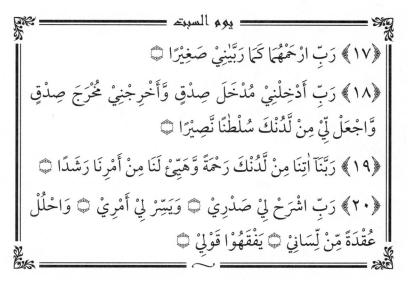

(21) *My Lord, increase me in knowledge.*

(22) *Adversity has afflicted me and You are the Most Merciful of those who show mercy.*

(23) *My Lord, leave me not childless, even though You are the Best of heirs.*

(24) *My Lord, cause me to land at a blessed landing-place, for You are the Best of all who bring to land.*

ʿĪsā (Jesus) عليه السلام, or another prophet. In either case, they refused to submit to a tyrant who was forcing paganism on his subjects. They left behind everything as they took refuge in a cave to safeguard their īmān. And in doing so, they set an example for the youth today to follow.

(20) [*Ṭā-Hā*, 20:25-28]
This was the duʿāʾ of Prophet Mūsā عليه السلام when he was commanded to go to the Pharaoh and deliver the message of Allah to the tyrant.

(21) [*Ṭā-Hā*, 20:114]
The knowledge referred to here is the revealed knowledge, the one that increases one's consciousness of Allah. As a ḥadīth points out, this knowledge is the legacy of the prophets. This is the knowledge that guarantees success in this world and in the Hereafter, for it alone has the ability to answer the fundamental questions regarding the purpose of life and provide sure guidance.

The knowledge of the physical world, obtained through observation, experimentation, and reasoning, on the other hand, can be useful or harmful, depending upon the orientation and purpose of the person employing that knowledge. Thus science and technology have been used to serve the machinery of oppression and exploitation as well as to benefit humanity. See also duʿāʾ 45 below.

(22) [*Al-Anbiyāʾ*, 21:83]
This is the famous duʿāʾ of Sayyidnā Ayyūb (Job) عليه السلام. We do not know the exact nature of his affliction but we do know that it was a severe test and that he was cured after making this duʿāʾ. His →

﴿٢١﴾ رَبِّ زِدْنِي عِلْمًا ۝

﴿٢٢﴾ أَنِّي مَسَّنِيَ الضُّرُّ وَأَنْتَ أَرْحَمُ الرّٰحِمِيْنَ ۝

﴿٢٣﴾ رَبِّ لَا تَذَرْنِي فَرْدًا وَّأَنْتَ خَيْرُ الْوَارِثِيْنَ ۝

﴿٢٤﴾ رَبِّ أَنْزِلْنِي مُنْزَلًا مُّبٰرَكًا وَّأَنْتَ خَيْرُ الْمُنْزِلِيْنَ ۝

21. Rabbi zidnī ʿilma.

22. Annī massaniyaḍ-ḍurru wa anta Arḥamur-rāḥimīn.

23. Rabbi lā tadharnī fardan wa anta Khayrul-wārithīn.

24. Rabbi anzilnī munzalam mubārakan wa anta Khayrul-munzilīn.

---

patience has been praised in the Qur'ān: "Truly We found him full of patience" (*Ṣād*, 38:44).

A very important lesson to learn from this story is that in this world afflictions can affect both believers and non-believers. What distinguishes the former from the latter is not the fact of affliction but their response to it. The believers submit to the Will of Allah and turn to Him with supplication. The non-believers, on the other hand, can only complain and wonder "why me?" The faith of the first group gives them the strength to face the difficulties. The ordeals bring them closer to Allah سبحانه وتعالى.

According to Imām Jaʿfar aṣ-Ṣādiq, it is recommended to make this duʿā' whenever a person is sick or is facing any hardships.

(23) [*Al-Anbiyā'*, 21:89]
This was the duʿā' of Sayyidnā Zakariyyā (Zachariah) عليه السلام. It was granted and he was bestowed with Sayyidnā Yaḥyā (John) عليه السلام. He had prayed to be granted a child who would be his heir. That desire was human. However, it is part of the prophetic wisdom to remember that ultimately Allah سبحانه وتعالى is the inheritor of the entire world. Hence the second part of this duʿā'.

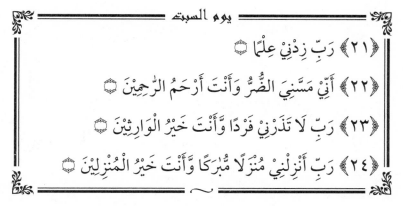

(25) My Lord, I seek refuge with You from the promptings of the shayṭāns and I seek refuge with You my Lord from that they come to me.

(26) Our Lord, we believe, so forgive us, and have mercy on us. You are the Best One to show mercy.

(27) Our Lord, turn away from us the punishment of Hell; surely its punishment is a persisting affliction.

---

(24) [*Al-Mu'minūn*, 23:29]
Allah سبحانه وتعالى taught this duʿā' to Sayyidnā Nūḥ (Noah) عليه السلام to say after boarding the Ark that saved him and the believers with him from the Flood.

(25) [*Al-Mu'minūn*, 23:97-98]
This duʿā' is often invoked for protection from the mischief of Shayṭān (Satan). It is also highly recommended for guarding against losing one's temper and giving in to fits. Additionally, it is very effective against other assaults of the devils. A variant of this duʿā' is reported for protection against nightmares. That duʿā' is:

> أَعُوْذُ بِكَلِمَاتِ اللهِ التَّامَّةِ مِنْ غَضَبِهِ وَشَرِّ عِبادِهِ، وَمِنْ هَمَزَاتِ الشَّيَاطِيْنِ وَأَنْ يَحْضُرُوْنِ
>
> I seek refuge with Allah's Perfect Words from Allah's wrath, and from the evils of His slaves, and from the promptings of the shayṭāns and from that they come to me.

Sayyidnā ʿAbdullāh ibn ʿAmr رضي الله عنه used to teach this to his older children. And for younger children he used to write it as an amulet and let them wear it around their necks.

(26) [*Al-Mu'minūn*, 23:109]
The Qur'ān mentions this as the duʿā' of the people who were ridiculed in this world by the unbelievers. In a glimpse of the Hereafter in the verses just preceding this we see the ridiculers futilely pleading that they be given another chance, while Allah سبحانه وتعالى says this regarding those making this duʿā': "I have rewarded them today for →

﴿٢٥﴾ رَبِّ أَعُوْذُ بِكَ مِنْ هَمَزٰتِ الشَّيٰطِيْنِ ۝ وَأَعُوْذُ بِكَ رَبِّ
أَنْ يَّحْضُرُوْنِ ۝

﴿٢٦﴾ رَبَّنَآ اٰمَنَّا فَاغْفِرْ لَنَا وَارْحَمْنَا وَأَنْتَ خَيْرُ الرّٰحِمِيْنَ ۝

﴿٢٧﴾ رَبَّنَا اصْرِفْ عَنَّا عَذَابَ جَهَنَّمَ إِنَّ عَذَابَهَا كَانَ غَرَامًا ۝

25. Rabbi aʿūdhu bika min hamazātish-shayāṭīn(i). Wa aʿūdhu bika Rabbi an yaḥḍurūn.

26. Rabbanā āmannā fagh-fir lanā war-ḥamnā wa anta Khayrur-rāḥimīn.

27. Rabbanaṣ-rif ʿannā ʿadhāba jahannam(a), inna ʿadhābahā kāna gharāma.

---

how patient they have been: they are the ones who are triumphant" (Al-Mu'minūn, 23:111).

When the going gets tough because of peer pressure, powerful media, or the campaigns of the world powers against them, the believers can get a lot of relief through this duʿā'.

(27) [*Al-Furqān*, 25:65]
This is the duʿā' of the people who have been honored with the title "ʿIbādur Raḥmān" (Servants of the Most Merciful). It is an attribute of such people that they are always concerned about the Hereafter and are always seeking protection against Hell.

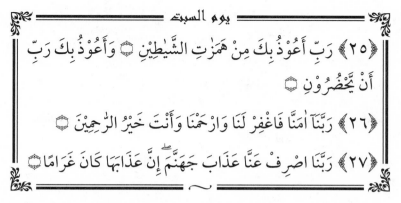

(28) Our Lord, grant us the delight of our eyes in our spouses and our offspring and make us a model for the God-fearing.

(29) My Lord, grant me that I should be grateful for Your favor that You have bestowed on me and on my parents, and that I do the good deeds that You are pleased with. And admit me through Your mercy among Your pious servants.

(30) My Lord, I am needy of whatever good You send down for me.

(31) My Lord, help me against the mischievous people.

---

(28) [*Al-Furqān*, 25:74]
delight of eyes: heartfelt joy.

This is the key duʿā' for marital bliss and for raising happy, loving, model Muslim families. There is a clear message here that *taqwā* (Allah consciousness and fear of Allah) is the true foundation on which one can hope to build a happy family life.

The second part of the duʿā' can also be translated as "make us leaders of the pious." In the context of the family, since a man is the leader of his family, the duʿā' really is for the piety of one's family and not for one's leadership. In the general sense the duʿā' is for attaining such piety that we become a model and inspiration for other pious people.

(29) [*An-Naml*, 27:19]
This was the duʿā' of Sayyidnā Sulaymān (Solomon) عليه السلام.

We need Allah's help even in showing gratitude for His favors. Further, good deeds in themselves are not sufficient. We need good deeds that will be accepted by Allah. It is possible that our good deeds carry no weight in the sight of Allah because of some inherent defect or flaw that only He knows.

(30) [*Al-Qaṣaṣ*, 28:24]
This was the duʿā' of Sayyidnā Mūsā عليه السلام when he reached Madyan to escape from a death sentence from the Pharaoh for accidentally killing an Egyptian. He was hungry, tired, penniless, and a total →

﴿٢٨﴾ رَبَّنَا هَبْ لَنَا مِنْ أَزْوَاجِنَا وَذُرِّيّٰتِنَا قُرَّةَ أَعْيُنٍ وَّاجْعَلْنَا
لِلْمُتَّقِيْنَ إِمَامًا ۝

﴿٢٩﴾ رَبِّ أَوْزِعْنِيْ أَنْ أَشْكُرَ نِعْمَتَكَ الَّتِيْ أَنْعَمْتَ عَلَيَّ وَعَلٰى
وَالِدَيَّ وَأَنْ أَعْمَلَ صَالِحًا تَرْضٰهُ وَأَدْخِلْنِيْ بِرَحْمَتِكَ فِيْ عِبَادِكَ
الصّٰلِحِيْنَ ۝

﴿٣٠﴾ رَبِّ إِنِّيْ لِمَآ أَنْزَلْتَ إِلَيَّ مِنْ خَيْرٍ فَقِيْرٌ ۝

﴿٣١﴾ رَبِّ انْصُرْنِيْ عَلَى الْقَوْمِ الْمُفْسِدِيْنَ ۝

28. Rabbanā hab lanā min azwājinā wa dhurriyyātinā qurrata aʿyunin waj-ʿalnā lil-muttaqīna imāma.

29. Rabbi awziʿnī an ashkura niʿmatakal-latī anʿamta ʿalayya wa ʿalā wālidayya wa an aʿmala ṣāliḥan tarḍāhu wa adkhilnī biraḥmatika fī ʿibādikaṣ-ṣāliḥīn.

30. Rabbi innī limā anzalta ilayya min khayrin faqīr.

31. Rabbin-ṣurnī ʿalal-qawmil-mufsidīn.

---

stranger in this town. Allah سبحانه وتعالى provided for him a home and a spouse and he lived there for a decade.

Anyone in a total state of destitution may derive immense strength from saying this duʿā' while remembering the condition of Sayyidnā Mūsā عليه السلام at that time.

(31) [*Al-ʿAnkabūt,* 29:30]

This was the duʿā' of Sayyidnā Lūṭ (Lot) عليه السلام against a nation of homosexuals who refused to mend their ways and openly challenged him. This duʿā' is pertinent against all mischievous people, including the kind against whom it was originally invoked.

(32) Our Lord, Your mercy and knowledge encompass everything, therefore forgive those who repent and follow Your Way and shield them from the punishment of the Hell.

(33) Our Lord, admit them to the Gardens of Eternity that You have promised to them and to the righteous among their fathers, their wives, and their posterity. You are the Powerful, the Wise. And shield them from (all) ills; and any whom You do shield from ills that Day, on them surely You have bestowed mercy. And that is the supreme achievement, indeed.

(34) And grant for my benefit goodness in my progeny. Truly I have turned to You repentant and truly I am one of those who submit to You.

(35) I have been overpowered so help me.

(36) Our Lord, forgive us and those of our brethren who preceded us in faith, and do not allow any spite to remain in our hearts toward

---

(32-33) [*Ghāfir*, 40:7-9]
This is a duʿā' for the believers made by the angels carrying the Throne (*ʿArsh*) of Allah سبحانه وتعالى.

(34) [*Al-Aḥqāf*, 46:15]

(35) [*Al-Qamar*, 54:10]
This was the duʿā' of Sayyidnā Nūḥ عليه السلام after 950 years of preaching to a stubborn people. This duʿā' is also appropriate when a person feels overwhelmed by great hardships, calamities, serious illness, or enemies.

(36) [*Al-Ḥashr*, 59:10]
This Qur'ānic duʿā' must inform our attitudes regarding our pious predecessors. That includes the Companions and their Followers. Having rancor, malice, or hatred against other believers, especially the pious predecessors, is a serious disease. This duʿā', when made sincerely, can cure it.

﴿٣٢﴾ رَبَّنَا وَسِعْتَ كُلَّ شَيْءٍ رَّحْمَةً وَّعِلْمًا فَاغْفِرْ لِلَّذِيْنَ تَابُوْا
وَاتَّبَعُوْا سَبِيْلَكَ وَقِهِمْ عَذَابَ الْجَحِيْمِ ۝

﴿٣٣﴾ رَبَّنَا وَأَدْخِلْهُمْ جَنّٰتِ عَدْنِ ِالَّتِيْ وَعَدْتَّهُمْ وَمَنْ صَلَحَ
مِنْ اٰبَائِهِمْ وَأَزْوَاجِهِمْ وَذُرِّيّٰتِهِمْ ۚ إِنَّكَ أَنْتَ الْعَزِيْزُ الْحَكِيْمُ ۝
وَقِهِمُ السَّيِّئَاتِ ۚ وَمَنْ تَقِ السَّيِّئَاتِ يَوْمَئِذٍ فَقَدْ رَحِمْتَهٗ ۚ وَذٰلِكَ هُوَ
الْفَوْزُ الْعَظِيْمُ ۝

﴿٣٤﴾ وَأَصْلِحْ لِيْ فِيْ ذُرِّيَّتِيْ ۖ إِنِّيْ تُبْتُ إِلَيْكَ وَإِنِّيْ مِنَ
الْمُسْلِمِيْنَ ۝

﴿٣٥﴾ أَنِّيْ مَغْلُوْبٌ فَانْتَصِرْ ۝

﴿٣٦﴾ رَبَّنَا اغْفِرْ لَنَا وَلِإِخْوَانِنَا الَّذِيْنَ سَبَقُوْنَا بِالْإِيْمَانِ وَلَا

32. Rabbanā wasiʿta kulla shay'in raḥmatan wa ʿilman fagh-fir lilladhīna tābū wat-tabaʿū sabīlaka wa qihim ʿadhābal-jaḥīm.

33. Rabbanā wa adkhilhum jannāti ʿadninil-latī waʿadttahum wa man ṣalaḥa min ābā'ihim wa azwājihim wa dhurriyyātihim. Innaka antal-ʿAzīzul-Ḥakīm(u). Wa qihimus-sayyi'āt(i). Wa man taqis-sayyi'āti yawma'idhin fa qad raḥimtah(ū). Wa dhālika huwal-fawzul-ʿaẓīm.

34. Wa aṣliḥ lī fī dhurriyyatī, innī tubtu ilayka wa innī minal-muslimīn.

35. Annī maghlūbun fan-taṣir.

36. Rabbanagh-fir lanā wa li'ikhwāninal-ladhīna sabaqūnā bil-īmāni wa lā tajʿal fī qulūbinā ghillan lilladhīna āmanū Rabbanā

the believers, our Lord, surely You are Full of Kindness, Most Merciful.

(37) Our Lord, in You we put our trust, and to You do we turn in repentance, and to You is the eventual destiny.

(38) Our Lord, make us not a prey for those who disbelieve, and forgive us, our Lord. Indeed You alone are the Exalted in Might, the Wise.

(39) Our Lord, perfect our light for us, and forgive us. Surely You have power over all things.

(40) O my Lord, forgive me, my parents, all who enter my house in a state of belief, and (all) believing men and believing women.

---

(37) [*Al-Mumtaḥinah*, 60:4]

(38) [*Al-Mumtaḥinah*, 60:5]

(39) [*At-Taḥrīm*, 66:8]
This will be the duʿā' of the Prophet ﷺ and the believers on the Day of Resurrection, when "Allah will not disgrace the Prophet ﷺ and the believers with him" (*At-Taḥrīm*, 66:8). A report from Sayyidnā Abū Umāmah رضي الله عنه gives details of distribution of light in the Hereafter. Keeping it in mind will help us understand the importance of this duʿā'. It states:

> Then you will be transferred from the graves to the Plain of Gathering where there will be different stages and spots to stand or wait. Then there will come a stage when some faces will brighten up and others will be darkened by the Divine command. An intense darkness will prevail and nobody will be able to see anything. Thereafter light will be distributed.

Another report of Ibn Abī Ḥātim, quoted by Ibn Kathīr, narrates on the authority of Sayyidnā ʿAbdullāh ibn Masʿūd رضي الله عنه:

> Each believer will receive the light commensurate with his deeds. Some will have light as large as a mountain, some as a →

تَجْعَلْ فِيْ قُلُوْبِنَا غِلًّا لِّلَّذِيْنَ اٰمَنُوْا رَبَّنَآ إِنَّكَ رَءُوْفٌ رَّحِيْمٌ ۝

﴿٣٧﴾ رَبَّنَا عَلَيْكَ تَوَكَّلْنَا وَإِلَيْكَ أَنَبْنَا وَإِلَيْكَ الْمَصِيْرُ ۝

﴿٣٨﴾ رَبَّنَا لَا تَجْعَلْنَا فِتْنَةً لِّلَّذِيْنَ كَفَرُوْا وَاغْفِرْ لَنَا رَبَّنَآ ۚ إِنَّكَ أَنْتَ الْعَزِيْزُ الْحَكِيْمُ ۝

﴿٣٩﴾ رَبَّنَآ أَتْمِمْ لَنَا نُوْرَنَا وَاغْفِرْ لَنَآ ۚ إِنَّكَ عَلٰى كُلِّ شَيْءٍ قَدِيْرٌ ۝

﴿٤٠﴾ رَبِّ اغْفِرْ لِيْ وَلِوَالِدَيَّ وَلِمَنْ دَخَلَ بَيْتِيَ مُؤْمِنًا وَّلِلْمُؤْمِنِيْنَ وَالْمُؤْمِنَاتِ۔

innaka Ra'ūfun Raḥīm.

37. Rabbanā ʿalayka tawakkalnā wa ilayka anabnā wa ilaykal-maṣīr.

38. Rabbanā lā tajʿalnā fitnatan lilladhīna kafarū wagh-fir lanā rabbanā, innaka antal-ʿAzīzul-Ḥakīm.

39. Rabbanā atmim lanā nūranā wagh-fir lanā, innaka ʿalā kulli shay'in qadīr.

40. Rabbigh-fir lī wa liwālidayya wa liman dakhala baytiya mu'minan wa lil-mu'minīna wal-mu'mināt.

---

date tree, some as big as the height of a man. The least among them will have a light as big as his index finger; it will light at times and extinguish at other times.

The hypocrites and the disbelievers will not receive any light.

The crossing of the Bridge will take place afterwards and those without light will not be able to cross it safely (*Maʿārif al-Qur'ān*).

(40) [*Nūḥ*, 71:28]
This was the duʿā' of Sayyidnā Nūḥ عليه السلام before the Flood.

(41) O Allah, wash away my sins with snow and hail water and purify my heart of sins as a white garment is cleansed of soil. And distance my sins as far away from me as You have distanced the east from the west.

(42) O Allah, bestow on my soul its taqwā. Purify it, for You are the Best of those who can purify it. You alone are its Guardian and Master.

(43) O Allah, we ask You for every good that Your prophet Muḥammad ﷺ asked You for.

(44) O Allah, we beg You for the means of Your forgiveness, for the deeds that will lead to salvation, for safety from all sins, for a share in

---

(41) [ʿĀ'ishah. *Ṣaḥīḥ al-Bukhārī* #5898]
The cold snow and hail water are needed to extinguish the heat and fire inherent in sins. The desired result is that one's heart will be as completely cleansed of sins as a freshly laundered white garment.

It goes without saying that a person making this duʿā' with sincerity and full understanding can never take pleasure from sins. Thus this powerful duʿā' is an antidote against the sin-is-fun pop culture. The person making this duʿā' sees his sins and mistakes as dark spots on a white cloth and the Sharīʿah's injunctions against sins as a blessing not a burden.

(42) [Zayd ibn Arqam. *Ṣaḥīḥ Muslim* #4899]
Taqwā means piety, having fear of displeasing Allah, and Allah consciousness. The Prophet ﷺ made this duʿā' for himself. If he needed taqwā and Allah's help in acquiring it, what does that tell us about our needs in this regard?

This duʿā' is a reminder that we perpetually need purification of the heart, and that this can only come with Allah's help.

(43) [Abū Umāmah al-Bāhilī. *Sunan at-Tirmidhī* #3443]
Sayyidnā Abū Umāmah رضي الله عنه says that he heard many duʿā's from the Prophet ﷺ but could not remember them. So he requested the Prophet ﷺ to teach him an all-inclusive, concise, and comprehensive duʿā'. This beautiful duʿā' was a response to that request. →

﴿٤١﴾ اَللّٰهُمَّ اغْسِلْ خَطَايَايَ بِمَاءِ الثَّلْجِ وَالْبَرَدِ، وَنَقِّ قَلْبِيْ مِنَ الْخَطَايَا كَمَا يُنَقَّى الثَّوْبُ الْأَبْيَضُ مِنَ الدَّنَسِ، وَبَاعِدْ بَيْنِي وَبَيْنَ خَطَايَايَ كَمَا بَاعَدْتَّ بَيْنَ الْمَشْرِقِ وَالْمَغْرِبِ۔

﴿٤٢﴾ اَللّٰهُمَّ اٰتِ نَفْسِيْ تَقْوَاهَا، وَزَكِّهَا أَنْتَ خَيْرُ مَنْ زَكَّاهَا، أَنْتَ وَلِيُّهَا وَمَوْلَاهَا۔

﴿٤٣﴾ اَللّٰهُمَّ إِنَّا نَسْأَلُكَ مِنْ خَيْرِ مَا سَأَلَكَ مِنْهُ نَبِيُّكَ مُحَمَّدٌ صَلَّى اللّٰهُ عَلَيْهِ وَسَلَّمَ۔

﴿٤٤﴾ إِنَّا نَسْأَلُكَ عَزَائِمَ مَغْفِرَتِكَ، وَمُنْجِيَاتِ أَمْرِكَ، وَالسَّلَامَةَ مِنْ كُلِّ إِثْمٍ، وَّالْغَنِيْمَةَ مِنْ كُلِّ بِرٍّ، وَّالْفَوْزَ بِالْجَنَّةِ،

41. Allāhummagh-sil khaṭāyāya bimā'ith-thalji wal-barad(i), wa naqqi qalbī minal-khaṭāyā kamā yunaqqath-thawbul-'abyaḍu minad-danas(i), wa bāʿid baynī wa bayna khaṭāyāya kamā bāʿadtta baynal-mashriqi wal-maghrib.

42. Allāhumma āti nafsī taqwāhā, wa zakkihā anta khayru man zakkāhā, anta Waliyyuhā wa Mawlāhā.

43. Allāhumma innā nas'aluka min khayri mā sa'alaka minhu nabiyyuka Muḥammadun ṣallAllāhu ʿalayhi wa sallam.

44. Innā nas'aluka ʿazā'ima maghfiratik(a), wa munjiyāti amrik(a), was-salāmata min kulli ithm(in), wal-ghanīmata min

---

We seek all the good that he sought. We seek protection against all the evil that he sought protection against. We want to lovingly follow each one of his footsteps, and we hope to find his company in the Hereafter.

every piety, for attainment of Paradise, and for freedom from Hell.

(45) O Allah, I beg You for beneficial knowledge.

(46) O Allah, forgive my sins, both unintentional and intentional.

(47) O Allah, forgive my errors, my ignorance, my excesses in my affairs, and those of my wrongs that you know better than I.

(48) O Allah, forgive my sins that I committed earnestly and those that I committed in jest.

(49) O Allah, the Turner of hearts, keep our hearts turned to your obedience.

(50) O Allah, give me guidance and keep me firm (on the path of guidance).

---

(44) [ʿAbdullāh ibn Masʿūd. *Mustadrak Ḥākim* #157/1957]

(45) [Jābir ibn ʿAbdillāh. *Kanz al-ʿUmmāl* #3787]
Obviously not all knowledge turns out to be beneficial, either because its contents lack usefulness or because we fail to derive benefit from it. This duʿā' is for protection against both of these possibilities. This point is further emphasized in another ḥadīth that includes the duʿā': "O Allah I seek Your protection against knowledge that does not benefit" (Duʿā' 54). See also duʿā' 21.

(46) [ʿUthmān ibn Abil-ʿĀṣ. *Musnad Aḥmad* #17229]
While intentional sins are certainly more serious, those committed unintentionally and carelessly are also nothing to be relaxed about. When on one occasion an exchange between the Companions resulted in the raising of their voices in the presence of the Prophet ﷺ, Allah سبحانه وتعالى warned them that such acts could destroy their good deeds, without their even realizing it (*Al-Ḥujurāt*, 49:1). Similarly a ḥadīth points out that sometimes a person utters a word carelessly and does not think much about it but it earns for him the wrath of Allah until the Day of Judgment.

(47) [Abū Mūsā al-Ashʿarī. *Ṣaḥīḥ al-Bukhārī* #5920] →

وَالنَّجَاةَ مِنَ النَّارِ۔

﴿٤٥﴾ اَللّٰهُمَّ إِنِّيْ أَسْأَلُكَ عِلْمًا نَّافِعًا۔

﴿٤٦﴾ اَللّٰهُمَّ اغْفِرْ لِيْ ذَنْبِيْ خَطَئِيْ وَعَمَدِيْ۔

﴿٤٧﴾ اَللّٰهُمَّ اغْفِرْ لِيْ خَطِيْئَتِيْ وَجَهْلِيْ، وَإِسْرَافِيْ فِيْ أَمْرِيْ، وَمَا أَنْتَ أَعْلَمُ بِهٖ مِنِّيْ۔

﴿٤٨﴾ اَللّٰهُمَّ اغْفِرْ لِيْ جِدِّيْ وَهَزْلِيْ۔

﴿٤٩﴾ اَللّٰهُمَّ مُصَرِّفَ الْقُلُوْبِ صَرِّفْ قُلُوْبَنَا عَلٰى طَاعَتِكَ۔

﴿٥٠﴾ اَللّٰهُمَّ اهْدِنِيْ وَسَدِّدْنِيْ۔

kulli birr(in), wal-fawza bil-janna(ti), wan-najāta minan-Nār.

45. Allāhumma innī as'aluka ʿilman nāfiʿa.

46. Allāhummagh-fir lī dhambī khaṭa'ī wa ʿamadī.

47. Allāhummagh-fir lī khaṭī'atī wa jahlī, wa isrāfī fī amrī, wa mā anta aʿlamu bihī minnī.

48. Allāhummagh-fir lī jiddī wa hazlī.

49. Allāhumma Muṣarrifal-qulūbi ṣarrif qulūbanā ʿalā ṭāʿatik.

50. Allāhummah-dinī wa saddidnī.

---

(48) [Abū Mūsā al-Ashʿarī. *Ṣaḥīḥ Muslim* #4896]

(49) [ʿAbdullāh ibn ʿAmr ibn al-ʿĀṣ. *Ṣaḥīḥ Muslim* #4798]
A person sincerely seeking Allah's help in His obedience will, inshā Allah, find his heart in it.

(51) O Allah, I beg You for guidance, piety, chastity, and contentment.

(52) O Allah, put in order for me my religion, which is my protection. Put in order for me my material world in which lies my livelihood. Put in order for me my life to come to which is my return. Make life a means of increase for me in all that is good, and death a respite for me from every evil.

(53) O Allah, forgive my sins, have mercy on me, give me health and safety, and provide me with sustenance.

(54) O Allah, I seek Your protection from helplessness, lethargy, cowardice, senility, debt, and sinfulness; from the punishment of Fire, the ordeal of Fire, the tribulation of the grave, the punishment in the grave, and the evil tribulations of affluence and of poverty; from the evil tribulation of the Anti-Christ; from the tests of life and death;

---

(50) [ʿAlī ibn Abī Ṭālib. *Ṣaḥīḥ Muslim* #4904]
This duʿā', with the addition of "وَ قِنِي شَرَّ نَفْسِي" is also the short duʿā' of *istikhārah* that one should make when faced with quick decision-making and there is no time for *Istikhārah* ṣalāt.

(51) [ʿAbdullāh ibn Masʿūd. *Ṣaḥīḥ Muslim* #4898]
Making this duʿā' often, with full understanding, may also be a strong antidote to the hedonistic pop culture, which promotes the exactly opposite values.

This duʿā' implies that piety and chastity are linked with contentment and that all three require Divine guidance.

(52) [Abū Hurayrah. *Ṣaḥīḥ Muslim* #4897]
Without the *dīn* (religion) we are totally lost here and in the Hereafter.

(53) [Ṭāriq al-Ashjaʿī. *Ṣaḥīḥ Muslim* #4865]
This duʿā' teaches us that seeking forgiveness for our sins invites Allah's mercy, which in turn assures both protection and provisions. As other aḥādith remind us, anyone looking for a way out of

﴿٥١﴾ اَللّٰهُمَّ إِنِّيْ أَسْأَلُكَ الْهُدٰى وَالتُّقٰى وَالْعَفَافَ وَالْغِنٰى۔

﴿٥٢﴾ اَللّٰهُمَّ أَصْلِحْ لِيْ دِيْنِيَ الَّذِيْ هُوَ عِصْمَةُ أَمْرِيْ، وَأَصْلِحْ لِيْ دُنْيَايَ الَّتِيْ فِيْهَا مَعَاشِيْ، وَأَصْلِحْ لِيْ اٰخِرَتِيَ الَّتِيْ فِيْهَا مَعَادِيْ، وَاجْعَلِ الْحَيٰوةَ زِيَادَةً لِّيْ فِيْ كُلِّ خَيْرٍ، وَّاجْعَلِ الْمَوْتَ رَاحَةً لِّيْ مِنْ كُلِّ شَرٍّ۔

﴿٥٣﴾ اَللّٰهُمَّ اغْفِرْ لِيْ وَارْحَمْنِيْ وَعَافِنِيْ وَارْزُقْنِيْ۔

﴿٥٤﴾ اَللّٰهُمَّ إِنِّيْ أَعُوْذُ بِكَ مِنَ الْعَجْزِ، وَالْكَسَلِ، وَالْجُبْنِ، وَالْهَرَمِ، وَالْمَغْرَمِ، وَالْمَأْثَمِ، وَمِنْ عَذَابِ النَّارِ وَفِتْنَةِ النَّارِ، وَفِتْنَةِ الْقَبْرِ وَعَذَابِ الْقَبْرِ، وَشَرِّ فِتْنَةِ الْغِنٰى، وَشَرِّ فِتْنَةِ الْفَقْرِ، وَمِنْ شَرِّ فِتْنَةِ الْمَسِيْحِ الدَّجَّالِ، وَمِنْ فِتْنَةِ الْمَحْيَا وَالْمَمَاتِ،

51. Allāhumma innī as'alukal-hudā wat-tuqā wal-ʿafāfa wal-ghinā.

52. Allāhumma aṣliḥ lī dīniyal-ladhī huwa ʿiṣmatu amrī, wa aṣliḥ lī dunyāyal-latī fīhā maʿāshī, wa aṣliḥ lī ākhiratiyal-latī fīhā maʿādī, waj-ʿalil-ḥayāta ziyādatan lī fī kulli khayr(in), waj-ʿalil-mawta rāḥatan lī min kulli sharr.

53. Allāhummagh-fir lī war-ḥamnī wa ʿāfinī war-zuqnī.

54. Allāhumma innī aʿūdhu bika minal-ʿajz(i), wal-kasal(i), wal-jubn(i), wal-haram(i), wal-maghram(i), wal-ma'tham(i), wa min ʿadhābin-nāri wa fitnatin-nār(i), wa fitnatil-qabri wa ʿadhābil-qabr(i), wa sharri fitnatil-ghinā, wa sharri fitnatil-faqr(i), wa min sharri fitnatil-masīḥid-dajjāl(i), wa min fitnatil-maḥyā

from the hardness of heart, heedlessness, economic dependence, humiliation, indigence, unbelief, transgression, dissension, and seeking fame and showing off; from deafness, dumbness, lunacy, leprosy, and all painful diseases; from the burden of debt, worries, grief, stinginess, and coercion of the people; from reaching debilitating old age; and from the tribulations of this world, the knowledge that does not benefit, the heart that does not submit to Allah, the soul that is never satiated, and the du'ā' that is not accepted.

---

his or her difficulties should engage in *istighfār* (seeking forgiveness from Allah) profusely.

(54) [Composite: Anas ibn Mālik. *Mustadrak Ḥākim* #144/1944; 'Ā'ishah. *Ṣaḥīḥ al-Bukhārī* #5898; Ibid. *Ṣaḥīḥ al-Bukhārī* #789; Anas ibn Mālik. *Ṣaḥīḥ al-Bukhārī* #2679; Sa'd ibn Abī Waqqāṣ. *Ṣaḥīḥ al-Bukhārī* #2610; Zayd ibn Arqam. *Ṣaḥīḥ Muslim* #4899]

helplessness and lethargy: *'ajz* refers to lack of ability; *kasal* refers to lack of willingness. This is a du'ā' that we always are both able and willing to do good.

One day Prophet Muḥammad ﷺ saw Abū Umāmah رَضِيَ اللهُ عَنْهُ sitting in the masjid when it was not time for ṣalāt. Upon inquiry he said, "Worries and debt have afflicted me." Prophet Muḥammad ﷺ replied, "Shall I not teach you words that when you say them Allah will drive away your worries and discharge your debt?" Then he taught him to say the following du'ā' every morning and evening:

اَللّٰهُمَّ إِنِّيْ أَعُوْذُ بِكَ مِنَ الْهَمِّ وَالْحَزَنِ وَأَعُوْذُ بِكَ مِنَ الْعَجْزِ وَالْكَسَلِ وَأَعُوْذُ بِكَ مِنَ الْجُبْنِ وَالْبُخْلِ وَأَعُوْذُ بِكَ مِنْ غَلَبَةِ الدَّيْنِ وَقَهْرِ الرِّجَالِ.

Abū Umāmah رَضِيَ اللهُ عَنْهُ reports that he did as told and Allah سُبْحَانَهُ وَتَعَالَىٰ removed his worries and his debt was paid.

وَمِنَ الْقَسْوَةِ، وَالْغَفْلَةِ، وَالْعَيْلَةِ، وَالذِّلَّةِ، وَالْمَسْكَنَةِ، وَالْكُفْرِ، وَالْفُسُوْقِ، وَالشِّقَاقِ، وَالسُّمْعَةِ وَالرِّيَاءِ، وَمِنَ الصَّمَمِ وَالْبَكَمِ، وَالْجُنُوْنِ وَالْجُذَامِ وَسَيِّئِ الْأَسْقَامِ، وَضَلَعِ الدَّيْنِ، وَمِنَ الْهَمِّ وَالْحَزَنِ، وَالْبُخْلِ، وَغَلَبَةِ الرِّجَالِ، وَمِنْ أَنْ أُرَدَّ إِلٰى أَرْذَلِ الْعُمُرِ، وَفِتْنَةِ الدُّنْيَا، وَمِنْ عِلْمٍ لَّا يَنْفَعُ، وَمِنْ قَلْبٍ لَّا يَخْشَعُ، وَمِنْ نَّفْسٍ لَّا تَشْبَعُ، وَمِنْ دَعْوَةٍ لَّا يُسْتَجَابُ لَهَا۔

wal-mamāt(i), wa minal-qaswa(ti), wal-ghafla(ti), wal-ʿayla(ti), wadh-dhilla(ti), wal-maskana(ti), wal-kufr(i), wal-fusūq(i), wash-shiqāq(i), was-sumʿati war-riyā'(i), wa minaṣ-ṣamami wal-bakam(i), wal-junūni wal-judhāmi wa sayyi'il-'asqām(i), wa ḍalaʿid-dayn(i), wa minal-hammi wal-ḥazan(i), wal-bukhl(i), wa ghalabatir-rijāl(i), wa min an uradda ilā ardhalil-ʿumur(i), wa fitnatid-dunyā, wa min ʿilmin lā yanfaʿ(u), wa min qalbin lā yakhshaʿ(u), wa min nafsin lā tashbaʿ(u), wa min daʿwatin lā yustajābu lahā.

SUNDAY

In the Name of Allah, the Most Compassionate, the Most Merciful

(55) My Lord, help me and do not help my enemies against me. Aid me to victory and do not aid my enemies against me. Use Your plan for me and do not use Your plan against me. Guide me and make it easy for me to follow the guidance. Aid me to victory against those who act wrongfully toward me. My Lord, make me one who is most grateful to You, who constantly remembers You, who is full of fear toward You, who is fully obedient to You, who is humble before You, who is earnest in supplication to You, and who always turns to You. My Lord, accept my repentance, wash away my sin, grant my supplication, establish my evidence, make my speech upright, guide my heart, and throw out malice from my bosom.

(56) O Allah, forgive us. Have mercy on us. Be pleased with us. Accept from us. Admit us to Paradise and protect us from Hell. And set right all our affairs.

(57) O Allah, join our hearts, mend our relationships, and guide us to the paths of peace. Bring us out of darkness into light and keep us away from manifest and concealed obscenities. Bless us in our

---

(55) [ʿAbdullāh ibn ʿAbbās. *Sunan at-Tirmidhī* #3474]
do not use Your plan against me: This may happen with a person who is engaged in worship to Allah but his worship is rejected because of its lack of sincerity while he thinks it is accepted (*Tuḥfah al-Aḥwadhī*).
establish my evidence: against Your enemies in this world and the Hereafter and in front of the angels in the grave (*Tuḥfah al-Aḥwadhī*).

(56) [Abū Umāmah al-Bāhilī. *Sunan Ibn Mājah* #3826]

(57) [ʿAbdullāh ibn Masʿūd. *Sunan Abī Dāwūd* #825]
According to Sayyidnā ʿAbdullāh ibn Masʿūd رضي الله عنه, Prophet

بِسْمِ اللهِ الرَّحْمَنِ الرَّحِيمِ

﴿٥٥﴾ رَبِّ أَعِنِّيْ وَلَا تُعِنْ عَلَيَّ، وَانْصُرْنِيْ وَلَا تَنْصُرْ عَلَيَّ، وَامْكُرْ لِيْ وَلَا تَمْكُرْ عَلَيَّ، وَاهْدِنِيْ وَيَسِّرْ لِيَ الْهُدٰى، وَانْصُرْنِيْ عَلٰى مَنْ بَغٰى عَلَيَّ. رَبِّ اجْعَلْنِيْ لَكَ شَكَّارًا، لَّكَ ذَكَّارًا، لَّكَ رَهَّابًا، لَّكَ مِطْوَاعًا، لَّكَ مُخْبِتًا، إِلَيْكَ أَوَّاهًا مُّنِيْبًا. رَبِّ تَقَبَّلْ تَوْبَتِيْ، وَاغْسِلْ حَوْبَتِيْ، وَأَجِبْ دَعْوَتِيْ، وَثَبِّتْ حُجَّتِيْ، وَسَدِّدْ لِسَانِيْ، وَاهْدِ قَلْبِيْ، وَاسْلُلْ سَخِيْمَةَ صَدْرِيْ۔

﴿٥٦﴾ اَللّٰهُمَّ اغْفِرْ لَنَا، وَارْحَمْنَا، وَارْضَ عَنَّا، وَتَقَبَّلْ مِنَّا، وَأَدْخِلْنَا الْجَنَّةَ، وَنَجِّنَا مِنَ النَّارِ، وَأَصْلِحْ لَنَا شَأْنَنَا كُلَّهُ۔

﴿٥٧﴾ اَللّٰهُمَّ أَلِّفْ بَيْنَ قُلُوْبِنَا، وَأَصْلِحْ ذَاتَ بَيْنِنَا، وَاهْدِنَا سُبُلَ السَّلَامِ، وَنَجِّنَا مِنَ الظُّلُمَاتِ إِلَى النُّوْرِ، وَجَنِّبْنَا الْفَوَاحِشَ مَا

55. Rabbi a'innī wa lā tu'in 'alayy(a), wan-ṣurnī wa lā tanṣur 'alayy(a), wam-kur lī wa lā tamkur 'alayy(a), wah-dinī wa yassir liyal-hudā, wan-ṣurnī 'alā mam baghā 'alayy(a). Rabbij-'alnī laka shakkāra(n), laka dhakkāra(n), laka rahhāba(n), laka miṭwā'a(n), laka mukhbita(n), ilayka awwāham munība(n). Rabbi taqabbal tawbatī, wagh-sil ḥawbatī, wa ajib da'watī, wa thabbit ḥujjatī, wa saddid lisānī, wah-di qalbī, was-lul sakhīmata ṣadrī.

56. Allāhummagh-fir lanā, war-ḥamnā, war-ḍa 'annā, wa taqabbal minnā, wa adkhilnal-Janna(ta), wa najjinā minan-Nār(i), wa aṣliḥ lanā sha'nanā kullah.

57. Allāhumma allif bayna qulūbinā, wa aṣliḥ dhāta bayninā,

ears, our eyes, our hearts, our spouses, and our offspring. Accept our repentance. Indeed, You are the Most Forgiving, the Most Merciful. Make us grateful for Your blessings, so we receive them with due praise. And perfect them for us.

(58) O Allah, I beg You for steadfastness in religious affairs. I beg You for determination to follow the guidance. I beg You to enable me to show gratitude for Your bounties and to worship You with the best devotion. I beg You for a truthful tongue, a sound heart, and an upright character. I seek Your protection from the evil of all that only You are aware of. I beg You for the good that only You know. And I seek forgiveness from You for what You know (of my sins). Surely, You are the All-Knowing of the hidden.

(59) O Allah, forgive what I did earlier and what I did later; what I did secretly and what I did publicly; and whatever you know more than I.

Muḥammad ﷺ used to teach this duʿā' to his Companions for saying in the ṣalāt before the ending salām.

(58) [Shaddād ibn 'Aws. *Sunan at-Tirmidhī* #3329; Ibid. *Mustadrak Ḥākim* #72/1872]

sound heart: one that is protected from corrupted beliefs and evil desires (*Tuḥfah al-Aḥwadhī*).

Prophet Muḥammad ﷺ used to say this duʿā' in the last sitting of the fourth rakʿah before the ending salām. It is reported that after teaching this duʿā' to Sayyidnā Shaddād ibn Aws رضي الله عنه, Prophet Muḥammad ﷺ said: "When you see people collecting gold and silver as treasures, consider this duʿā' as your treasure."

(59) [ʿAbdullāh ibn ʿUmar. *Mustadrak Ḥākim* #134/1934]

According to Sayyidnā ʿAlī رضي الله عنه Prophet Muḥammad ﷺ used to say this duʿā' after finishing the ṣalāt.

ظَهَرَ مِنْهَا وَمَا بَطَنَ، وَبَارِكْ لَنَا فِيْ أَسْمَاعِنَا وَأَبْصَارِنَا وَقُلُوْبِنَا وَأَزْوَاجِنَا وَذُرِّيَّاتِنَا، وَتُبْ عَلَيْنَا، إِنَّكَ أَنْتَ التَّوَّابُ الرَّحِيْمُ، وَاجْعَلْنَا شَاكِرِيْنَ لِنِعْمَتِكَ، مُثْنِيْنَ بِهَا قَابِلِيْهَا، وَأَتِمَّهَا عَلَيْنَا۔

﴿٥٨﴾ اَللّٰهُمَّ إِنِّيْ أَسْأَلُكَ الثَّبَاتَ فِي الْأَمْرِ، وَأَسْأَلُكَ عَزِيْمَةَ الرُّشْدِ، وَأَسْأَلُكَ شُكْرَ نِعْمَتِكَ، وَحُسْنَ عِبَادَتِكَ، وَأَسْأَلُكَ لِسَانًا صَادِقًا، وَّقَلْبًا سَلِيْمًا، وَّخُلُقًا مُّسْتَقِيْمًا، وَّأَعُوْذُ بِكَ مِنْ شَرِّ مَا تَعْلَمُ، وَأَسْأَلُكَ مِنْ خَيْرِ مَا تَعْلَمُ، وَأَسْتَغْفِرُكَ مِمَّا تَعْلَمُ، إِنَّكَ أَنْتَ عَلَّامُ الْغُيُوْبِ۔

﴿٥٩﴾ اَللّٰهُمَّ اغْفِرْ لِيْ مَا قَدَّمْتُ وَمَا أَخَّرْتُ، وَمَا أَسْرَرْتُ وَمَا أَعْلَنْتُ، وَمَا أَنْتَ أَعْلَمُ بِهٖ مِنِّيْ۔

wah-dinā subulas-salām(i), wa najjinā minaẓ-ẓulumāti ilan-nūr(i), wa jannibnal-fawāḥisha mā ẓahara minhā wa mā baṭan(a), wa bārik lanā fī asmāʿinā wa abṣārinā wa qulūbinā wa azwājinā wa dhurriyyātinā, wa tub ʿalaynā, innaka antat-Tawwābur-Raḥīm(u), waj-ʿalnā shākirīna liniʿmatik(a), muthnīna bihā qābilīhā, wa atimmahā ʿalaynā.

58. Allāhumma innī as'alukath-thabāta fil-'amr(i), wa as'aluka ʿazīmatar-rushd(i), wa as'aluka shukra niʿmatik(a), wa ḥusna ʿibādatik(a), wa as'aluka lisānan ṣādiqa(n), wa qalban salīma(n), wa khuluqam mustaqīma(n), wa aʿūdhu bika min sharri mā taʿlam(u), wa as'aluka min khayri mā taʿlam(u), wa astaghfiruka mimmā taʿlam(u), innaka anta ʿAllāmul-ghuyūb.

59. Allāhummagh-fir lī mā qaddamtu wa mā akh-khart(u), wa mā asrartu wa mā aʿlant(u), wa mā Anta aʿlamu bihī minnī.

(60) O Allah, grant us that fear of You which You may drive between us and our disobedience to You. Grant us that obedience to You with which You may lead us to Paradise. Give us that faith with which You will lighten the worldly hardships for us. Grant us the use of our ears, eyes, and other faculties as long as You keep us alive. And make these our survivors. Make our revenge target (only) those who oppress us. Help us to victory over the one who displays enmity to us. Do not let our misfortunes hit our religion. Do not make this world our greatest concern and the sum total of our knowledge. And do not impose over us one who shows no mercy to us.

(61) O Allah, increase (Your grace) for us and do not curtail it; give us honor and do not humiliate us; give us and do not deprive us; favor us and do not favor others over us; make us be pleased with You and be pleased with us.

---

(60) [ʿAbdullāh ibn ʿUmar. *Riyāḍ aṣ-Ṣāliḥīn* #834; *Sunan at-Tirmidhī* #3434]
make these our survivors: In other words may we enjoy all our faculties until we breathe our last.
Make our revenge target (only) those who oppress us: Make our revenge be limited solely to those who oppress us, and don't make us among those who transgress in seeking their revenge and attack the innocents as well, as was customary in the Jāhiliyyah period, lest we end up being wrongdoers after having been wronged (*Tuḥfah al-Aḥwadhī*).

This distinguishes revenge in Islam, which is always concerned with justice, from that in Jāhiliyyah societies, ancient and modern, which are totally devoid of this concern.
Do not let our misfortunes hit our religion: Misfortunes in religion include false beliefs, consumption of ḥarām, and disruption of worship (*Tuḥfah al-Aḥwadhī*).
Do not make this world our greatest concern: Do not make our supreme goal and concern the obtaining of wealth and personal glory; rather make our major concern to be working for the Hereafter. This also recognizes that there are a few concerns regarding livelihood that one cannot do without and that are permitted, recommended, or even obligatory (*Tuḥfah al-Aḥwadhī*). →

﴿٦٠﴾ اَللّٰهُمَّ اقْسِمْ لَنَا مِنْ خَشْيَتِكَ مَا تَحُوْلُ بِهٖ بَيْنَنَا وَبَيْنَ
مَعَاصِيْكَ، وَمِنْ طَاعَتِكَ مَا تُبَلِّغُنَا بِهٖ جَنَّتَكَ، وَمِنَ الْيَقِيْنِ
مَا تُهَوِّنُ بِهٖ عَلَيْنَا مَصَائِبَ الدُّنْيَا، وَمَتِّعْنَا بِأَسْمَاعِنَا وَأَبْصَارِنَا
وَقُوَّاتِنَا مَا أَحْيَيْتَنَا، وَاجْعَلْهُ الْوَارِثَ مِنَّا، وَاجْعَلْ ثَأْرَنَا عَلٰى
مَنْ ظَلَمَنَا، وَانْصُرْنَا عَلٰى مَنْ عَادَانَا، وَلَا تَجْعَلْ مُصِيْبَتَنَا فِيْ
دِيْنِنَا، وَلَا تَجْعَلِ الدُّنْيَا أَكْبَرَ هَمِّنَا، وَلَا مَبْلَغَ عِلْمِنَا، وَلَا تُسَلِّطْ
عَلَيْنَا مَنْ لَّا يَرْحَمُنَا۔

﴿٦١﴾ اَللّٰهُمَّ زِدْنَا وَلَا تَنْقُصْنَا، وَأَكْرِمْنَا وَلَا تُهِنَّا، وَأَعْطِنَا وَلَا
تَحْرِمْنَا، وَاٰثِرْنَا وَلَا تُؤْثِرْ عَلَيْنَا، وَأَرْضِنَا وَارْضَ عَنَّا۔

60. Allāhummaq-sim lanā min khashyatika mā taḥūlu bihī baynanā wa bayna maʿāṣīk(a), wa min ṭāʿatika mā tuballighunā bihī jannatak(a), wa minal-yaqīni mā tuhawwinu bihī ʿalaynā maṣā'ibad-dunyā, wa mattiʿnā bi'asmāʿinā wa abṣārinā wa quwwātinā mā aḥyaytanā, waj-ʿalhul-wāritha minnā, waj-ʿal tha'ranā ʿalā man ẓalamanā, wan-ṣurnā ʿalā man ʿādānā, wa lā tajʿal muṣībatanā fī dīninā, wa lā tajʿalid-dunyā akbara hamminā, wa lā mablagha ʿilminā, wa lā tusalliṭ ʿalaynā man lā yarḥamunā.

61. Allāhumma zidnā wa lā tanquṣnā, wa akrimnā wa lā tuhinnā, wa aʿṭinā wa lā taḥrimnā, wa āthirnā wa lā tu'thir ʿalaynā, wa arḍinā war-ḍa ʿannā.

It was a practice of Prophet Muḥammad ﷺ to end his sittings with the Companions with this duʿā'.

(61) [ʿUmar ibn al-Khaṭṭāb. *Sunan at-Tirmidhī* #3097]
The text of this duʿā' does not provide any object for *zidnā* and

(62) O Allah, inspire me with the right guidance for me.

(63) O Allah, protect me from the evil of my self and give me the determination to do what is most right in my affairs.

(64) O Allah, I beg You for protection in this world and in the Hereafter.

(65) O Allah, I beg You to enable me to do good deeds, to shun bad deeds, and to love the poor. (I beg You to) forgive me and have mercy on me. And when You plan tribulations for a people cause me to die without being put to trial. I beg for Your love, and the love of the one who loves You, and the love of such deeds that will bring me closer to Your love.

---

tanquṣnā (increase and curtail). This is for generalization; we seek increase in every good and decrease in none.

(62) [ʿImrān ibn Ḥuṣayn. *Sunan at-Tirmidhī* #3405]
This very profound duʿā' demands reflection. A person who is sincerely seeking guidance from Allah ﷻ has taken the first and the most important step in getting it, since Allah ﷻ is the source of all guidance. Whenever we are faced with a decision, we should resort to this duʿā'. Additionally we can suggest this to a non-Muslim who is in search of the true religion. If he or she sincerely makes this duʿā' Allah ﷻ will open his or her heart to Islam, as has been the experience of numerous new Muslims.

(63) [ʿImrān ibn Ḥuṣayn. *Musnad Aḥmad* #19141]
There are two major sources of corruption that lead one astray. One is external and the other is internal. The external is the Shayṭān and his followers among the jinns and the humans. The internal is our own ego and our lusts and desires. We should seek Allah's protection against both. This duʿā' is for the latter.

(64) [Abū Hurayrah. *Kanz al-ʿUmmāl* #3201]
ʿĀfiyah means health, safety, and protection from all harmful objects. Prophet Muḥammad ﷺ said that the most beloved duʿā' in the sight of Allah is the one for *ʿāfiyah* (*Sunan at-Tirmidhī*). →

﴿٦٢﴾ اَللّٰهُمَّ أَلْهِمْنِي رُشْدِيْ۔

﴿٦٣﴾ اَللّٰهُمَّ قِنِيْ شَرَّ نَفْسِيْ وَاعْزِمْ لِيْ عَلٰى أَرْشَدِ أَمْرِيْ۔

﴿٦٤﴾ اَللّٰهُمَّ إِنِّيْ أَسْأَلُكَ الْعَافِيَةَ فِي الدُّنْيَا وَالْاٰخِرَةِ۔

﴿٦٥﴾ اَللّٰهُمَّ إِنِّيْ أَسْأَلُكَ فِعْلَ الْخَيْرَاتِ، وَتَرْكَ الْمُنْكَرَاتِ، وَحُبَّ الْمَسَاكِيْنِ، وَأَنْ تَغْفِرَ لِيْ وَتَرْحَمَنِيْ، وَإِذَا أَرَدْتَّ بِقَوْمٍ فِتْنَةً فَتَوَفَّنِيْ غَيْرَ مَفْتُوْنٍ، وَّأَسْأَلُكَ حُبَّكَ وَحُبَّ مَنْ يُّحِبُّكَ، وَحُبَّ عَمَلٍ يُّقَرِّبُنِيْ إِلٰى حُبِّكَ۔

62. Allāhumma alhimnī rushdī.

63. Allāhumma qinī sharra nafsī waʿ-zim lī ʿalā arshadi amrī.

64. Allāhumma innī as'alukal-ʿāfiyata fid-dunyā wal-ākhirah.

65. Allāhumma innī as'aluka fiʿlal-khayrāt(i), wa tarkal-munkarāt(i), wa ḥubbal-masākīn(i), wa an taghfira lī wa tarḥamanī, wa idhā aradtta biqawmin fitnatan fa tawaffanī ghayra maftūn(in), wa as'aluka ḥubbaka wa ḥubba man yuḥibbuk(a), wa ḥubba ʿamalin yuqarribunī ilā ḥubbik.

---

(65) [Muʿādh ibn Jabal. *Sunan at-Tirmidhī* #3159; Thawbān ibn Bajdad. *Mustadrak Ḥākim* #132/1932]

Your love: Here it could mean both my love for You and Your love for me (*Tuḥfah al-Aḥwadhī*).

This duʿā' was made by Prophet Muḥammad ﷺ at a special occasion when Allah ﷻ invited him to make a duʿā'. The details reported in *Sunan at-Tirmidhī* are as follows:

Once the Prophet ﷺ was overtaken by sleep in the middle of his *Tahajjud* ṣalāt (nightly prayer) whereby he experienced a vision in which he had a conversation with Allah ﷻ. Allah ﷻ asked

(66) O Allah, make Your love dearer to me than myself, my family, and cold water.

(67) O Allah, provide me with Your love and the love of those whose love will benefit me with You. O Allah, whatever you provided to me of the things that I love, make them a source of strength for me in pursuing what You love. O Allah, and whatever you kept away from me of the things that I crave, make their absence free up time that I can devote to whatever You love.

(68) O Turner of hearts, keep my heart steadfast on Your religion.

(69) O Allah, I beg You for the faith that will not be shaken, the bless-

---

him, what were the high-ranking angels discussing. He responded that he did not know. This happened three times. After that, the Prophet ﷺ in his vision felt His Palm on his chest and shoulders and suddenly everything became clear to him. Allah سبحانه وتعالى repeated the question and this time the Prophet ﷺ said that they were discussing the actions that expiate sins. Allah سبحانه وتعالى asked, "What are they?" He replied, "Walking (to the masjid) to attend congregational ṣalāt, sitting in the masjid after the ṣalāt, and perfecting the wuḍū' in difficult conditions." Allah سبحانه وتعالى asked, "What else?" The Prophet ﷺ said, "Feeding others, talking gently, and praying at night when the people are asleep." Then, Allah سبحانه وتعالى said, "Ask." And in response, the Prophet ﷺ made this duʿā'. After narrating this incident, the Prophet ﷺ told his Companions, "This (vision) is certainly true, so remember it (i.e. this vision and all its lessons) and teach it."

(66) [Abū ad-Dardā'. *Sunan at-Tirmidhī* #3412]
Refreshing cold water on a hot summer day in the desert is one of the great comforts of this world. Our duʿā' is that our love for Allah سبحانه وتعالى should be greater than our love for this comfort.

(67) [ʿAbdullāh ibn Yazīd al-Khaṭamī al-Anṣārī. *Sunan at-Tirmidhī* #3413]
Of the things of this world that we love, there will be some that we get and others that we cannot. This wonderful duʿā' can set our perspective right so neither our achievements nor our failures in →

﴿٦٦﴾ اَللّٰهُمَّ اجْعَلْ حُبَّكَ أَحَبَّ إِلَيَّ مِنْ نَفْسِيْ وَأَهْلِيْ وَمِنَ الْمَاءِ الْبَارِدِ۔

﴿٦٧﴾ اَللّٰهُمَّ ارْزُقْنِيْ حُبَّكَ وَحُبَّ مَنْ يَّنْفَعُنِيْ حُبُّهٗ عِنْدَكَ. اَللّٰهُمَّ مَا رَزَقْتَنِيْ مِمَّا أُحِبُّ فَاجْعَلْهُ قُوَّةً لِّيْ فِيْمَا تُحِبُّ. اَللّٰهُمَّ وَمَا زَوَيْتَ عَنِّيْ مِمَّا أُحِبُّ فَاجْعَلْهُ فَرَاغًا لِّيْ فِيْمَا تُحِبُّ۔

﴿٦٨﴾ يَا مُقَلِّبَ الْقُلُوْبِ ثَبِّتْ قَلْبِيْ عَلٰى دِيْنِكَ۔

﴿٦٩﴾ اَللّٰهُمَّ إِنِّيْ أَسْأَلُكَ إِيْمَانًا لَّا يَرْتَدُّ وَنَعِيْمًا لَّا يَنْفَدُ

66. Allāhummaj-ʿal ḥubbaka aḥabba ilayya min nafsī wa ahlī wa minal-mā'il-bārid.

67. Allāhummar-zuqnī ḥubbaka wa ḥubba man yanfaʿunī ḥubbuhū ʿindak(a). Allāhumma mā razaqtanī mimmā uḥibbu faj-ʿalhu quwwatan lī fīmā tuḥibb(u). Allāhumma wa mā zawayta ʿannī mimmā uḥibbu faj-ʿalhu farāghan lī fīmā tuḥibb.

68. Yā Muqallibal-qulūbi thabbit qalbī ʿalā dīnik.

69. Allāhumma innī as'aluka īmānan lā yartaddu wa naʿīman

---

getting the desired things distract us from the love of Allah ﷻ. By subordinating all our loves to the love of Allah ﷻ, we achieve inner peace and contentment.

(68) [Anas ibn Mālik. *Sunan at-Tirmidhī* #2066]
We should always be alert to the horrible possibility that our hearts turn away from the religion under the influence of Shayṭān or our own inclinations towards evil. That is why we seek Allah's help against that. It is reported by Um Salamah رضي الله عنها that the Prophet ﷺ used to make this duʿā' very frequently.

ings that will not end, and the company of our Prophet Muḥammad ﷺ in the highest section of the eternal Paradise.

(70) O Allah, I ask You for sound health with faith, faith with good manners, success here followed by success in the Hereafter, mercy from You, health and safety, and Your forgiveness and pleasure.

(71) O Allah, cause me to benefit from what You have taught me and teach me what will benefit me.

(72) O Allah, with Your knowledge of the unseen, and Your absolute power over the creations, let me live in this world as long as You know my living is good for me, and give me death when You know death is better for me. I beg You for Your fear in secret and in public and sincere talk in times of joy and anger. I beg You for endless blessings and perpetual comfort of my eyes. I beg You that I become pleased with fate. (I beg You) for a cool, comfortable life after

---

(69) [ʿAbdullāh ibn Masʿūd. *Kanz al-ʿUmmāl* #5088; Ibid. *Mustadrak Ḥākim* #128/1928]

This duʿā' has a very moving background. One night the Prophet ﷺ was walking with his Companions when they passed by ʿAbdullāh ibn Masʿūd ؓ who was reciting the Qur'ān in his nafl ṣalāt. As they stopped to listen, the Prophet ﷺ commented that ʿAbdullāh recited the Qur'ān so tenderly as it was revealed. As ʿAbdullāh finished his ṣalāt and was making supplications, the Prophet ﷺ exclaimed twice: "Ask and you will be given!" Sayyidnā ʿAbdullāh ibn Masʿūd ؓ was later asked what duʿā' he was making at that time. He replied with this one.

(70) [Abū Hurayrah. *Mustadrak Ḥākim* #119/1919]

(71) [Anas ibn Mālik. *Mustadrak Ḥākim* #79/1879]

ʿIlm (knowledge) gets value from possibilities of action. To benefit from ʿilm is to act according to it. Further, truly beneficial knowledge is one that benefits one in the Hereafter. The definition also includes the knowledge that benefits one in this world and which in turn leads to the former (*Tuḥfah al-Aḥwadhī*).

وَمُرَافَقَةَ نَبِيِّنَا مُحَمَّدٍ صَلَّى اللهُ عَلَيْهِ وَسَلَّمَ فِيْ أَعْلَىٰ دَرَجَةِ الْجَنَّةِ جَنَّةِ الْخُلْدِ۔

﴿٧٠﴾ اَللّٰهُمَّ إِنِّيْ أَسْأَلُكَ صِحَّةً فِيْ إِيْمَانٍ، وَّإِيْمَانًا فِيْ حُسْنِ خُلُقٍ، وَّنَجَاحًا يَّتْبَعُهٗ فَلَاحٌ، وَّرَحْمَةً مِّنْكَ وَعَافِيَةً، وَّمَغْفِرَةً مِّنْكَ وَرِضْوَانًا۔

﴿٧١﴾ اَللّٰهُمَّ انْفَعْنِيْ بِمَا عَلَّمْتَنِيْ وَعَلِّمْنِيْ مَا يَنْفَعُنِيْ۔

﴿٧٢﴾ اَللّٰهُمَّ بِعِلْمِكَ الْغَيْبَ وَقُدْرَتِكَ عَلَى الْخَلْقِ أَحْيِنِيْ مَا عَلِمْتَ الْحَيٰوةَ خَيْرًا لِّيْ، وَتَوَفَّنِيْ إِذَا عَلِمْتَ الْوَفَاةَ خَيْرًا لِّيْ. وَأَسْأَلُكَ خَشْيَتَكَ فِي الْغَيْبِ وَالشَّهَادَةِ، وَكَلِمَةَ الْإِخْلَاصِ فِي الرِّضٰى وَالْغَضَبِ. وَأَسْأَلُكَ نَعِيْمًا لَّا يَنْفَدُ وَقُرَّةَ عَيْنٍ لَّا تَنْقَطِعُ، وَأَسْأَلُكَ الرِّضَاءَ بِالْقَضَاءِ، وَبَرْدَ الْعَيْشِ بَعْدَ الْمَوْتِ،

lā yanfadu wa murāfaqata nabiyyinā Muḥammadin ṣallAllāhu ʿalayhi wa sallama fī aʿlā darajatil-Jannati Jannatil-khuld.

70. Allāhumma innī as'aluka ṣiḥḥatan fī īmān(in), wa īmānan fī ḥusni khuluq(in), wa najāḥan yatbaʿuhū falāḥ(un), wa raḥmatam minka wa ʿāfiya(tan), wa maghfiratam minka wa riḍwāna.

71. Allāhumman-faʿnī bimā ʿallamtanī wa ʿallimnī mā yanfaʿunī.

72. Allāhumma biʿilmikal-ghayba wa qudratika ʿalal-khalqi aḥyinī mā ʿalimtal-ḥayāta khayran lī, wa tawaffanī idhā ʿalimtal-wafāta khayran lī. Wa as'aluka khashyataka fil-ghaybi wash-shahāda(ti), wa kalimatal-'ikhlāṣi fir-riḍā wal-ghaḍab(i). Wa as'aluka naʿīman

death; the delight of the sight of Your Countenance (after death); and the longing to meet You (before death). I seek Your protection against deeply hurting ordeals and tribulations that lead one astray. O Allah, adorn us with the beauty of faith and make us properly guided guides for other people.

(73) O Allah, I beg You for all the good, immediate and in the future; that of which I know and that of which I know not.

(74) O Allah, I beg You for every good that Your servant and prophet ﷺ asked You for. O Allah, I beg You for Paradise and all words or actions that may bring me closer to it. I beg You that You make every decree of fate good for me. And I beg You that whatever decisions You make for me, make their end good.

(75) O Allah, make the end of all our affairs the best and save us

---

(72) [ʿAmmār ibn Yāsir. *Sunan an-Nasāʾī* #1289]
joy and anger: This refers to both us and the people we are dealing with. Their joy or anger with us should not make us deviate from telling the truth any more than our joy or anger with them should.
adorn us: Beauty of the soul is superior to that of the body. Those who get it (though *īmān*) will also get the beauty of the body in the Hereafter.
properly guided guides: Those who know and follow the path of guidance themselves in addition to calling others to it.

Prophet Muḥammad ﷺ used to say this duʿā' in ṣalāt after *at-taḥiyyāt*.

(73) [ʿĀ'ishah. *Sunan Ibn Mājah* #3836]

(74) [ʿĀ'ishah. *Sunan Ibn Mājah* #3836; Ibid. *Mustadrak Ḥākim* #114/1914]
A famous ḥadīth says that everything that Allah سبحانه وتعالى brings about is good for the believer. If it is a blessing he is thankful for it and if it is a hardship he shows patience in facing it. In both cases the end result is good for him. Is there a contradiction between that ḥadīth and this duʿā'? Not at all. The ḥadīth describes the attitude of a true believer. The duʿā' here is that we develop that attitude

وَلَذَّةَ النَّظَرِ إِلىٰ وَجْهِكَ، وَالشَّوْقَ إِلىٰ لِقَائِكَ، وَأَعُوْذُ بِكَ مِنْ ضَرَّاءَ مُضِرَّةٍ وَّفِتْنَةٍ مُّضِلَّةٍ. اَللّٰهُمَّ زَيِّنَّا بِزِيْنَةِ الْإِيْمَانِ وَاجْعَلْنَا هُدَاةً مُّهْتَدِيْنَ۔

﴿٧٣﴾ اَللّٰهُمَّ إِنِّيْ أَسْأَلُكَ مِنَ الْخَيْرِ كُلِّهٖ، عَاجِلِهٖ وَاٰجِلِهٖ، مَا عَلِمْتُ مِنْهُ وَمَا لَمْ أَعْلَمْ۔

﴿٧٤﴾ اَللّٰهُمَّ إِنِّيْ أَسْأَلُكَ مِنْ خَيْرِ مَا سَأَلَكَ عَبْدُكَ وَنَبِيُّكَ. اَللّٰهُمَّ إِنِّيْ أَسْأَلُكَ الْجَنَّةَ وَمَا قَرَّبَ إِلَيْهَا مِنْ قَوْلٍ أَوْ عَمَلٍ، وَّأَسْأَلُكَ أَنْ تَجْعَلَ كُلَّ قَضَاءٍ قَضَيْتَهٗ لِيْ خَيْرًا، وَّأَسْأَلُكَ مَا قَضَيْتَ لِيْ مِنْ أَمْرٍ أَنْ تَجْعَلَ عَاقِبَتَهٗ رُشْدًا۔

﴿٧٥﴾ اَللّٰهُمَّ أَحْسِنْ عَاقِبَتَنَا فِي الْأُمُوْرِ كُلِّهَا، وَأَجِرْنَا مِنْ

lā yanfadu wa qurrata ʿaynin lā tanqaṭiʿ(u), wa as'alukar-riḍā'a bil-qaḍā'(i), wa bardal-ʿayshi baʿdal-mawt(i), wa ladh-dhatan-naẓari ilā wajhik(a), wash-shawqa ilā liqā'ik(a), wa aʿūdhu bika min ḍarrā'a muḍirratin wa fitnatim muḍilla(tin). Allāhumma zayyinnā bizīnatil-īmāni waj-ʿalnā hudātam muhtadīn.

73. Allāhumma innī as'aluka minal-khayri kullih(ī), ʿājilihī wa ājilih(ī), mā ʿalimtu minhu wa mā lam aʿlam.

74. Allāhumma innī as'aluka min khayri mā sa'alaka ʿabduka wa nabiyyuk(a). Allāhumma innī as'alukal-Jannata wa mā qarraba ilayhā min qawlin aw ʿamal(in), wa as'aluka an tajʿala kulla qaḍā'in qaḍaytahū lī khayra(n), wa as'aluka mā qaḍayta lī min amrin an tajʿala ʿāqibatahū rushda.

75. Allāhumma aḥsin ʿāqibatanā fil-'umūri kullihā, wa ajirnā min

from disgrace in this world and punishment in the Hereafter.

(76) O Allah, protect me with Islam while I am standing, protect me with Islam while I am sitting, and protect me with Islam while I am lying down. And let not an enemy or a jealous person take delight from my plight. O Allah, I ask You for all the good whose treasures are in Your Hands, and I ask You for that good which is totally in Your Hands.

(77) O Allah, do not leave any of our sins except that you forgive them, nor any of our worries except that you remove them, nor any of our debts except that you discharge them, nor any of our needs from this world and the Hereafter except that you satisfy them. O the Most Merciful of those who show mercy.

(78) O Allah, help us in Your remembrance, in gratitude to You, and in reaching excellence in Your worship.

(79) O Allah, make me content with what You have provided for me and bless me in it, and be my protector in everything that is out of

---

and conviction that will help us in all the ups and downs of this life (*Fayḍ al-Qadīr*).

(75) [Busr ibn Arṭāt al-Qurashī. *Musnad Aḥmad* #16970]

(76) [Composite: ʿAbdullāh ibn Masʿūd. *Kanz al-ʿUmmāl* #3679; ʿUmar ibn al-Khaṭṭāb. *Kanz al-ʿUmmāl* #5035]
all the good whose treasures are in Your Hands: All good is actually in the hands of Allah, even though due to normal chains of causations in this world it may appear to be coming to us from the hands of others.
that good which is totally in Your Hands: It refers to the good that clearly has no worldly sources.

(77) [Anas ibn Mālik. *Majmaʿ az-Zawā'id* #17266]

(78) [Abū Hurayrah. *Kanz al-ʿUmmāl* #3700; Muʿādh ibn Jabal. *Sunan Abī Dāwūd* #1301]
Prophet Muḥammad ﷺ taught the singular version of this duʿā'

خِزْيِ الدُّنْيَا وَعَذَابِ الْآخِرَةِ۔

﴿٧٦﴾ اَللّٰهُمَّ احْفَظْنِيْ بِالْإِسْلَامِ قَائِمًا، وَّاحْفَظْنِيْ بِالْإِسْلَامِ قَاعِدًا، وَّاحْفَظْنِيْ بِالْإِسْلَامِ رَاقِدًا، وَّلَا تُشْمِتْ بِيْ عَدُوًّا وَّلَا حَاسِدًا. اَللّٰهُمَّ إِنِّيْ أَسْأَلُكَ مِنْ كُلِّ خَيْرٍ خَزَائِنُهُ بِيَدِكَ۔ وَأَسْأَلُكَ مِنَ الْخَيْرِ الَّذِيْ هُوَ بِيَدِكَ كُلِّهٖ۔

﴿٧٧﴾ اَللّٰهُمَّ لَا تَدَعْ لَنَا ذَنْبًا إِلَّا غَفَرْتَهٗ، وَلَا هَمًّا إِلَّا فَرَّجْتَهٗ، وَلَا دَيْنًا إِلَّا قَضَيْتَهٗ، وَلَا حَاجَةً مِّنْ حَوَائِجِ الدُّنْيَا وَالْآخِرَةِ إِلَّا قَضَيْتَهَا يَا أَرْحَمَ الرَّاحِمِيْنَ۔

﴿٧٨﴾ اَللّٰهُمَّ أَعِنَّا عَلٰى ذِكْرِكَ وَشُكْرِكَ وَحُسْنِ عِبَادَتِكَ۔

﴿٧٩﴾ اَللّٰهُمَّ قَنِّعْنِيْ بِمَا رَزَقْتَنِيْ وَبَارِكْ لِيْ فِيْهِ، وَاخْلُفْ عَلٰى

khizyid-dunyā wa ʿadhābil-ākhirah.

76. Allāhummaḥ-faẓnī bil-'Islāmi qā'ima(n), waḥ-faẓnī bil-'Islāmi qāʿida(n), waḥ-faẓnī bil-'Islāmi rāqida(n), wa lā tushmit bī ʿaduwwan wa lā ḥāsida(n). Allāhumma innī as'aluka min kulli khayrin khazā'inuhū biyadik(a). Wa as'aluka minal-khayril-ladhī huwa biyadika kullih.

77. Allāhumma lā tadaʿ lanā dhamban illā ghafartah(ū), wa lā hamman illā farrajtah(ū), wa lā daynan illā qaḍaytah(ū), wa lā ḥājatam min ḥawā'ijid-dunyā wal-ākhirati illā qaḍaytahā yā arḥamar-rāḥimīn.

78. Allāhumma aʿinnā ʿalā dhikrika wa shukrika wa ḥusni ʿibādatik.

79. Allāhumma qanniʿnī bimā razaqtanī wa bārik lī fīh(i), wakh-

my sight.

(80) O Allah, I ask You for a clean life, a graceful death, and a return (to You) which is neither humiliating nor disgracing.

(81) O Allah, I am weak; replace my weakness with strength in my pursuits of Your pleasure. Pull me by my forelocks toward good. Make Islam the ultimate object of my pleasure. I am lowly, so give me honor. And I am needy, so provide for me.

(82) O Allah, I beg You for the best of petitions and invocations, thorough success, best deeds, best recompense, best life, and best death. Grant me firmness. Make my scales heavy and my faith genuine. Elevate my ranks, accept my ṣalāt, and forgive my sins. I solicit of You high ranks in Paradise. Āmīn. O Allah, I beg You for the good: its beginnings and endings, its most comprehensive forms, its first and its last, and its outward and inward manifestations. O Allah, I beg You for the good of my accomplishments, my deeds, and my actions. The good of that which is hidden and that which is exposed.

---

to Sayyidnā Muʿādh ibn Jabal رضي الله عنه as a very special gift and advised him to say it after every ṣalāt (*Sunan Abī Dāwūd*).

(79) [ʿAbdullāh ibn ʿAbbās. *Mustadrak Ḥākim* #78/1878]

(80) [ʿAbdullāh ibn ʿUmar. *Mustadrak Ḥākim* #186/1986]
A clean life is a life of purity and virtue. Such a person is happy and contented. He is pleased with Allah's decrees and Allah is pleased with him.

(81) [Buraydah al-Aslamī. *Mustadrak Ḥākim* #131/1931; Ibid. *Al-Jāmiʿ aṣ-Ṣaghīr* #2882]

(82) [Um Salamah. *Kanz al-ʿUmmāl* #3820; Ibid. *Mustadrak Ḥākim* #111/1911]

كُلِّ غَائِبَةٍ لِّيْ بِخَيْرٍ۔

﴿٨٠﴾ اَللّٰهُمَّ إِنِّيْ أَسْأَلُكَ عِيْشَةً نَّقِيَّةً، وَّمِيْتَةً سَوِيَّةً، وَّمَرَدًّا غَيْرَ مُخْزِيٍّ وَّلَا فَاضِحٍ۔

﴿٨١﴾ اَللّٰهُمَّ إِنِّيْ ضَعِيْفٌ فَقَوِّ فِيْ رِضَاكَ ضُعْفِيْ، وَخُذْ إِلَى الْخَيْرِ بِنَاصِيَتِيْ، وَاجْعَلِ الْإِسْلَامَ مُنْتَهٰى رِضَائِيْ، وَإِنِّيْ ذَلِيْلٌ فَأَعِزَّنِيْ، وَإِنِّيْ فَقِيْرٌ فَارْزُقْنِيْ۔

﴿٨٢﴾ اَللّٰهُمَّ إِنِّيْ أَسْأَلُكَ خَيْرَ الْمَسْأَلَةِ، وَخَيْرَ الدُّعَاءِ، وَخَيْرَ النَّجَاحِ، وَخَيْرَ الْعَمَلِ، وَخَيْرَ الثَّوَابِ، وَخَيْرَ الْحَيٰوةِ، وَخَيْرَ الْمَمَاتِ، وَثَبِّتْنِيْ، وَثَقِّلْ مَوَازِيْنِيْ، وَحَقِّقْ إِيْمَانِيْ، وَارْفَعْ دَرَجَاتِيْ، وَتَقَبَّلْ صَلَاتِيْ، وَاغْفِرْ خَطِيْئَتِيْ، وَأَسْأَلُكَ الدَّرَجَاتِ الْعُلٰى مِنَ الْجَنَّةِ، اٰمِيْنَ. اَللّٰهُمَّ إِنِّيْ أَسْأَلُكَ فَوَاتِحَ

luf ʿalā kulli ghā'ibatin lī bikhayr.

80. Allāhumma innī as'aluka ʿīshatan naqiyya(tan), wa mītatan sawiyya(tan), wa maraddan ghayra makhziyyin wa lā fāḍiḥ.

81. Allāhumma innī ḍaʿīfun fa qawwi fī riḍāka ḍuʿfī, wa khudh ilal-khayri bināṣiyatī, waj-ʿalil-'Islāma muntahā riḍā'ī, wa innī dhalīlun fa aʿizzanī, wa innī faqīrun far-zuqnī.

82. Allāhumma innī as'aluka khayral-mas'ala(ti), wa khayrad-duʿā'(i), wa khayran-najāḥ(i), wa khayral-ʿamal(i), wa khayrath-thawāb(i), wa khayral-ḥayā(ti), wa khayral-mamāt(i), wa thabbitnī, wa thaqqil mawāzīnī, wa ḥaqqiq īmānī, war-faʿ darajātī, wa taqabbal ṣalātī, wagh-fir khaṭī'atī, wa as'alukad-darajātil-ʿulā minal-Jannat(i), Āmīn(a). Allāhumma innī as'aluka fawātiḥal-

(83) O Allah, make my sustenance the most plentiful in my old age and during the last days of my life.

(84) O Allah, make the last part of my life its best, my last deed my best one, and the day I meet You my best day. O Protector of Islam and its followers, keep me firm on it until I meet you.

I seek from You my contentment and that of my family.

---

(83) [ʿĀ'ishah. *Mustadrak Ḥākim* #187/1987]

(84) [Composite: Anas ibn Mālik. *Majmaʿ az-Zawā'id* #17267; Abū Ṣirmah. *Musnad Aḥmad* #15194]
This is part of a beautiful duʿā' made by a Bedouin. Prophet Muḥammad ﷺ heard him and loved these words so much that he gave him a gift of gold. The complete duʿā', that won this Prophetic "gold medal," was:

يَا مَنْ لَا تَرَاهُ الْعُيُوْنُ وَلَا تُخَالِطُهُ الظُّنُوْنُ وَلَا يَصِفُهُ الْوَاصِفُوْنَ، وَلَا تُغَيِّرُهُ الْحَوَادِثُ، وَلَا يَخْشَى الدَّوَائِرَ، يَعْلَمُ مَثَاقِيْلَ الْجِبَالِ وَمَكَايِيْلَ الْبِحَارِ، وَعَدَدَ قَطْرِ الْأَمْطَارِ وَعَدَدَ وَرَقِ الْأَشْجَارِ، وَعَدَدَ مَا أَظْلَمَ عَلَيْهِ اللَّيْلُ وَأَشْرَقَ عَلَيْهِ النَّهَارُ، وَلَا تُوَارِيْ مِنْهُ سَمَاءٌ سَمَاءً، وَلَا أَرْضٌ أَرْضًا، وَلَا بَحْرٌ مَّا فِيْ قَعْرِهٖ، وَلَا جَبَلٌ مَّا فِيْ وَعْرِهٖ، اجْعَلْ خَيْرَ عُمُرِيْ آخِرَهٗ، وَخَيْرَ عَمَلِيْ خَوَاتِيْمَهٗ، وَخَيْرَ أَيَّامِيْ يَوْمَ أَلْقَاكَ فِيْهِ

O the One Whom eyes cannot see, conjectures cannot grasp, and describers cannot describe; Whom events cannot affect and Who does not fear calamities; Who knows the weights of the mountains and the volumes of the oceans and the counts of the raindrops and of the tree leaves, and the counts of everything on which night brings darkness and day brings the light; (O the One from Whom) a heaven cannot hide another heaven, nor the earth can hide another earth, nor an ocean can hide what is in its depths, nor a mountain can hide what is behind its ruggedness—make the last part of my life its best, my last deed my best one, and the day I meet You my best day.

→

الْخَيْرِ وَخَوَاتِمَهُ، وَجَوَامِعَهُ، وَأَوَّلَهُ وَاٰخِرَهُ، وَظَاهِرَهُ وَبَاطِنَهُ. اَللّٰهُمَّ إِنِّيْ أَسْأَلُكَ خَيْرَ مَا اٰتِيْ، وَخَيْرَ مَا أَفْعَلُ، وَخَيْرَ مَا أَعْمَلُ، وَخَيْرَ مَا بَطَنَ، وَخَيْرَ مَا ظَهَرَ.

﴿٨٣﴾ اَللّٰهُمَّ اجْعَلْ أَوْسَعَ رِزْقِكَ عَلَيَّ عِنْدَ كِبَرِ سِنِّيْ وَانْقِطَاعِ عُمُرِيْ.

﴿٨٤﴾ وَاجْعَلْ خَيْرَ عُمُرِيْ اٰخِرَهُ، وَخَيْرَ عَمَلِيْ خَوَاتِيْمَهُ، وَخَيْرَ أَيَّامِيْ يَوْمَ أَلْقَاكَ فِيْهِ. يَا وَلِيَّ الْإِسْلَامِ وَأَهْلِهِ ثَبِّتْنِيْ بِهٖ حَتّٰى أَلْقَاكَ. أَسْأَلُكَ غِنَايَ وَغِنٰى مَوْلَايَ.

khayri wa khawātimah(ū), wa jawāmiʿah(ū), wa awwalahū wa ākhirah(ū), wa ẓāhirahū wa bāṭinah(ū). Allāhumma innī as'aluka khayra mā ātī, wa khayra mā afʿal(u), wa khayra mā aʿmal(u), wa khayra mā baṭan(a), wa khayra mā ẓahar.

83. Allāhummaj-ʿal awsaʿa rizqika ʿalayya ʿinda kibari sinnī wanqiṭāʿi ʿumurī.

84. Waj-ʿal khayra ʿumurī ākhirah(ū), wa khayra ʿamalī khawātīmah(ū), wa khayra ayyāmī yawma alqāka fīh(i). Yā Waliyyal-'Islāmi wa ahlihī thabbitnī bihī ḥattā alqāk(a). As'aluka ghināya wa ghinā mawlāy.

One marvels at the level of consciousness of Allah (*maʿrifah*) of a Bedouin inspired in him by his contact with the Prophet ﷺ. May Allah ﷻ grant us some of that.

The concern for a good ending is the paramount concern of a believer. Sayydinā Abū Bakr رضي الله عنه was asked why he made this duʿā' despite being a Companion of the highest status. He replied,

(85) O Allah, I seek Your protection from undesirable age and mischief of the heart. I seek Your refuge, by virtue of Your Honor as there is no god except You, from that You should lead me astray. (I seek Your refuge) from severe trials, wretchedness, bad fate, and taunts from the enemies. From the evil of what I did and what I did not. From the loss of Your blessings and the removal of Your protection. From Your sudden punishment and from all (that can warrant) Your wrath. From the mischief of my hearing, sight, speech, heart, and seed. From oppressing others or being oppressed, from being crushed or falling, from drowning or being burnt. Or that Shayṭān should confuse me at the time of my death. Or that I should die as a fugitive from jihad or that I should die due to a venomous bite.

"(Sometimes) a servant keeps on doing pious deeds for a lifetime but they are ended with the deeds of the people of the Fire. And (sometimes) a servant keeps on doing sinful deeds for a lifetime but they are ended with the deeds of the people of the Garden" (*Kanz al-ʿUmmāl*).

We can never be complacent with our piety today. We must strive to maintain īmān and taqwā to the finish.

(85) [Composite: ʿUmar ibn al-Khaṭṭāb. *Sunan an-Nasāʾī* #5402; ʿAbdullāh ibn ʿAbbās. *Ṣaḥīḥ Muslim* #4894; Abū Hurayrah. *Ṣaḥīḥ al-Bukhārī* #5871; ʿĀʾishah. *Ṣaḥīḥ Muslim* #4891; ʿAbdullāh ibn ʿUmar. *Ṣaḥīḥ Muslim* #4922; Shakal ibn Ḥumayd. *Sunan at-Tirmidhī* #3414; Abū Hurayrah. *Kanz al-ʿUmmāl* #3688; Abul-Yasr. *Sunan Abī Dāwūd* #1328]

From the evil of what I did and what I did not: We seek protection against the evil of our actions as well as inactions.

that Shayṭān should confuse me: Shayṭān makes his most determined effort to mislead a believer at the time of his death. He reminds his associates that if they don't get the person then, they will never get him. The Satanic effort consists in confusing or distracting the dying person so he or she does not die in a state of īmān or perform repentance before death. At a minimum it aims at causing despair in the person so he will have no hope of Allah's mercy as he meets Him (*ʿAwn al-Maʿbūd*). →

﴿٨٥﴾ اَللّٰهُمَّ إِنِّيْ أَعُوْذُ بِكَ مِنْ سُوْءِ الْعُمُرِ وَفِتْنَةِ الصَّدْرِ، وَأَعُوْذُ بِعِزَّتِكَ لَا إِلٰهَ إِلَّا أَنْتَ أَنْ تُضِلَّنِيْ، وَمِنْ جَهْدِ الْبَلَاءِ، وَدَرَكِ الشَّقَاءِ، وَسُوْءِ الْقَضَاءِ، وَشَمَاتَةِ الْأَعْدَاءِ، وَمِنْ شَرِّ مَا عَمِلْتُ، وَمِنْ شَرِّ مَا لَمْ أَعْمَلْ، وَمِنْ زَوَالِ نِعْمَتِكَ، وَتَحَوُّلِ عَافِيَتِكَ، وَفُجَاءَةِ نِقْمَتِكَ، وَجَمِيْعِ سَخَطِكَ، وَمِنْ شَرِّ سَمْعِيْ، وَمِنْ شَرِّ بَصَرِيْ، وَمِنْ شَرِّ لِسَانِيْ، وَمِنْ شَرِّ قَلْبِيْ، وَمِنْ شَرِّ مَنِيِّيْ، وَمِنْ أَنْ أَظْلِمَ أَوْ أُظْلَمَ، وَمِنَ الْهَدَمِ، وَمِنَ التَّرَدِّيْ، وَمِنَ الْغَرَقِ وَالْحَرَقِ، وَأَنْ يَّتَخَبَّطَنِيَ الشَّيْطَانُ عِنْدَ الْمَوْتِ، وَمِنْ أَنْ أَمُوْتَ فِيْ سَبِيْلِكَ مُدْبِرًا، وَّأَنْ أَمُوْتَ لَدِيْغًا۔

85. Allāhumma innī aʿūdhu bika min sūʾil-ʿumuri wa fitnatiṣ-ṣadr(i), wa aʿūdhu biʿizzatika lā ilāha illā anta an tuḍillanī, wa min jahdil-balāʾ(i), wa darakish-shaqāʾ(i), wa sūʾil-qaḍāʾ(i), wa shamātatil-ʾaʿdāʾ(i), wa min sharri mā ʿamilt(u), wa min sharri mā lam aʿmal, wa min zawāli niʿmatik(a), wa taḥawwuli ʿāfiyatik(a), wa fujāʾati niqmatik(a), wa jamīʿi sakhaṭik(a), wa min sharri samʿī, wa min sharri baṣarī, wa min sharri lisānī, wa min sharri qalbī, wa min sharri maniyyī, wa min an aẓlima aw uẓlam(a), wa minal-hadam(i), wa minat-taraddī, wa minal-gharaqi wal-ḥaraq(i), wa an yatakhabbaṭaniyash-shayṭānu ʿindal-mawt(i), wa min an amūta fī sabīlika mudbira(n), wa an amūta ladīgha.

Prophet Muḥammad ﷺ made this duʿāʾ only to teach the ummah, as he was clearly immune from Satanic attacks.

This duʿāʾ also includes pleas for protection from many forms of sudden and painful deaths. For more on that, see commentary for duʿāʾ 206.

MONDAY

In the Name of Allah, the Most Compassionate, the Most Merciful

(86) O Allah, make me one who is highly grateful. Make me one who is patient and perseverant. Make me small in my own eyes but great in the eyes of others.

(87) O Allah, put blessings, beauty, and calm in our land. Do not deprive me of the blessings of what You have given me and do not subject me to a trial in what You have withheld from me.

(88) O Allah, You have given me a good physique; favor me with good morals and manners as well. Extinguish the anger in my heart and, as long as You keep me alive, save me from such trying situations that can lead me astray.

(89) O Allah, instruct me in the evidence of faith at the time of death.

(90) O Lord, I beg You for the good of this day and the good of what will come after it.

---

(86) [Buraydah al-Aslamī. *Kanz al-ʿUmmāl* #3675]

one who is highly grateful: Gratefulness is an act of the tongue as well as the heart. We must feel gratitude for the blessings of Allah سُبْحَانَهُ وَتَعَالَىٰ in our heart and we should also express it in words.

small in my eyes but great in the eyes of others: Getting respect from others has its obvious advantages; life may be difficult for the person who gets respect from no one. Further, one needs this respect to discharge his responsibilities toward them as a believer, like enjoining good and forbidding evil. However, it can also lead to pride and arrogance, which are deadly diseases of the heart. Therefore we ask for being small in our own eyes before asking for being great in the eyes of others.

(87) [Composite: Samurah ibn Jundub and Ubayy ibn Kaʿb. *Majmaʿ az-Zawāʾid* #17425, 17359]

In other words my deprivations in this world should not become my tribulations. →

بِسْمِ اللَّهِ الرَّحْمَٰنِ الرَّحِيمِ

﴿٨٦﴾ اَللّٰهُمَّ اجْعَلْنِيْ شَكُوْرًا، وَّاجْعَلْنِيْ صَبُوْرًا، وَّاجْعَلْنِيْ فِيْ عَيْنِيْ صَغِيْرًا وَّفِيْ أَعْيُنِ النَّاسِ كَبِيْرًا۔

﴿٨٧﴾ اَللّٰهُمَّ ضَعْ فِيْ أَرْضِنَا بَرَكَتَهَا وَزِيْنَتَهَا وَسَكَنَهَا۔ وَلَا تَحْرِمْنِيْ بَرَكَةَ مَا أَعْطَيْتَنِيْ، وَلَا تَفْتِنِّيْ فِيْمَا أَحْرَمْتَنِيْ۔

﴿٨٨﴾ اَللّٰهُمَّ أَحْسَنْتَ خَلْقِيْ فَأَحْسِنْ خُلُقِيْ۔ وَأَذْهِبْ غَيْظَ قَلْبِيْ وَأَجِرْنِيْ مِنْ مُّضِلَّاتِ الْفِتَنِ مَا أَحْيَيْتَنَا۔

﴿٨٩﴾ اَللّٰهُمَّ لَقِّنِيْ حُجَّةَ الْإِيْمَانِ عِنْدَ الْمَمَاتِ۔

﴿٩٠﴾ رَبِّ أَسْأَلُكَ خَيْرَ مَا فِيْ هٰذَا الْيَوْمِ وَخَيْرَ مَا بَعْدَهٗ۔

86. Allāhummaj-ʿalnī shakūra(n), waj-ʿalnī ṣabūra(n), waj-ʿalnī fī ʿaynī ṣaghīran wa fī aʿyunin-nāsi kabīra.

87. Allāhumma ḍaʿ fī arḍinā barakatahā wa zīnatahā wa sakanahā. Wa lā taḥrimnī barakata mā aʿṭaytanī, wa lā taftinnī fīmā aḥramtanī.

88. Allāhumma aḥsanta khalqī fa aḥsin khuluqī. Wa adh-hib ghayẓa qalbī wa ajirnī mim muḍillātil-fitani mā aḥyaytanā.

89. Allāhumma laqqinī ḥujjatal-īmāni ʿindal-mamāt.

90. Rabbi as'aluka khayra mā fī hādhal-yawmi wa khayra mā baʿdah.

---

(88) [Composite: ʿAbdullāh ibn Masʿūd. *Musnad Aḥmad* #3632; Um Salamah. *Musnad Aḥmad* #25364]

The first part of this duʿā' (اَللّٰهُمَّ أَحْسَنْتَ خَلْقِيْ فَأَحْسِنْ خُلُقِيْ) is also to be

(91) O Allah, I beseech You for the good of this day: its victory, its success, its light, its blessing, and its guidance.

(92) O Allah, I ask You for forgiveness and security in my religion and in my worldly affairs, in my family and in my property. O Allah, conceal those things of mine that are worth concealing and give calm to my fears. O Allah, guard me (from all sides): in front and behind, on my right and on my left, and from above me. And I seek refuge in Your greatness from receiving unexpected harm from below.

(93) O the Living, the Eternal, I beg through Your mercy. Set right all of my affairs and do not leave me under the control of my ego (nafs) for even the blink of an eye.

(94) In the name of the light of Your Countenance that lights the heavens and the earth and in the name of every right of Yours and

---

recited when one sees himself or herself in the mirror. It contains two important messages. First, a good physique or good appearance is a blessing of Allah ﷻ. It will be foolish if anyone tried to take credit for that. Second, good morals and manners are more important. They are our actions. And in the Hereafter the actions we performed, not the gifts we received, will determine our fate. So instead of gloating over the first, we seek the second.

(89) [Abū Hurayrah. *Kanz al-ʿUmmāl* #3286]
This is another important duʿā' for breathing our last in a state of īman. It is the overriding concern of a believer that he or she should die in a state of īman, for otherwise a lifetime of good deeds may come to nothing. Therefore protecting our faith is a lifelong struggle. The ḥadīth that teaches this duʿā' sheds further light on the importance of this matter. "None of you should say, 'O Allah, instruct me in my evidence at the time of death', as the non-believer is also instructed in his evidence. Rather you should say, 'O Allah! Instruct me in the evidence of faith at the time of death.'"

(90) [ʿAbdullāh ibn Masʿūd. *Sunan at-Tirmidhī* #3312]
At night, one should say: رَبِّ أَسْأَلُكَ خَيْرَ مَا فِي هَذِهِ اللَّيْلَةِ وَخَيْرَ مَا بَعْدَهَا →

﴿٩١﴾ اَللّٰهُمَّ إِنِّيْ أَسْأَلُكَ خَيْرَ هٰذَا الْيَوْمِ فَتْحَهُ وَنَصْرَهُ وَنُوْرَهُ وَبَرَكَتَهُ وَهُدَاهُ۔

﴿٩٢﴾ اَللّٰهُمَّ إِنِّيْ أَسْأَلُكَ الْعَفْوَ وَالْعَافِيَةَ فِيْ دِيْنِيْ وَدُنْيَايَ وَأَهْلِيْ وَمَالِيْ. اَللّٰهُمَّ اسْتُرْ عَوْرَاتِيْ وَاٰمِنْ رَوْعَاتِيْ. اَللّٰهُمَّ احْفَظْنِيْ مِنْ بَيْنِ يَدَيَّ وَمِنْ خَلْفِيْ، وَعَنْ يَّمِيْنِيْ وَعَنْ شِمَالِيْ، وَمِنْ فَوْقِيْ، وَأَعُوْذُ بِعَظَمَتِكَ أَنْ أُغْتَالَ مِنْ تَحْتِيْ۔

﴿٩٣﴾ يَا حَيُّ يَا قَيُّوْمُ بِرَحْمَتِكَ أَسْتَغِيْثُ، أَصْلِحْ لِيْ شَأْنِيْ كُلَّهُ، وَلَا تَكِلْنِيْ إِلٰى نَفْسِيْ طَرْفَةَ عَيْنٍ۔

﴿٩٤﴾ أَسْأَلُكَ بِنُوْرِ وَجْهِكَ الَّذِيْ أَشْرَقَتْ لَهُ السَّمٰوٰتُ

91. Allāhumma innī as'aluka khayra hādhal-yawmi fatḥahū wa naṣrahū wa nūrahū wa barakatahū wa hudāh.

92. Allāhumma innī as'alukal-ʿafwa wal-ʿāfiyata fī dīnī wa dunyāya wa ahlī wa mālī. Allāhummas-tur ʿawrātī wa āmin rawʿātī. Allāhummaḥ-faẓnī mim bayni yadayya wa min khalfī, wa ʿan yamīnī wa ʿan shimālī, wa min fawqī, wa aʿūdhu biʿaẓamatika an ughtāla min taḥtī.

93. Yā Ḥayyu yā Qayyūmu biraḥmatika astaghīth(u), aṣliḥ lī sha'nī kullah(ū), wa lā takilnī ilā nafsī ṭarfata ʿayn.

94. As'aluka binūri Wajhikal-ladhī ashraqat lahus-samāwātu wal-'arḍu wa bikulli ḥaqqin huwa laka wa biḥaqqis-sā'ilīna ʿalayka an

(O Lord, I beg You for the good of this night and the good of what comes after it.)

(in the name of) the right on You that You have granted to the beggars, I beseech You to forgive me and protect me from the Fire through Your Power.

(95) O Allah, make the first part of this day good, the middle part success, and the last part salvation. I ask from You the good of this world and the Hereafter, O the Most Merciful of those who show mercy.

(96) O Allah, forgive my sins, expel my Shayṭān, and redeem my pledge. Make my scales heavy and make me from among the highest class (in the Hereafter).

(97) O Allah, save me from Your punishment on the day You raise Your servants to life again.

(98) O Allah, Lord of the seven heavens and whatever comes under their shadows. Lord of the earths and whatever they bear. Lord of

---

(91) [Abū Mālik al-Ashʿarī. *Sunan Abī Dāwūd* #4421]
Ibn ʿUlān in *Futūhāt ar-Rabbāniyyah* writes: In the generalized sense *fatḥ* means achievement of goals. *Naṣr* means help against overt and covert enemies. *Nūr* is the light from Allah that allows one to see the Right Path. *Barakah* means perpetuation of obedience. *Hudā* means guidance to steadfastness that leads one to a beautiful ending.

(92) [ʿAbdullāh ibn ʿUmar. *Sunan Abī Dāwūd* #4412]
receiving unexpected harm from below: *Ightiyāl* means being killed by deception at a place where nobody can see you. According to Wakīʿ ibn al-Jarrāḥ, "ughtāla min taḥtī" means being killed in an earthquake.

Prophet Muḥammad ﷺ used to say this duʿā' every morning and evening.

(93) [Anas ibn Mālik. *Mustadrak Ḥākim* #200/2000]
According to a ḥadīth, this duʿā' contains *al-Ism al-Aʿẓam*, one of the special names of Allah that, when invoked while making a duʿā', tremendously increase its chances of acceptance. This duʿā' should be made profusely at the time of difficulties, as was the practice of →

وَالأَرْضِ وَبِكُلِّ حَقٍّ هُوَ لَكَ وَبِحَقِّ السَّائِلِيْنَ عَلَيْكَ أَنْ تُقِيْلَنِي وَأَنْ تُجِيْرَنِيْ مِنَ النَّارِ بِقُدْرَتِكَ۔

﴿٩٥﴾ اَللّٰهُمَّ اجْعَلْ أَوَّلَ هٰذَا النَّهَارِ صَلَاحًا، وَّأَوْسَطَهٗ فَلَاحًا، وَّاٰخِرَهٗ نَجَاحًا. أَسْأَلُكَ خَيْرَ الدُّنْيَا وَالْاٰخِرَةِ، يَا أَرْحَمَ الرَّاحِمِيْنَ۔

﴿٩٦﴾ اَللّٰهُمَّ اغْفِرْ لِيْ ذَنْبِيْ، وَاخْسِئْ شَيْطَانِيْ، وَفُكَّ رِهَانِيْ، وَثَقِّلْ مِيْزَانِيْ، وَاجْعَلْنِيْ فِي النَّدِيِّ الْأَعْلٰى۔

﴿٩٧﴾ اَللّٰهُمَّ قِنِيْ عَذَابَكَ يَوْمَ تَبْعَثُ عِبَادَكَ۔

﴿٩٨﴾ اَللّٰهُمَّ رَبَّ السَّمٰوٰتِ السَّبْعِ وَمَا أَظَلَّتْ، وَرَبَّ

tuqīlanī wa an tujīranī minan-nāri biqudratik.

95. Allāhummaj-ʿal awwala hādhan-nahāri ṣalāḥa(n), wa awsaṭahū falāḥa(n), wa ākhirahū najāḥa(n). As'aluka khayrad-dunyā wal-ākhira(ti), yā Arḥamar-rāḥimīn.

96. Allāhummagh-fir lī dhambī, wakh-si' shayṭānī, wa fukka rihānī, wa thaqqil mīzānī, waj-ʿalnī fin-nadiyyil-'aʿlā.

97. Allāhumma qinī ʿadhābaka yawma tabʿathu ʿibādak.

98. Allāhumma Rabbas-samāwātis-sabʿi wa mā aẓallat, wa Rabbal-

---

the Prophet ﷺ. He also urged his daughter Sayyidah Fāṭimah رضي الله عنها to make this duʿā' every morning and evening.

(94) [Abū Umāmah al-Bāhilī. *Muʿjam al-Kabīr (Ṭabarānī)* #265/8]
right of beggars: We do not have any built-in, autonomous right

the devils and whatever they mislead. Be a Protector for me from the mischiefs of Your entire creation lest any of them do evil or oppress me. Strong is Your protection and blessed is Your name.

(99) There is no god except You, You have no partner. Glorified are You, O Allah, I seek forgiveness from You for my sin and I beseech You for Your mercy.

(100) O Allah, forgive my sin, make my home ample for me, and bless me in my sustenance.

(101) O Allah, make me one of those who turn to You and repent much, and make me one of those who stay very clean and very pure.

(102) O Allah, forgive me, guide me, provide for me, and give me protection. And guide me with Your Will to the right thing in whatever is controversial.

---

over Allah ﷻ. No one can demand anything from Allah ﷻ or force Him to grant anything. However, Allah ﷻ has through His Own kindness and compassion, granted us the privilege of making pleas to Him and He accepts them when they are made sincerely and obediently. It is this that has been referred to here.

(95) [ʿAbdur-Raḥmān ibn Abzā. *Muṣannaf ibn Abī Shaybah* #29268]

(96) [Abū al-Azhar al-Anmārī. *Sunan Abī Dāwūd* #4395; Ibid. *Mustadrak Ḥākim* #182/1982]
my Shayṭān: any shayṭān from the jinns or humans who targets the person making this duʿā'.
redeem my pledge: This refers to the verse: "Every man is in pledge for his deeds" (*Aṭ-Ṭūr*, 52:21). So the duʿā' is that we discharge all our obligations toward Allah ﷻ and His creations so our pledge is redeemed.
highest class: the group of the highest ranking angels in the court of Allah. The duʿā' is for getting their company.

(97) [Ḥafṣah. *Sunan Abī Dāwūd* #4388]
Prophet Muḥammad ﷺ used to say this duʿā' after the ṣalāt.

الْأَرَضِيْنَ وَمَا أَقَلَّتْ، وَرَبَّ الشَّيَاطِيْنِ وَمَا أَضَلَّتْ، كُنْ لِّيْ جَارًا مِّنْ شَرِّ خَلْقِكَ أَجْمَعِيْنَ أَنْ يَّفْرُطَ عَلَيَّ أَحَدٌ مِّنْهُمْ أَوْ أَنْ يَّطْغٰى، عَزَّ جَارُكَ وَتَبَارَكَ اسْمُكَ۔

﴿٩٩﴾ لَا إِلٰهَ إِلَّا أَنْتَ لَا شَرِيْكَ لَكَ سُبْحَانَكَ. اَللّٰهُمَّ إِنِّيْ أَسْتَغْفِرُكَ لِذَنْبِيْ وَأَسْأَلُكَ رَحْمَتَكَ۔

﴿١٠٠﴾ اَللّٰهُمَّ اغْفِرْ لِيْ ذَنْبِيْ، وَوَسِّعْ لِيْ فِيْ دَارِيْ، وَبَارِكْ لِيْ فِيْ رِزْقِيْ۔

﴿١٠١﴾ اَللّٰهُمَّ اجْعَلْنِيْ مِنَ التَّوَّابِيْنَ وَاجْعَلْنِيْ مِنَ الْمُتَطَهِّرِيْنَ۔

﴿١٠٢﴾ اَللّٰهُمَّ اغْفِرْ لِيْ، وَاهْدِنِيْ، وَارْزُقْنِيْ، وَعَافِنِيْ، وَاهْدِنِيْ لِمَا اخْتُلِفَ فِيْهِ مِنَ الْحَقِّ بِإِذْنِكَ۔

'araḍīna wa mā aqallat, wa Rabbash-shayāṭīni wa mā aḍallat, kun lī jāram min sharri khalqika ajmaʿīna an yafruṭa ʿalayya aḥadum minhum aw an yaṭghā, ʿazza jāruka wa tabārakas-muk.

99. Lā ilāha illā anta lā sharīka laka subḥānak(a). Allāhumma innī astaghfiruka lidhambī wa as'aluka raḥmatak.

100. Allāhummagh-fir lī dhambī, wa wassiʿ lī fī dārī, wa bārik lī fī rizqī.

101. Allāhummaj-ʿalnī minat-tawwābīna waj-ʿalnī minal-mutaṭahhirīn.

102. Allāhummagh-fir lī, wah-dinī, war-zuqnī, wa ʿāfinī, wah-dinī limakh-tulifa fīhi minal-ḥaqqi bi-'idhnik.

(103) O Allah, put Light in my heart, Light in my sight, Light in my hearing, Light to my right, Light to my left, Light behind me, and Light in front of me. (O Allah,) bestow upon me Light. (O Allah,) put Light in my muscles, Light in my flesh, Light in my blood, Light in my hair, Light in my skin, Light in my tongue, and Light in my soul. Make my Light great and make me all Light. And put Light above me and Light below me. O Allah, give me Light.

(104) O Allah, open for us the doors to Your mercy and give us easy access to the doors to Your provisions.

(105) O Allah, protect me from the cursed Shayṭān.

(106) O Allah, I beg You for Your favor.

---

(98) [Khālid ibn al-Walīd. *Majmaʿ az-Zawāʾid* #17063]
This duʿāʾ was taught to Sayyidnā Khālid ibn al-Walīd رضي الله عنه by Prophet Muḥammad ﷺ to cure his insomnia.

(99) [ʿĀʾishah. *Kanz al-ʿUmmāl* #23417]

(100) [Abū Hurayrah. *Kanz al-ʿUmmāl* #3633]
This duʿāʾ should also be recited when making wuḍūʾ.

(101) [ʿUmar ibn al-Khaṭṭāb. *Sunan at-Tirmidhī* #50]
This duʿāʾ is also to be said after making wuḍūʾ.

(102) [Composite: ʿĀʾishah. *Sunan an-Nasāʾī* #5440; Ibid. *Ṣaḥīḥ Muslim* #1289]
When faced with controversies and confusions, we seek Allah's help to get a clear vision of the reality. A person earnestly resorting to this duʿāʾ is also protected from the ego trips which lead even the knowledgeable people astray in the heat of controversies.

(103) [ʿAbdullāh ibn ʿAbbās. *Ṣaḥīḥ al-Bukhārī* #5841; *Ṣaḥīḥ Muslim* #1279]
According to the aḥādith, this duʿāʾ should be made while going to the masjid for Fajr ṣalāt. The darkness of the surroundings at that time reminds us of the general darkness of the human condition. Those who wake up and walk to the masjid at this time are true seekers of light. We seek it from Allah سبحانه وتعالى, as He is the only source of light. There is no light and there is no enlightenment without

﴿١٠٣﴾ اَللّٰهُمَّ اجْعَلْ فِيْ قَلْبِيْ نُوْرًا، وَّفِيْ بَصَرِيْ نُوْرًا، وَّفِيْ سَمْعِيْ نُوْرًا، وَّعَنْ يَّمِيْنِيْ نُوْرًا، وَّعَنْ شِمَالِيْ نُوْرًا، وَّخَلْفِيْ نُوْرًا، وَّمِنْ أَمَامِيْ نُوْرًا، وَّاجْعَلْ لِّيْ نُوْرًا، وَّفِيْ عَصَبِيْ نُوْرًا، وَّفِيْ لَحْمِيْ نُوْرًا، وَّفِيْ دَمِيْ نُوْرًا، وَّفِيْ شَعْرِيْ نُوْرًا، وَّفِيْ بَشَرِيْ نُوْرًا، وَّفِيْ لِسَانِيْ نُوْرًا، وَّاجْعَلْ فِيْ نَفْسِيْ نُوْرًا، وَّأَعْظِمْ لِيْ نُوْرًا، وَّاجْعَلْنِيْ نُوْرًا، وَّاجْعَلْ مِنْ فَوْقِيْ نُوْرًا، وَّمِنْ تَحْتِيْ نُوْرًا. اَللّٰهُمَّ أَعْطِنِيْ نُوْرًا۔

﴿١٠٤﴾ اَللّٰهُمَّ افْتَحْ لَنَا أَبْوَابَ رَحْمَتِكَ، وَسَهِّلْ لَنَا أَبْوَابَ رِزْقِكَ۔

﴿١٠٥﴾ اَللّٰهُمَّ اعْصِمْنِيْ مِنَ الشَّيْطَانِ الرَّجِيْمِ۔

﴿١٠٦﴾ اَللّٰهُمَّ إِنِّيْ أَسْأَلُكَ مِنْ فَضْلِكَ۔

103. Allāhummaj-ʿal fī qalbī nūra(n), wa fī baṣarī nūra(n), wa fī samʿī nūra(n), wa ʿan yamīnī nūra(n), wa ʿan shimālī nūra(n), wa khalfī nūra(n), wa min amāmī nūra(n), waj-ʿal lī nūra(n), wa fī ʿaṣabī nūra(n), wa fī laḥmī nūra(n), wa fī damī nūra(n), wa fī shaʿrī nūra(n), wa fī basharī nūra(n), wa fī lisānī nūra(n), waj-ʿal fī nafsī nūra(n), wa aʿẓim lī nūra(n), waj-ʿalnī nūra(n), waj-ʿal min fawqī nūra(n), wa min taḥtī nūra(n). Allāhumma aʿṭinī nūra.

104. Allāhummaf-taḥ lanā abwāba raḥmatik(a), wa sahhil lanā abwāba rizqik.

105. Allāhummaʿ-ṣimnī minash-shayṭānir-rajīm.

106. Allāhumma innī as'aluka min faḍlik.

(107) O Allah, forgive all of my sins and mistakes. O Allah, elevate me, give me life and provisions, and guide me to pious deeds and morals. Certainly no one leads to the pious deeds and morals and no one protects from the evil ones except You.

(108) O Allah, I beg You for provisions that are pure, knowledge that is beneficial, and deeds that will be accepted.

(109) O Allah, I am Your slave, son of Your male servant, and son of Your female servant. My forelock is in Your Hand. Your command for me prevails. Your Judgment concerning me is just. I beseech You through every name You have, by which You have called Yourself, or which You have sent down in Your Book, or which You taught to any one of Your creations, or which You preferred to keep to Yourself among Your guarded secrets, to make the Great Qur'ān the springtime of my heart, the light of my eyes, the remedy of my

---

Him. "And he for whom Allah has not appointed light, for him there is no light" (*An-Nūr*, 24:40).

(104) [Abū Ḥumayd. *Musnad Aḥmad #15477; Al-Ḥizb al-Aʿẓam*]
The first part of this duʿā' is also to be recited when entering a masjid. A masjid is the house of Allah ﷻ. We enter it with the plea that we are engulfed in His mercy.

(105) [Abū Hurayrah. *Sunan Ibn Mājah #765*]

(106) [Abū Ḥumayd. *Ṣaḥīḥ Muslim #1165*]
A person exiting the masjid should put his left foot out first and say this duʿā'. *Faḍl* refers to the bounties of this world.

(107) [Abū Ayyūb al-Anṣārī. *Mustadrak Ḥākim #1540/5942;* Abū Umāmah al-Bāhilī. *Muʿjam al-Kabīr (Ṭabarānī)*]
forgive all of my sins and mistakes: The reference to sins in the duʿā's of the Prophet ﷺ should not be interpreted literally. We must remember that he was sinless. These refer to the leaving out of the most preferred option, not the commission of a sin as such.

(108) [Um Salamah. *Muʿjam al-Kabīr (Ṭabarānī)*]

﴿١٠٧﴾ اَللّٰهُمَّ اغْفِرْ لِيْ خَطَايَايَ وَذُنُوْبِيْ كُلَّهَا. اَللّٰهُمَّ أَنْعِشْنِيْ، وَأَحْيِنِيْ، وَارْزُقْنِيْ، وَاهْدِنِيْ لِصَالِحِ الأَعْمَالِ وَالأَخْلَاقِ، إِنَّهٗ لَا يَهْدِيْ لِصَالِحِهَا وَلَا يَصْرِفُ سَيِّئَهَا إِلَّا أَنْتَ.

﴿١٠٨﴾ اَللّٰهُمَّ إِنِّيْ أَسْأَلُكَ رِزْقًا طَيِّبًا، وَّعِلْمًا نَّافِعًا، وَّعَمَلًا مُّتَقَبَّلًا.

﴿١٠٩﴾ اَللّٰهُمَّ إِنِّيْ عَبْدُكَ وَابْنُ عَبْدِكَ وَابْنُ أَمَتِكَ، نَاصِيَتِيْ بِيَدِكَ، مَاضٍ فِيَّ حُكْمُكَ، عَدْلٌ فِيَّ قَضَاؤُكَ. أَسْأَلُكَ بِكُلِّ اسْمٍ هُوَ لَكَ، سَمَّيْتَ بِهٖ نَفْسَكَ، أَوْ أَنْزَلْتَهٗ فِيْ كِتَابِكَ، أَوْ عَلَّمْتَهٗ أَحَدًا مِّنْ خَلْقِكَ، أَوِ اسْتَأْثَرْتَ بِهٖ فِيْ عِلْمِ الْغَيْبِ عِنْدَكَ، أَنْ تَجْعَلَ الْقُرْاٰنَ الْعَظِيْمَ رَبِيْعَ قَلْبِيْ، وَنُوْرَ بَصَرِيْ، وَجِلَاءَ حُزْنِيْ،

107. Allāhummagh-fir lī khaṭāyāya wa dhunūbī kullahā. Allāhumma anʿashnī, wa aḥyinī, war-zuqnī, wah-dinī liṣāliḥil-'aʿmāli wal-'akhlāq(i), innahū lā yahdī liṣāliḥihā wa lā yaṣrifu sayyi'ahā illā Ant.

108. Allāhumma innī as'aluka rizqan ṭayyiba(n), wa ʿilman nāfiʿan, wa ʿamalam mutaqabbala.

109. Allāhumma innī ʿabduka wab-nu ʿabdika wab-nu amatik(a), nāṣiyatī biyadik(a), māḍin fiyya ḥukmuk(a), ʿadlun fiyya qaḍā'uk(a). As'aluka bikullis-min huwa lak(a), sammayta bihī nafsak(a), aw anzaltahū fī kitābik(a), aw ʿallamtahū aḥadam min khalqik(a), awis-ta'tharta bihī fī ʿilmil-ghaybi ʿindak(a), an tajʿalal-Qur'ānal-ʿaẓīma rabīʿa qalbī, wa nūra baṣarī, wa jilā'a ḥuznī, wa dhahāba hammī.

grief, and the dispeller of my anxiety.

(110) O Allah, Lord of Jibrīl (Gabriel), Mīkā'īl (Michael), Isrāfīl, and Lord of Ibrāhīm (Abraham), Ismā'īl (Ishmael), and Is-ḥāq (Isaac), grant me safety and do not impose anyone of Your creations upon me with such a thing as would be intolerable for me.

(111) O Allah, protect me from what You declared ḥarām (unlawful) through the sufficiency of what You made halāl (lawful). And make me, by Your benevolence, independent of all besides You.

(112) O Allah, You hear my speech and behold my situation. You know my secret and open matters. None of my affairs is concealed from You. And I am the miserable, needy, suppliant, succor-seeking, fearful and anxious person who confesses his sins. I beg of You—the begging of the destitute. I implore You—the imploring of an abased sinner. And I make du'ā' to You—the du'ā' of the fearful afflicted

---

(109) ['Abdullāh ibn Mas'ūd. *Mu'jam al-Kabīr (Ṭabarānī)*]
Sayyidnā 'Abdullāh ibn Mas'ūd ﵁ reports that the Prophet ﷺ said, "Whenever a Muslim is suffering from a worry or grief and he makes this du'ā', Allah will remove his worry and replace his grief with joy." The Companions said, "Should we not learn these words?" He replied, "Certainly. It is only proper for anyone who listens to these words to learn them." Also see du'ā' 172.

(110) [*Muṣannaf ibn Abī Shaybah* #29171]

(111) ['Alī ibn Abī Ṭālib. *Sunan at-Tirmidhī* #3486]
Sayyidnā 'Alī ﵁ was approached by a a slave who needed money to win his freedom. He did not have money to help the person; instead he taught him these words, saying that the Prophet ﷺ said, "If one is under the burden of a mountain of debt, Allah will help him discharge it when he supplicates to Him thus."

(112) [Composite: 'Abdullāh ibn 'Abbās and 'Abdullāh ibn Ja'far. *Kanz al-'Ummāl* #3614, 3613]
O Allah, You hear my speech . . . and the Best of all who give: The Prophet ﷺ made this du'ā' on the day of 'Arafah during his last

وَذَهَابَ هَمِّيْ۔

﴿١١٠﴾ اَللّٰهُمَّ إِلٰهَ جِبْرَئِيْلَ وَمِيْكَائِيْلَ وَإِسْرَافِيْلَ، وَإِلٰهَ إِبْرَاهِيْمَ وَإِسْمٰعِيْلَ وَإِسْحٰقَ، عَافِنِيْ وَلَا تُسَلِّطَنَّ أَحَدًا مِّنْ خَلْقِكَ عَلَيَّ بِشَيْءٍ لَّا طَاقَةَ لِيْ بِهٖ۔

﴿١١١﴾ اَللّٰهُمَّ اكْفِنِيْ بِحَلَالِكَ عَنْ حَرَامِكَ، وَأَغْنِنِيْ بِفَضْلِكَ عَمَّنْ سِوَاكَ۔

﴿١١٢﴾ اَللّٰهُمَّ إِنَّكَ تَسْمَعُ كَلَامِيْ، وَتَرٰى مَكَانِيْ، وَتَعْلَمُ سِرِّيْ وَعَلَانِيَتِيْ، لَا يَخْفٰى عَلَيْكَ شَيْءٌ مِّنْ أَمْرِيْ، وَأَنَا الْبَائِسُ الْفَقِيْرُ، الْمُسْتَغِيْثُ الْمُسْتَجِيْرُ، الْوَجِلُ الْمُشْفِقُ الْمُقِرُّ الْمُعْتَرِفُ بِذَنْبِهٖ۔ أَسْأَلُكَ مَسْأَلَةَ الْمِسْكِيْنِ، وَأَبْتَهِلُ إِلَيْكَ ابْتِهَالَ الْمُذْنِبِ الذَّلِيْلِ، وَأَدْعُوْكَ دُعَاءَ الْخَائِفِ الضَّرِيْرِ،

110. Allāhumma ilāha Jibra'īla wa Mīkā'īla wa Isrāfīl(a), wa ilāha Ibrāhīma wa Ismāʿīla wa Isḥāq(a), ʿāfinī wa lā tusalliṭanna aḥadam min khalqika ʿalayya bishay'in lā ṭāqata lī bih.

111. Allāhummak-finī biḥalālika ʿan ḥarāmik(a), wa aghninī bifaḍlika ʿamman siwāk.

112. Allāhumma innaka tasmaʿu kalāmī, wa tarā makānī, wa taʿlamu sirrī wa ʿalāniyatī, lā yakhfā ʿalayka shay'um min amrī, wa anal-bā'isul-faqīr(u), al-mustaghīthul-mustajīr(u), al-wajilul-mushfiqul-muqirrul-muʿtarifu bidhambih(ī). As'aluka mas'alatal-miskīn(i), wa abtahilu ilaykab-tihālal-mudhnibidh-dhalīl(i), wa adʿūka duʿā'al-khā'ifiḍ-ḍarīr(i), wa duʿā'a man khaḍaʿat laka raqabatuh(ū), wa fāḍat laka ʿabratuh(ū), wa dhalla

person, whose neck is bowed down before You, whose eyes pour out tears before You, whose body is humbled before You, and whose nose cleaves to the ground for You. O Allah, do not make me frustrated in my supplication to You. And be Compassionate and Merciful to me. O, the Best of those who are asked, and the Best of all who give. O Allah, I place my complaint before You for my weakness, lack of means, and my insignificance in the eyes of people. O the Most Merciful of those who show mercy, to whom will You entrust me? To an enemy who will oppress me or to the hands of a sympathetic friend whom You have entrusted my affair? (O Allah,) if You are not displeased with me then I do not care for such things. Still, Your protection will be the easier for me.

(113) O Allah, we beg You for yearning hearts that are humble and that turn to Your path.

(114) O Allah, I beg You for the faith that settles deep in my heart, a true conviction so that I understand that nothing can afflict me beyond what You have decreed for me, and satisfaction with the pro-

---

Ḥajj. At this time all of Arabia had come under the domination of Islam. About 124,000 companions performed Ḥajj with him.

O Allah, I place my complaint . . . Still, Your protection will be the easier for me: This duʿā' was made on one of the saddest days in the life of Prophet Muḥammad ﷺ. It was June 619 CE when he visited Ṭā'if, a hill station near Makkah. The pagans of Ṭā'if not only mocked his invitation to believe in the one true God, they also sent their urchins to throw stones at him until his shoes filled with blood. In great distress the Prophet ﷺ turned to Allah with this duʿā'. Slightly more than a decade later, the entire area came under the rule of Islam.

Thus, of the two duʿā's that *Munājāt* has put together here, one was said at the height of his worldly achievements; the other at one of the lowest points in his life. Yet they have exactly the same tone. The juxtaposition is extremely significant. It points out that in the best of times, just as in the worst of times, Prophet Muḥammad ﷺ was the same servant of Allah.

وَدُعَاءَ مَنْ خَضَعَتْ لَكَ رَقَبَتُهُ، وَفَاضَتْ لَكَ عَبْرَتُهُ، وَذَلَّ لَكَ جِسْمُهُ، وَرَغِمَ لَكَ أَنْفُهُ. اَللّٰهُمَّ لَا تَجْعَلْنِيْ بِدُعَائِكَ شَقِيًّا، وَّكُنْ بِيْ رَءُوْفًا رَّحِيْمًا، يَّا خَيْرَ الْمَسْئُوْلِيْنَ، وَيَا خَيْرَ الْمُعْطِيْنَ.
اَللّٰهُمَّ إِلَيْكَ أَشْكُوْ ضُعْفَ قُوَّتِيْ، وَقِلَّةَ حِيْلَتِيْ، وَهَوَانِيْ عَلَى النَّاسِ، يَا أَرْحَمَ الرَّاحِمِيْنَ إِلٰى مَنْ تَكِلُنِيْ؟ إِلٰى عَدُوٍّ يَّتَهَجَّمُنِيْ، أَمْ إِلٰى قَرِيْبٍ مَّلَّكْتَهُ أَمْرِيْ؟ إِنْ لَّمْ تَكُنْ سَاخِطًا عَلَيَّ فَلَا أُبَالِيْ، غَيْرَ أَنَّ عَافِيَتَكَ أَوْسَعُ لِيْ.

﴿١١٣﴾ اَللّٰهُمَّ إِنَّا نَسْأَلُكَ قُلُوْبًا أَوَّاهَةً مُّخْبِتَةً مُّنِيْبَةً فِيْ سَبِيْلِكَ.

﴿١١٤﴾ اَللّٰهُمَّ إِنِّيْ أَسْأَلُكَ إِيْمَانًا يُّبَاشِرُ قَلْبِيْ، وَيَقِيْنًا صَادِقًا حَتّٰى أَعْلَمَ أَنَّهُ لَا يُصِيْبُنِيْ إِلَّا مَا كَتَبْتَ لِيْ، وَرِضًى مِّنَ الْمَعِيْشَةِ

laka jismuh(ū), wa raghima laka anfuh(ū). Allāhumma lā tajʿalnī biduʿā'ika shaqiyya(n), wa kum bī Ra'ūfan Raḥīma(n), yā Khayral-mas'ūlīn(a), wa yā Khayral-muʿṭīn(a). Allāhumma ilayka ashkū ḍuʿfa quwwatī, wa qillata ḥīlatī, wa hawānī ʿalan-nās(i). Yā Arḥamar-rāḥimīna ilā man takilunī? Ilā ʿaduwwin yatahajjamunī, am ilā qarībim mallaktahū amrī? In lam takun sākhiṭan ʿalayya fa lā ubālī, ghayra anna ʿāfiyataka awsaʿu lī.

113. Allāhumma innā nas'aluka qulūban awwāhatam mukhbitatam munībatan fī sabīlik.

114. Allāhumma innī as'aluka īmānan yubāshiru qalbī, wa yaqīnan ṣādiqan ḥattā aʿlama annahū lā yuṣībunī illā mā katabta lī, wa riḍam minal-maʿīshati bimā qasamta lī.

vision which You have apportioned for me.

(115) O Allah, praise belongs to You just as You say, and better than how we say it.

(116) O Allah, I seek Your protection from bad morals, deeds, desires, and diseases. We seek Your protection from the evil of everything for which Your Prophet Muḥammad ﷺ sought Your protection. And from a bad neighbor where we live, for a bad neighbor in travel moves away. And from domination of the enemy and the ridicule of the enemies. And from hunger; indeed, it is a bad bedfellow. And from betrayal of trust, for it is a bad intimate. And from that we should turn back on our feet, or that we should be persecuted into separation from our religion. And from tribulations both open and hidden, from the bad day, the bad night, the bad moment, and the bad companion.

---

(113) [ʿAbdullāh ibn Masʿūd. *Mustadrak Ḥākim* #157/1957]

(114) [ʿAbdullāh ibn ʿUmar. *Kanz al-ʿUmmāl* #3657; Ibid. *Majmaʿ az-Zawāʾid* #17410]

(115) [ʿAlī ibn Abī Ṭālib. *Sunan at-Tirmidhī* #3442]

(116) [Composite: Quṭbah ibn Mālik. *Kanz al-ʿUmmāl* #3671; Abū Umāmah al-Bāhilī. *Sunan at-Tirmidhī* #3443; Abū Hurayrah. *Mustadrak Ḥākim* #151/1951; ʿAbdullāh ibn ʿAmr ibn al-ʿĀṣ. *Sunan an-Nasāʾī* #5380; Abū Hurayrah. *Sunan an-Nasāʾī* #5373; Ibn Abī Mulaykah. *Ṣaḥīḥ al-Bukhārī* #6104; Zayd ibn Thābit. *Ṣaḥīḥ Muslim* #5112; ʿUqbah ibn ʿĀmir. *Muʿjam al-Kabīr (Ṭabarānī)* 17:294]

bad intimate: Biṭānah means intimate. Here it means the bad intention (of betraying) that settles deep into one's heart.

from that we should turn back . . . from our religion: Ibn Abī Mulaykah, raḥimahullāh, used to make this duʿāʾ after mentioning the famous ḥadīth according to which angels will force back some people from the Ḥawḍ of Kawthar on the Day of Judgment, explaining to the Prophet ﷺ that these people had turned back after him.

بِمَا قَسَمْتَ لِيْ۔

﴿١١٥﴾ اَللّٰهُمَّ لَكَ الْحَمْدُ كَالَّذِيْ تَقُوْلُ وَخَيْرًا مِّمَّا نَقُوْلُ۔

﴿١١٦﴾ اَللّٰهُمَّ إِنِّيْ أَعُوْذُ بِكَ مِنْ مُّنْكَرَاتِ الْأَخْلَاقِ وَالْأَعْمَالِ وَالْأَهْوَاءِ وَالْأَدْوَاءِ، نَعُوْذُ بِكَ مِنْ شَرِّ مَا اسْتَعَاذَ مِنْهُ نَبِيُّكَ مُحَمَّدٌ صَلَّى اللهُ عَلَيْهِ وَسَلَّمَ، وَمِنْ جَارِ السُّوْءِ فِيْ دَارِ الْمُقَامَةِ فَإِنَّ جَارَ الْبَادِيَةِ يَتَحَوَّلُ، وَغَلَبَةِ الْعَدُوِّ، وَشَمَاتَةِ الْأَعْدَاءِ، وَمِنَ الْجُوْعِ فَإِنَّهٗ بِئْسَ الضَّجِيْعُ، وَمِنَ الْخِيَانَةِ فَإِنَّهَا بِئْسَتِ الْبِطَانَةُ، وَأَنْ نَّرْجِعَ عَلٰى أَعْقَابِنَا، أَوْ نُفْتَنَ عَنْ دِيْنِنَا، وَمِنَ الْفِتَنِ مَا ظَهَرَ مِنْهَا وَمَا بَطَنَ، وَمِنْ يَّوْمِ السُّوْءِ، وَمِنْ لَّيْلَةِ السُّوْءِ، وَمِنْ سَاعَةِ السُّوْءِ، وَمِنْ صَاحِبِ السُّوْءِ۔

115. Allāhumma lakal-ḥamdu kālladhī taqūlu wa khayram mimmā naqūl.

116. Allāhumma innī aʿūdhu bika mim munkarātil-ʾakhlāqi wal-ʾaʿmāli wal-ʾahwāʾi wal-ʾadwāʾ(i), naʿūdhu bika min sharri mas-taʿādha minhu nabiyyuka Muḥammadun ṣallAllāhu ʿalayhi wa sallam(a), wa min jāris-sūʾi fī dāril-muqāmati fa inna jāral-bādiyati yataḥawwal(u), wa ghalabatil-ʿaduww(i), wa shamātatil-ʾaʿdāʾ(i), wa minal-jūʿi fa innahū biʾsaḍ-ḍajīʿ(u), wa minal-khiyānati fa innahā biʾsatil-biṭāna(tu), wa an narjiʿa ʿalā aʿqābinā, aw nuftana ʿan dīninā, wa minal-fitani mā ẓahara minhā wa mā baṭan(a), wa min yawmis-sūʾ(i), wa min laylatis-sūʾ(i), wa min sāʿatis-sūʾ(i), wa min ṣāḥibis-sūʾ.

TUESDAY

In the Name of Allah, the Most Compassionate, the Most Merciful

(117) O Allah, my ṣalāt, my sacrifice, my life, and my death are all for You. To You is my return and Yours is what I leave behind.

(118) O Allah, I beg You for all the good brought by winds.

(119) O Allah, make me such that I thank you greatly for Your blessings, I remember You much, I follow Your counsel, and I preserve Your commands. O Allah, our hearts, our foreheads, and our limbs are in Your Hand. You did not give us total control over any of them. Since You have done that with these then be their patron, and guide us to the path of rectitude.

(120) O Allah, make Your love the dearest and make Your fear the most frightening of all things to me. Cut off worldly needs from me by giving me the longing to meet You. And as You bring comfort to the eyes of the men of the world with their worldly possessions, bring

---

(117) [ʿAlī ibn Abī Ṭālib. *Sunan at-Tirmidhī* #3442]

(118) [ʿAlī ibn Abī Ṭālib. *Kanz al-ʿUmmāl* #3637]

(119) [Composite: Abū Hurayrah. *Sunan at-Tirmidhī* #3530; Jābir ibn ʿAbdillāh. *Kanz al-ʿUmmāl* #3644]

(120) [Al-Haytham ibn Mālik Aṭ-Ṭāʾī. *Kanz al-ʿUmmāl* #3648]

بِسْمِ اللّٰهِ الرَّحْمٰنِ الرَّحِيْمِ

﴿١١٧﴾ اَللّٰهُمَّ لَكَ صَلَاتِيْ وَنُسُكِيْ وَمَحْيَايَ وَمَمَاتِيْ، وَإِلَيْكَ مَآبِيْ، وَلَكَ رَبِّ تُرَاثِيْ۔

﴿١١٨﴾ اَللّٰهُمَّ إِنِّيْ أَسْأَلُكَ مِنْ خَيْرِ مَا تَجِيْءُ بِهِ الرِّيَاحُ۔

﴿١١٩﴾ اَللّٰهُمَّ اجْعَلْنِيْ أُعَظِّمُ شُكْرَكَ، وَأُكْثِرُ ذِكْرَكَ، وَأَتَّبِعُ نَصِيْحَتَكَ، وَأَحْفَظُ وَصِيَّتَكَ۔ اَللّٰهُمَّ إِنَّ قُلُوْبَنَا وَنَوَاصِيَنَا وَجَوَارِحَنَا بِيَدِكَ، لَمْ تُمَلِّكْنَا مِنْهَا شَيْئًا، فَإِذَا فَعَلْتَ ذٰلِكَ بِهِمَا فَكُنْ أَنْتَ وَلِيَّهُمَا، وَاهْدِنَا إِلٰى سَوَاءِ السَّبِيْلِ۔

﴿١٢٠﴾ اَللّٰهُمَّ اجْعَلْ حُبَّكَ أَحَبَّ الْأَشْيَاءِ إِلَيَّ، وَاجْعَلْ خَشْيَتَكَ أَخْوَفَ الْأَشْيَاءِ عِنْدِيْ، وَاقْطَعْ عَنِّيْ حَاجَاتِ الدُّنْيَا بِالشَّوْقِ إِلٰى لِقَائِكَ، وَإِذَا أَقْرَرْتَ أَعْيُنَ أَهْلِ الدُّنْيَا مِنْ دُنْيَاهُمْ

117. Allāhumma laka ṣalātī wa nusukī wa maḥyāya wa mamātī, wa ilayka ma'ābī, wa laka rabbi turāthī.

118. Allāhumma innī as'aluka min khayri mā tajī'u bihir-riyāḥ.

119. Allāhummaj-ʿalnī uʿaẓẓimu shukrak(a), wa ukthiru dhikrak(a), wa attabiʿu naṣīḥatak(a), wa aḥfaẓu waṣiyyatak(a). Allāhumma inna qulūbanā wa nawāṣiyanā wa jawāriḥanā biyadik(a), lam tumalliknā minhā shay'a(n), fa idhā faʿalta dhālika bihimā fa kun anta waliyyahumā, wah-dinā ilā sawā'is-sabīl.

120. Allāhummaj-ʿal ḥubbaka aḥabbal-'ashyā'i ilayy(a), waj-ʿal khashyataka akhwafal-'ashyā'i ʿindī, waq-ṭaʿ ʿannī ḥājātid-dunyā bish-shawqi ilā liqā'ik(a), wa idhā aqrarta aʿyuna ahlid-dunyā min

comfort to my eyes with Your obedience and worship.

(121) O Allah, I beg You for health, chastity, integrity, good character, and acceptance of fate.

(122) O Allah, to You is due all praise with thanks; it is only Your domain to do favors with grace. O Allah, I beseech You to enable me to perform the deeds loved by You, develop sincere reliance on You, and hold good expectations from You.

(123) O Allah, open my heart to the hearing of Your remembrance. Grant me obedience to You and to Your Messenger ﷺ *and (grant me) performance of deeds according to Your Book.*

(124) O Allah, make me fear You as if I see You all the time until I meet You. Make me blissful as a result of Your taqwā (Your fear and piety); do not make me wretched as a result of Your disobedience.

---

(121) ['Abdullāh ibn 'Amr ibn al-'Āṣ. *Kanz al-'Ummāl* #3650]

Health is the first item in this list because its absence affects a person's ability to worship Allah سبحانه وتعالى in addition to affecting his ability to enjoy this worldly life. The other qualities mentioned are all attributes of īmān. Like īmān itself, they can come to us through the blessings of Allah.

(122) [Composite: Ka'b ibn 'Ujrah and Abū Hurayrah. *Kanz al-'Ummāl* #3653, 3654]

It is important to hold good expectations from Allah سبحانه وتعالى, for Allah سبحانه وتعالى deals with a person according to his expectations. When a servant of Allah sincerely puts his trust and hopes in Him, Allah سبحانه وتعالى does not disappoint him.

(123) ['Alī ibn Abī Ṭālib. *Kanz al-'Ummāl* #3655]

open my heart: That is, when I perform dhikr by tongue or hear it from others, it should also reach the depths of my heart.

(124) [Abū Hurayrah. *Majma' az-Zawā'id* #17393]

فَأَقْرِرْ عَيْنِي مِنْ عِبَادَتِكَ۔

﴿١٢١﴾ اَللّٰهُمَّ إِنِّيْ أَسْأَلُكَ الصِّحَّةَ، وَالْعِفَّةَ، وَالْأَمَانَةَ، وَحُسْنَ الْخُلُقِ، وَالرِّضَا بِالْقَدَرِ۔

﴿١٢٢﴾ اَللّٰهُمَّ لَكَ الْحَمْدُ شُكْرًا وَّلَكَ الْمَنُّ فَضْلًا۔ اَللّٰهُمَّ إِنِّيْ أَسْأَلُكَ التَّوْفِيْقَ لِمَحَابِّكَ مِنَ الْأَعْمَالِ، وَصِدْقَ التَّوَكُّلِ عَلَيْكَ، وَحُسْنَ الظَّنِّ بِكَ۔

﴿١٢٣﴾ اَللّٰهُمَّ افْتَحْ مَسَامِعَ قَلْبِيْ لِذِكْرِكَ، وَارْزُقْنِيْ طَاعَتَكَ، وَطَاعَةَ رَسُوْلِكَ، وَعَمَلًا بِكِتَابِكَ۔

﴿١٢٤﴾ اَللّٰهُمَّ اجْعَلْنِيْ أَخْشَاكَ كَأَنِّيْ أَرَاكَ أَبَدًا حَتّٰى أَلْقَاكَ، وَأَسْعِدْنِيْ بِتَقْوَاكَ وَلَا تُشْقِنِيْ بِمَعْصِيَتِكَ۔

dunyāhum fa aqrir ʿaynī min ʿibādatik.

121. Allāhumma innī as'alukaṣ-ṣiḥḥa(ta), wal-ʿiffa(ta), wal-'amāna(ta), wa ḥusnal-khuluq(i), war-riḍā bil-qadar.

122. Allāhumma lakal-ḥamdu shukran wa lakal-mannu faḍla(n). Allāhumma innī as'alukat-tawfīqa limaḥābbika minal-'aʿmāl(i), wa ṣidqat-tawakkuli ʿalayk(a), wa ḥusnaẓ-ẓanni bik.

123. Allāhummaf-taḥ masāmiʿa qalbī lidhikrik(a), war-zuqnī ṭāʿatak(a), wa ṭāʿata Rasūlik(a), wa ʿamalam biKitābik.

124. Allāhummaj-ʿalnī akhshāka ka'annī arāka abadan ḥattā alqāk(a), wa asʿidnī bitaqwāka wa lā tushqinī bimaʿṣiyatik.

(125) O Allah, extend Your graciousness to me by turning all difficulties into ease, for to make a difficulty easy is very easy for You. And I ask You for ease and forgiveness in the world and in the Hereafter. O Allah, forgive me for indeed You are the Generous Forgiver.

(126) O Allah, purify my heart from hypocrisy, my deeds from ostentation and pretension, my tongue from lies, and my eyes from wrongful glances. For, indeed, You know what the eyes deceptively glance at and what the hearts conceal.

(127) O Allah, grant me profusely weeping eyes that comfort the heart with tears that flow out of Your fear—before the time comes when eyes will be shedding blood and teeth will become embers.

(128) O Allah, grant me security with Your power, admit me to

---

(125) [Composite: Abū Hurayrah and Abū Saʿīd al-Khudrī. *Kanz al-ʿUmmāl* #3658, 3659]

(126) [Um Maʿbad al-Khuzāʿiyyah. *Kanz al-ʿUmmāl* #3660]

(127) [ʿAbdullāh ibn ʿUmar. *Kanz al-ʿUmmāl* #3661]
A believer is a soft-hearted person who sheds much tears here out of the fear of Allah.
before the time: This refers to the state of sinners and disbelievers in the Hereafter.

(128) [ʿAbdullāh ibn ʿUmar. *Kanz al-ʿUmmāl* #3662]

﴿١٢٥﴾ اَللّٰهُمَّ الْطُفْ بِيْ فِيْ تَيْسِيْرِ كُلِّ عَسِيْرٍ، فَإِنَّ تَيْسِيْرَ كُلِّ عَسِيْرٍ عَلَيْكَ يَسِيْرٌ، وَّأَسْأَلُكَ الْيُسْرَ وَالْمُعَافَاةَ فِي الدُّنْيَا وَالْاٰخِرَةِ۔ اَللّٰهُمَّ اعْفُ عَنِّيْ فَإِنَّكَ عَفُوٌّ كَرِيْمٌ۔

﴿١٢٦﴾ اَللّٰهُمَّ طَهِّرْ قَلْبِيْ مِنَ النِّفَاقِ، وَعَمَلِيْ مِنَ الرِّيَاءِ، وَلِسَانِيْ مِنَ الْكَذِبِ، وَعَيْنِيْ مِنَ الْخِيَانَةِ، فَإِنَّكَ تَعْلَمُ خَائِنَةَ الْأَعْيُنِ وَمَا تُخْفِي الصُّدُوْرُ۔

﴿١٢٧﴾ اَللّٰهُمَّ ارْزُقْنِيْ عَيْنَيْنِ هَطَّالَتَيْنِ، تَشْفِيَانِ الْقَلْبَ بِذُرُوْفِ الدُّمُوْعِ مِنْ خَشْيَتِكَ، قَبْلَ أَنْ تَكُوْنَ الدُّمُوْعُ دَمًا وَّالْأَضْرَاسُ جَمْرًا۔

﴿١٢٨﴾ اَللّٰهُمَّ عَافِنِيْ فِيْ قُدْرَتِكَ، وَأَدْخِلْنِيْ فِيْ رَحْمَتِكَ،

125. Allāhummal-ṭuf bī fī taysīri kulli ʿasīr(in), fa inna taysīra kulli ʿasīrin ʿalayka yasīr(un), wa as'alukal-yusra wal-muʿāfāta fid-dunyā wal-ākhira(ti). Allāhummaʿ-fu ʿannī fa innaka ʿAfuwwun Karīm.

126. Allāhumma ṭahhir qalbī minan-nifāq(i), wa ʿamalī minar-riyā'(i), wa lisānī minal-kadhib(i), wa ʿaynī minal-khiyāna(ti), fa innaka taʿlamu khā'inatal-'aʿyuni wa mā tukhfiṣ-ṣudūr.

127. Allāhummar-zuqnī ʿaynayni haṭṭālatayn(i), tashfiyānil-qalba bidhurūfid-dumūʿi min khashyatik(a), qabla an takūnad-dumūʿu daman wal-'aḍrāsu jamra.

128. Allāhumma ʿāfinī fī qudratik(a), wa adkhilnī fī raḥmatik(a),

Your mercy, let me spend my entire life in Your obedience, let my life end with my best deed, and make Paradise its reward.

(129) O Allah, the Soother of worry, the Remover of grief, the Grantor of the duʿāʾ of the helpless, the Giver of mercy and compassion in the world and the Hereafter, You alone can have true mercy on me. So show such mercy to me that will totally free me from the need of others' mercy.

(130) O Allah, I beg You for a surprise blessing and seek Your protection from a sudden misfortune.

(131) O Allah, Your name is as-Salām (Giver of Peace); peace comes only from You and returns to You. I beg You, O the Majestic and Benevolent, that You accept our duʿā's, grant us what we long

---

(129) [ʿĀ'ishah. *Mustadrak Ḥākim* #98/1898]

(130) [Anas ibn Mālik. *ʿAmal al-Yawm wal-Laylah (Ibn as-Sunnī)* #39]
We do not know what a new day brings with it. So we should be making this duʿāʾ every morning and evening, as was the practice of Prophet Muḥammad ﷺ. He said that anyone who makes this duʿāʾ every morning and evening will be saved from sudden calamities during that day or night.

(131) [Abū Saʿīd al-Khudrī. *Majmaʿ az-Zawā'id* #16998]
free us from . . . who do not need us: This is an interdependent world. That makes communities, societies, and civilization itself possible. When two parties have mutual and roughly equal needs for each other, the result is an equitable exchange. On the other hand, one-sided dependence is the source of all exploitation. We seek Allah's help in getting out of it and we must do all we can to end such a relationship.

وَاقْضِ أَجَلِيْ فِيْ طَاعَتِكَ، وَاخْتِمْ لِيْ بِخَيْرِ عَمَلِيْ، وَاجْعَلْ ثَوَابَهُ الْجَنَّةَ.

﴿١٢٩﴾ اَللّٰهُمَّ فَارِجَ الْهَمِّ، كَاشِفَ الْغَمِّ، مُجِيْبَ دَعْوَةِ الْمُضْطَرِّيْنَ، رَحْمٰنَ الدُّنْيَا وَالْاٰخِرَةِ وَرَحِيْمَهُمَا، أَنْتَ تَرْحَمُنِيْ فَارْحَمْنِيْ بِرَحْمَةٍ تُغْنِيْنِيْ بِهَا عَنْ رَّحْمَةِ مَنْ سِوَاكَ.

﴿١٣٠﴾ اَللّٰهُمَّ إِنِّيْ أَسْأَلُكَ مِنْ فُجَاءَةِ الْخَيْرِ، وَأَعُوْذُ بِكَ مِنْ فُجَاءَةِ الشَّرِّ.

﴿١٣١﴾ اَللّٰهُمَّ أَنْتَ السَّلَامُ وَمِنْكَ السَّلَامُ وَإِلَيْكَ يَعُوْدُ السَّلَامُ، أَسْأَلُكَ يَا ذَا الْجَلَالِ وَالْإِكْرَامِ أَنْ تَسْتَجِيْبَ لَنَا

waq-ḍi ajalī fī ṭāʿatik(a), wakh-tim lī bikhayri ʿamalī, waj-ʿal thawābahul-Jannah.

129. Allāhumma Fārijal-hamm(i), Kāshifal-ghamm(i), Mujība daʿwatil-muḍṭarrīn(a), Raḥmānad-dunyā wal-ākhirati wa raḥīmahumā, anta tarḥamunī far-ḥamnī biraḥmatin tughnīnī bihā ʿan raḥmati man siwāk.

130. Allāhumma innī as'aluka min fujā'atil-khayr(i), wa aʿūdhu bika min fujā'atish-sharr.

131. Allāhumma antas-Salāmu wa minkas-salāmu wa ilayka yaʿūdus-salām(u), as'aluka yā Dhal-jalāli wal-'ikrāmi an tastajība

for, and free us from needing those of Your creatures who do not need us.

(132) O Allah, choose and select for me.

(133) O Allah, make me happy with Your Will, and bless me in whatever You have destined for me so that I do not want to hasten what you delayed or to delay what you hastened.

(134) O Allah, there is no (real) life except that of the Hereafter.

(135) O Allah, give me life of a humble person and death of a humble person, and raise me on the Day of Judgment among humble persons.

(136) O Allah, make me among those who, when they commit an act of virtue, rejoice, and when they commit a mistake, seek forgiveness.

---

(132) [Abū Bakr. *Sunan at-Tirmidhī* #3438]
When a person is faced with a decision and there is no time for *Istikhārah* ṣalāt, this duʿā' can be said repeatedly instead.

(133) [ʿAbdullāh ibn ʿUmar. *Kanz al-ʿUmmāl* #9323]
This duʿā' is also recommended for saying when one is facing financial difficulties.

(134) [Anas ibn Mālik. *Ṣaḥīḥ al-Bukhārī* #2741]
The Prophet ﷺ said this when digging the trench in preparation for the Battle of the Trench. The Ansar were reciting:

نَحْنُ الَّذِينَ بَايَعُوا مُحَمَّدَا   عَلَى الْجِهَادِ مَا حَيِينَا أَبَدَا

And the Prophet ﷺ responded with:

اَللّٰهُمَّ لَا عَيْشَ إِلَّا عَيْشُ الْآخِرَهْ   فَأَكْرِمْ الْأَنْصَارَ وَالْمُهَاجِرَهْ

(135) [Anas ibn Mālik. *Sunan at-Tirmidhī* #2275]

(136) [ʿĀ'ishah. *Sunan Ibn Mājah* #3810]
Some scholars have commented: The best sin is the one followed →

دَعْوَتَنَا، وَأَنْ تُعْطِيَنَا رَغْبَتَنَا، وَأَنْ تُغْنِيَنَا عَمَّنْ أَغْنَيْتَهُ عَنَّا مِنْ خَلْقِكَ۔

﴿١٣٢﴾ اَللّٰهُمَّ خِرْ لِيْ وَاخْتَرْ لِيْ۔

﴿١٣٣﴾ اَللّٰهُمَّ أَرْضِنِيْ بِقَضَائِكَ، وَبَارِكْ لِيْ فِيْمَا قُدِّرَ لِيْ، حَتّٰى لَا أُحِبَّ تَعْجِيْلَ مَا أَخَّرْتَ، وَلَا تَأْخِيْرَ مَا عَجَّلْتَ۔

﴿١٣٤﴾ اَللّٰهُمَّ لَا عَيْشَ إِلَّا عَيْشُ الْاٰخِرَةِ۔

﴿١٣٥﴾ اَللّٰهُمَّ أَحْيِنِيْ مِسْكِيْنًا وَّأَمِتْنِيْ مِسْكِيْنًا وَّاحْشُرْنِيْ فِيْ زُمْرَةِ الْمَسَاكِيْنِ۔

﴿١٣٦﴾ اَللّٰهُمَّ اجْعَلْنِيْ مِنَ الَّذِيْنَ إِذَا أَحْسَنُوْا اسْتَبْشَرُوْا، وَإِذَا أَسَاءُوْا اسْتَغْفَرُوْا۔

lanā daʿwatanā, wa an tuʿṭiyanā raghbatanā, wa an tughniyanā ʿamman aghnaytahū ʿannā min khalqik.

132. Allāhumma khir lī wakh-tar lī.

133. Allāhumma arḍinī biqaḍā'ik(a), wa bārik lī fīmā quddira lī, ḥattā lā uḥibba taʿjīla mā akh-khart(a), wa lā ta'khīra mā ʿajjalt.

134. Allāhumma lā ʿaysha illā ʿayshul-ākhirah.

135. Allāhumma aḥyinī miskīnan wa amitnī miskīnan waḥ-shurnī fī zumratil-masākīn.

136. Allāhummaj-ʿalnī minal-ladhīna idhā aḥsanus-tabsharū, wa idhā asā'us-taghfarū.

by repentance, and the worst act of obedience is the one followed by pride *(Fayḍ al-Qadīr)*.

(137) O Allah, I beg You for Your special mercy with which You may guide my heart, arrange my affairs, end my disorder, improve my religion, discharge my debt, protect that part of me that is out of sight, elevate whatever is in sight, brighten my face, purify my deeds, inspire me with what is right for me, return to me what I cherish and love, and protect me from every evil.

(138) O Allah, grant me faith that is never shaken, belief so that there is no disbelief thereafter, and mercy by virtue of which I gain the distinction of honor granted by You in this life and the Hereafter.

(139) O Allah, I beg You for success in what is pre-determined, the hospitality reserved for Your martyrs, the life of the blissful, the company of prophets, and Your help against the enemies; verily You hear all duʿā's.

(137-143) [ʿAbdullāh ibn ʿAbbās. *Sunan at-Tirmidhī* #3341; *Muʿjam al-Kabīr (Ṭabarānī)* 10/284; *Kanz al-ʿUmmāl* #3608, 4988] All the duʿā's listed here from 137 to 143 are part of one comprehensive duʿā' that Prophet Muḥammad ﷺ said at the end of his nightly *Tahajjud* ṣalāt.

(137) special mercy: that ensues on its own without there being a cause for it. We seek Allah's mercy while recognizing that we can never deserve it through our own actions.
guide my heart: guide me to You and bring me closer to You.
out of sight: refers to a person's inner qualities: faith, morality, and character.
in sight: refers to our overt deeds.
purify my deeds: purify them of insincerity and the desire to get praise from other human beings (*Fayḍ al-Qadīr*).

(138) mercy by virtue of which: This again affirms that we gain higher ranks through Allah's mercy, not by dint of our actions.

(139) martyrs: The station of and the hospitality reserved for the Prophet ﷺ is higher than that of the martyrs. But it has been mentioned here to show that it is proper for the ummah to make this duʿā'.

﴿١٣٧﴾ اَللّٰهُمَّ إِنِّيْ أَسْأَلُكَ رَحْمَةً مِّنْ عِنْدِكَ تَهْدِيْ بِهَا قَلْبِيْ، وَتَجْمَعُ بِهَا أَمْرِيْ، وَتَلُمُّ بِهَا شَعْثِيْ، وَتُصْلِحُ بِهَا دِيْنِيْ، وَتَقْضِيْ بِهَا دَيْنِيْ، وَتَحْفَظُ بِهَا غَائِبِيْ، وَتَرْفَعُ بِهَا شَاهِدِيْ، وَتُبَيِّضُ بِهَا وَجْهِيْ، وَتُزَكِّيْ بِهَا عَمَلِيْ، وَتُلْهِمُنِيْ بِهَا رَشَدِيْ، وَتَرُدُّ بِهَا أُلْفَتِيْ، وَتَعْصِمُنِيْ بِهَا مِنْ كُلِّ سُوْءٍ.

﴿١٣٨﴾ اَللّٰهُمَّ أَعْطِنِيْ إِيْمَانًا لَّا يَرْتَدُّ، وَيَقِيْنًا لَّيْسَ بَعْدَهٗ كُفْرٌ، وَّرَحْمَةً أَنَالُ بِهَا شَرَفَ كَرَامَتِكَ فِي الدُّنْيَا وَالْاٰخِرَةِ.

﴿١٣٩﴾ اَللّٰهُمَّ إِنِّيْ أَسْأَلُكَ الْفَوْزَ فِي الْقَضَاءِ، وَنُزُلَ الشُّهَدَاءِ، وَعَيْشَ السُّعَدَاءِ، وَمُرَافَقَةَ الْأَنْبِيَاءِ، وَالنَّصْرَ عَلَى الْأَعْدَاءِ، إِنَّكَ سَمِيْعُ الدُّعَاءِ.

137. Allāhumma innī as'aluka raḥmatam min ʿindika tahdī bihā qalbī, wa tajmaʿu bihā amrī, wa talummu bihā shaʿthī, wa tuṣliḥu bihā dīnī, wa taqḍī bihā daynī, wa taḥfaẓu bihā ghā'ibī, wa tarfaʿu bihā shāhidī, wa tubayyiḍu bihā wajhī, wa tuzakkī bihā ʿamalī, wa tulhimunī bihā rashadī, wa taruddu bihā ulfatī, wa taʿṣimunī bihā min kulli sū'.

138. Allāhumma aʿṭinī īmānan lā yartadd(u), wa yaqīnan laysa baʿdahū kufr(un), wa raḥmatan anālu bihā sharafa karāmatika fid-dunyā wal-ākhirah.

139. Allāhumma innī as'alukal-fawza fil-qaḍā'(i), wa nuzulash-shuhadā'(i), wa ʿayshas-suʿadā'(i), wa murāfaqatal-'ambiyā'(i), wan-naṣra ʿalal-'aʿdā'(i), innaka Samīʿud-duʿā'.

(140) *O Allah, if there is any blessing that You have promised to any of Your creations or You are going to give it to any of Your servants, but I have been unable to conceive of it, and my efforts have fallen short of it, and my intentions and supplications have not reached it, then I also long for it and beg You for the same in the name of Your mercy, O Cherisher of the worlds.*

(141) *O Allah, I place my needs before You. Although my thoughts are deficient and my actions weak and wanting, I am in need of Your mercy. So, O the One Who decides all affairs and O the One Who heals the hearts, just as You keep the oceans apart from each other, so keep me away from the punishment of Hell and from seeking destruction (in the Hereafter, due to agonies of Hell) and (protect me) from the tribulations of the grave.*

(142) *O Allah, O the Maker of strong covenants whose every command is right. I beseech You for peace on the Appointed Day and for Paradise on the Day of Eternity along with those who are close to*

---

life of the blissful: i.e. in the Hereafter.
Your help: Allah's help sometimes comes overtly. At other times it comes internally whereby His servants' hearts are strengthened.
enemies: i.e. of the religion (*Fayḍ al-Qadīr*).

(140) In other words I am asking not only for all the good that I can think of but also for the good that I cannot even think of.

(141) **seeking destruction:** This refers to this verse: "Pray not that day for one destruction, but pray for many destructions!" (*Al-Furqān*, 25:14). People will be seeking self-destruction as an escape from the agonies of Hell but they will not get it.

The Prophet ﷺ said this du'ā' out of humbleness before Allah. No one should entertain any idea that prophets face questioning in the grave (Zamakhsharī in *Fayḍ al-Qadīr*).

(142) **strong covenant:** Literally, it means strong rope. It refers to the Qur'ān or the *dīn* as the Qur'ān says, "Hold fast to the rope of Allah" (*Āl-i-'Imrān*, 3:103).

﴿١٤٠﴾ اَللّٰهُمَّ مَا قَصَّرَ عَنْهُ رَأْيِيْ، وَضَعُفَ عَنْهُ عَمَلِيْ، وَلَمْ تَبْلُغْهُ نِيَّتِيْ وَمَسْأَلَتِيْ مِنْ خَيْرٍ وَّعَدْتَّهٗ أَحَدًا مِّنْ خَلْقِكَ، أَوْ خَيْرٍ أَنْتَ مُعْطِيْهِ أَحَدًا مِّنْ عِبَادِكَ، فَإِنِّيْ أَرْغَبُ إِلَيْكَ فِيْهِ، وَأَسْأَلُكَ بِرَحْمَتِكَ رَبَّ الْعٰلَمِيْنَ۔

﴿١٤١﴾ اَللّٰهُمَّ إِنِّيْ أُنْزِلُ بِكَ حَاجَتِيْ، وَإِنْ قَصَّرَ رَأْيِيْ وَضَعُفَ عَمَلِي افْتَقَرْتُ إِلٰى رَحْمَتِكَ. فَأَسْأَلُكَ يَا قَاضِيَ الْأُمُوْرِ، وَيَا شَافِيَ الصُّدُوْرِ، كَمَا تُجِيْرُ بَيْنَ الْبُحُوْرِ، أَنْ تُجِيْرَنِيْ مِنْ عَذَابِ السَّعِيْرِ، وَمِنْ دَعْوَةِ الثُّبُوْرِ، وَمِنْ فِتْنَةِ الْقُبُوْرِ۔

﴿١٤٢﴾ اَللّٰهُمَّ ذَا الْحَبْلِ الشَّدِيْدِ، وَالْأَمْرِ الرَّشِيْدِ، أَسْأَلُكَ الْأَمْنَ يَوْمَ الْوَعِيْدِ، وَالْجَنَّةَ يَوْمَ الْخُلُوْدِ، مَعَ الْمُقَرَّبِيْنَ الشُّهُوْدِ،

140. Allāhumma mā qaṣṣara ʿanhu ra'yī, wa ḍaʿufa ʿanhu ʿamalī, wa lam tablughhu niyyatī wa mas'alatī min khayrin waʿadttahū aḥadam min khalqik(a), aw khayrin anta muʿṭīhi aḥadam min ʿibādik(a), fa innī arghabu ilayka fīh(i), wa as'aluka biraḥmatika Rabbal-ʿālamīn.

141. Allāhumma innī unzilu bika ḥājatī, wa in qaṣṣara ra'yī wa ḍaʿufa ʿamalif-taqartu ilā raḥmatik(a). Fa as'aluka yā Qāḍiyal-'umūr(i), wa yā Shāfiyaṣ-ṣudūr(i), kamā tujīru baynal-buḥūr(i), an tujīranī min ʿadhābis-saʿīr(i), wa min daʿwatith-thubūr(i), wa min fitnatil-qubūr.

142. Allāhumma Dhal-ḥablish-shadīd(i), wal-'amrir-rashīd(i), as'alukal-'amna yawmal-waʿīd(i), wal-Jannata yawmal-khulūd(i),

You and will be watching you, are often busy in kneeling and prostrating before You, and who fulfill their covenants. Surely, You are the Merciful, the Most Loving, and indeed, You do what You will.

(143) O Allah, make us the ones who guide aright and are guided aright, who are neither misguided nor do they lead others astray. At peace with Your friends, at war with Your enemies. Loving with Your love those who love You. Despising with Your antagonism those of Your creatures who oppose You.

O Allah, this is the supplication and it is up to You to grant it. This is the effort and the reliance is on You.

(144) O Allah, do not leave me to my own devices even for the twinkling of an eye. Do not take back from me any good that You have granted me.

(145) O Allah, You are not a god who might have been devised by

---

Day of Eternity: Day of entering into the Eternal Garden or the Eternal Fire.

(143) As the ḥadīth points out, "Whoever loves for the sake of Allah and hates for the sake of Allah, he has perfected his imān."

(144) [ʿAbdullāh ibn ʿUmar. *Majmaʿ az-Zawā'id* #17409]

(145) [Ṣuhayb ar-Rūmī. *Kanz al-ʿUmmāl* #3676; Ibid. *Kanz al-ʿUmmāl* #3740.] Kaʿb al-Aḥbār narrated from Ṣuhayb ar-Rumī رضي الله عنه that the Prophet ﷺ used to make this duʿā'. He also added his comments that Prophet Dāwūd (David) عليه السلام used to do the same.

الرُّكَّعِ السُّجُوْدِ، الْمُوْفِيْنَ بِالْعُهُوْدِ، إِنَّكَ رَحِيْمٌ وَّدُوْدٌ، وَّإِنَّكَ تَفْعَلُ مَا تُرِيْدُ۔

﴿١٤٣﴾ اَللّٰهُمَّ اجْعَلْنَا هَادِيْنَ مُهْتَدِيْنَ، غَيْرَ ضَالِّيْنَ وَلَا مُضِلِّيْنَ، سِلْمًا لِّأَوْلِيَائِكَ وَحَرْبًا لِّأَعْدَائِكَ، نُحِبُّ بِحُبِّكَ مَنْ أَحَبَّكَ، وَنُعَادِيْ بِعَدَاوَتِكَ مَنْ خَالَفَكَ مِنْ خَلْقِكَ۔

اَللّٰهُمَّ هٰذَا الدُّعَاءُ وَعَلَيْكَ الْإِجَابَةُ، وَهٰذَا الْجُهْدُ وَعَلَيْكَ التُّكْلَانُ۔

﴿١٤٤﴾ اَللّٰهُمَّ لَا تَكِلْنِيْ إِلٰى نَفْسِيْ طَرْفَةَ عَيْنٍ، وَّلَا تَنْزِعْ مِنِّيْ صَالِحَ مَا أَعْطَيْتَنِيْ۔

﴿١٤٥﴾ اَللّٰهُمَّ إِنَّكَ لَسْتَ بِإِلٰهٍ إِسْتَحْدَثْنَاهُ، وَلَا بِرَبٍّ يَّبِيْدُ

maʿal-muqarrabīnash-shuhūd(i), ar-rukkaʿis-sujūd(i), al-mūfīna bil-ʿuhūd(i), innaka Raḥīmun Wadūd(un), wa innaka tafʿalu mā turīd.

143. Allāhummaj-ʿalnā hādīna muhtadīn(a), ghayra ḍāllīna wa lā muḍillīn(a), silman li'awliyā'ika wa ḥarban li'aʿdā'ik(a), nuḥibbu biḥubbika man aḥabbak(a), wa nuʿādī biʿadāwatika man khālafaka min khalqik.

Allāhumma hādhad-duʿā'u wa ʿalaykal-'ijāba(tu), wa hādhal-juhdu wa ʿalaykat-tuklān.

144. Allāhumma lā takilnī ilā nafsī ṭarfata ʿayn(in), wa lā tanziʿ minnī ṣāliḥa mā aʿṭaytanī.

145. Allāhumma innaka lasta bi'ilāhinis-taḥdathnāh(u), wa lā

us, nor are You a perishable lord invented by us. Nor do You have any partners that share in Your Authority. Nor is it that we had a different god before You whom we would be petitioning rather than You. And it is not that anyone helped You in our creation so we would associate him with You. You are, indeed, Blissful and Supreme.

(146) O Allah, You are the One Who created my soul and You are the One Who will take it back. Its death and life are in Your control. If You keep it alive then protect it. And if You give it death then grant it forgiveness. O Allah, I beg for ʿāfiyah.

(147) O Allah, enrich me with knowledge, grace me with forbearance, honor me with taqwa, and adorn me with peace and security.

---

(146) [ʿAbdullāh ibn ʿUmar. *Ṣaḥīḥ Muslim* #4887]
For the meaning of *al-ʿāfiyah*, see duʿāʾ 64. This duʿāʾ is also to be said before going to sleep.

(147) [ʿAbdullāh ibn ʿUmar. *Kanz al-ʿUmmāl* #3663]
Discussing this ḥadīth, *Fayḍ al-Qadīr* offers this very illuminating commentary on knowledge:

> This means the knowledge of the path of the Hereafter. Knowledge and worship are the core for which exist the books and lectures and sermons. It is for them that books were revealed and prophets were sent. It was for them that the heavens and the earth were created:
>
> (اَللهُ الَّذِي خَلَقَ سَبْعَ سَمَاوَاتٍ وَّمِنَ الْأَرْضِ مِثْلَهُنَّ يَتَنَزَّلُ الْأَمْرُ بَيْنَهُنَّ لِتَعْلَمُوْا أَنَّ اللهَ عَلَى كُلِّ شَيْءٍ قَدِيرٌ وَأَنَّ اللهَ قَدْ أَحَاطَ بِكُلِّ شَيْءٍ عِلْماً)
>
> Allah is He Who created seven heavens, and of the earth the like of them; the commandment continues to descend among them, that you may know that Allah has power over all things and that Allah indeed encompasses all things in (His) knowledge (*Aṭ-Ṭalāq*, 65:12).

→

ذِكْرُهُ ابْتَدَعْنَاهُ، وَلَا عَلَيْكَ شُرَكَاءُ يَقْضُوْنَ مَعَكَ، وَلَا كَانَ لَنَا قَبْلَكَ مِنْ إِلٰهٍ نَّلجَأُ إِلَيْهِ وَنَذَرُكَ، وَلَا أَعَانَكَ عَلىٰ خَلْقِنَا أَحَدٌ فَنُشْرِكُهُ فِيْكَ، تَبَارَكْتَ وَتَعَالَيْتَ۔

﴿١٤٦﴾ اَللَّهُمَّ خَلَقْتَ نَفْسِيْ وَأَنْتَ تَوَفَّاهَا. لَكَ مَمَاتُهَا وَمَحْيَاهَا. إِنْ أَحْيَيْتَهَا فَاحْفَظْهَا، وَإِنْ أَمَتَّهَا فَاغْفِرْ لَهَا. اَللَّهُمَّ إِنِّيْ أَسْأَلُكَ الْعَافِيَةَ۔

﴿١٤٧﴾ اَللّٰهُمَّ أَغْنِنِيْ بِالْعِلْمِ، وَزَيِّنِّيْ بِالْحِلْمِ، وَأَكْرِمْنِيْ بِالتَّقْوٰى، وَجَمِّلْنِيْ بِالْعَافِيَةِ۔

birabbin yabīdu dhikruhub-tadaʿnāh(u), wa lā ʿalayka shurakāʾu yaqḍūna maʿak(a), wa lā kāna lanā qablaka min ilāhin naljaʾu ilayhi wa nadharuk(a), wa lā aʿānaka ʿalā khalqinā aḥadun fa nushrikuhū fīk(a), tabārakta wa taʿālayt.

146. Allāhumma khalaqta nafsī wa anta tawaffāhā. Laka mamātuhā wa maḥyāhā. In aḥyaytahā faḥ-faẓhā, wa in amattahā fagh-fir lahā. Allāhumma innī asʾalukal-ʿāfiyah.

147. Allāhumma aghninī bil-ʿilm(i), wa zayyinnī bil-ḥilm(i), wa akrimnī bit-taqwā, wa jammilnī bil-ʿāfiyah.

This verse is sufficient proof of the grandeur of knowledge, especially the knowledge of the *maʿrifah* and *tawḥīd* (Allah consciousness and monotheism). Whoever has been given this knowledge is rich although he may have no money. And whoever is deprived of it is poor even though he may be wealthy.

(148) O Allah, may that period not reach me nor should they (my Companions) reach that period when the knowledgeable will not be followed and the gentle will get no regard. The hearts of the people of that age will be like the aʿājim while their language may be Arabic.

(149) O Allah, I seek from you an unbreakable promise. I am just a human being. So whichever believer I hurt or rebuke or hit or curse then change that for him into mercy, purification, and a means of closeness to You on the Day of Judgment.

(150) O Allah, I seek Your protection from leprosy, obstinacy, hy-

---

(148) [Abū Hurayrah. *Kanz al-ʿUmmāl* #3686]
Aʿājim is the plural of *aʿjam* meaning a non-Arab or a person who does not speak clearly. It is roughly the equivalent of "barbarian" in English.
hearts of the aʿājim: hearts with no moral values and full of hypocrisy and ostentation. (*Fayḍ al-Qadīr*)
their language may be Arabic: They will be very eloquent.

Because of cultural and historical barriers, the translation cannot do justice to this duʿā'. This duʿā', more than 1,400 years ago, forewarned about a period when savagery, cruelty, and hypocrisy will be assisted by eloquent and slick talk.

(149) [Abū Hurayrah. *Ṣaḥīḥ Muslim* #4707]
A duʿā' for those whom one might have hurt! Of course such a duʿā' could only come from the heart of the Prophet of Mercy ﷺ. This duʿā' is a further indication of his deep compassion for the ummah. Prophet Muḥammad ﷺ was far from using harsh words as the Qur'ān and the Sīrah very firmly establish. There were some expressions common among the Arabs to show displeasure and never meant literally. These have been referred to as *shatm* (rebuke) and *laʿn* (curse). For examples: "لَا أَشْبَعَ اللهُ بَطْنَكَ" ("May Allah not satiate your stomach!") and "تَرِبَتْ يَمِينُكَ" ("May your right hand be in dust!" meaning "you will not achieve goodness").

On the rare occasions when he had to admonish a believer, the admonishment would be based on the apparent act of the person involved, as the Prophet ﷺ was only responsible for taking →

﴿١٤٨﴾ اَللّٰهُمَّ لَا يُدْرِكْنِي زَمَانٌ، وَّلَا يُدْرِكُوْا زَمَانًا، لَّا يُتَّبَعُ فِيْهِ الْعَلِيْمُ وَلَا يُسْتَحْيٰى فِيْهِ مِنَ الْحَلِيْمِ، قُلُوْبُهُمْ قُلُوْبُ الْأَعَاجِمِ وَأَلْسِنَتُهُمْ أَلْسِنَةُ الْعَرَبِ۔

﴿١٤٩﴾ اَللّٰهُمَّ إِنِّيْ أَتَّخِذُ عِنْدَكَ عَهْدًا لَّنْ تُخْلِفَنِيْهِ، فَإِنَّمَا أَنَا بَشَرٌ، فَأَيُّمَا مُؤْمِنٍ اٰذَيْتُهٗ أَوْ شَتَمْتُهٗ أَوْ جَلَدْتُّهٗ أَوْ لَعَنْتُهٗ، فَاجْعَلْهَا لَهٗ صَلٰوةً وَّزَكٰوةً وَّقُرْبَةً تُقَرِّبُهٗ بِهَا إِلَيْكَ يَوْمَ الْقِيَامَةِ۔

﴿١٥٠﴾ اَللّٰهُمَّ إِنِّيْ أَعُوْذُ بِكَ مِنَ الْبَرَصِ وَمِنَ الشِّقَاقِ

148. Allāhumma lā yudriknī zamān(un), wa lā yudrikū zamāna(n), lā yuttabaʿu fīhil-ʿalīmu wa lā yustaḥyā fīhi minal-ḥalīm(i), qulūbuhum qulūbul-'aʿājimi wa alsinatuhum alsinatul-ʿarab.

149. Allāhumma innī attakhidhu ʿindaka ʿahdan lan tukhlifanīh(i), fa innamā ana bashar(un), fa ayyumā mu'minin ādhaytuhū aw shatamtuhū aw jaladttuhū aw laʿantuh(ū), faj-ʿalhā lahū ṣalātan wa zakātan wa qurbatan tuqarribuhū bihā ilayka yawmal-qiyāmah.

150. Allāhumma innī aʿūdhu bika minal-baraṣi wa minash-

---

action based on the apparent facts of the case. However if in reality they did not deserve it then this duʿā' would make the admonishment into a source of purification and mercy for them (Sharaḥ of Nawawī).

If we have unjustly hurt or wronged a person, we must make amends and seek forgiveness from them. This duʿā' will help in those situations where we did not remember or could not approach the wronged party.

pocrisy, bad morals, and the evil of all that only You are aware of. I seek Allah's protection from the state of the people of the Fire and from the Fire, and whatever words and actions bring one close to these. (I seek Your protection) from the evil of everything that is under Your control. I seek Your protection from the evil of this day and of that which will come after it. (I seek Your protection) from the evil of my self and the evil of Shayṭān and his polytheism. (I seek Your protection) from that we should perpetrate evil against ourselves or divert it to any Muslim. Or that I should commit a mistake or sin that You will not forgive. And from the constriction on the Day of Judgment.

---

(150) [Composite: Anas ibn Mālik. *Sunan Abī Dāwūd* #1329; Abū Hurayrah. *Sunan Abī Dāwūd* #1322; Shaddād ibn 'Aws. *Sunan at-Tirmidhī* #3329; Abū Hurayrah. *Sunan at-Tirmidhī* #3523; 'Ā'ishah. *Sunan Ibn Mājah* #3836; 'Alī ibn Abī Ṭālib. *Sunan Abī Dāwūd* #4393; Abū Mālik al-Ash'arī. *Sunan Abī Dāwūd* #4421; 'Abdullāh ibn 'Amr ibn al-'Āṣ. *Sunan at-Tirmidhī* #3452; Zayd ibn Thābit. *Musnad Aḥmad* #20678; 'Ā'ishah. *Sunan an-Nasā'ī* #1599]

obstinacy (shiqāq): opposing the truth (*'Awn al-Ma'būd*).

state of the people of Fire: hypocrisy and disbelief in this world and punishment in the Hereafter (*Tuḥfah al-Aḥwadhī*).

constriction: refers to the extreme hardships and difficulties of the Day of Judgment (*'Awn al-Ma'būd*).

وَالنِّفَاقِ وَسُوْءِ الْأَخْلَاقِ وَمِنْ شَرِّ مَا تَعْلَمُ. أَعُوْذُ بِاللهِ مِنْ
حَالِ أَهْلِ النَّارِ وَمِنَ النَّارِ وَمَا قَرَّبَ إِلَيْهَا مِنْ قَوْلٍ أَوْ عَمَلٍ،
وَّمِنْ شَرِّ مَا أَنْتَ اٰخِذٌ بِنَاصِيَتِهٖ. وَأَعُوْذُ بِكَ مِنْ شَرِّ مَا فِيْ هٰذَا
الْيَوْمِ وَشَرِّ مَا بَعْدَهٗ، وَمِنْ شَرِّ نَفْسِيْ، وَشَرِّ الشَّيْطَانِ وَشِرْكِهٖ،
وَأَنْ نَّقْتَرِفَ عَلٰى أَنْفُسِنَا سُوْءً أَوْ نَجُرَّهٗ إِلٰى مُسْلِمٍ، أَوْ أَكْتَسِبَ
خَطِيْئَةً أَوْ ذَنْبًا لَّا تَغْفِرُهٗ، وَمِنْ ضِيْقِ الْمَقَامِ يَوْمَ الْقِيَامَةِ۔

shiqāqi wan-nifāqi wa sū'il-'akhlāqi wa min sharri mā taʿlam(u). Aʿūdhu bilLāhi min ḥāli ahlin-nāri wa minan-nāri wa mā qarraba ilayhā min qawlin aw ʿamal(in), wa min sharri mā Anta ākhidhum bināṣiyatih(ī). Wa aʿūdhu bika min sharri mā fī hādhal-yawmi wa sharri mā baʿdah(ū), wa min sharri nafsī, wa sharrish-shayṭāni wa shirkih(ī), wa an naqtarifaʿalā anfusinā sū'an aw najurrahū ilā muslim(in), aw aktasiba khaṭī'atan aw dhamban lā taghfiruh(ū), wa min ḍīqil-maqāmi yawmal-qiyāmah.

WEDNESDAY

In the Name of Allah, the Most Compassionate, the Most Merciful

(151) O Allah, protect my chastity and make my matters easy for me.

(152) O Allah, I beseech You for completeness of wuḍū' (ablution) and ṣalāt, and perfection of Your pleasure (with me) and of Your forgiveness (for me).

(153) O Allah, grant me my book of accounts in my right hand.

(154) O Allah, wrap me in Your mercy and protect me from Your punishment.

(155) O Allah, make my feet firm on the Bridge on the day that feet will be shaking.

---

(151) [ʿAlī ibn Abī Ṭālib. *Kanz al-ʿUmmāl* #26690; *Al-Ḥizb al-Aʿẓam*]

(152) [ʿAlī ibn Abī Ṭālib. *Kanz al-ʿUmmāl* #26993]

(153) [ʿAlī ibn Abī Ṭālib. *Kanz al-ʿUmmāl* #26692]
This refers to this verse: "Then as for him who is given his book in his right hand, he will say: Lo! Read my book" (*Al-Ḥāqqah*, 69:19). These will be the believers who would be admitted to Paradise. On the other hand, those destined for Hell will be given their records in their left hands.

Islamic civilization emphasizes the right hand. We eat and drink with our right hand. We wear clothes and shoes beginning with the right side. We enter the masjid with our right foot first. And we pray to get our book of accounts in the Hereafter in our right hand.

(154) [ʿAlī ibn Abī Ṭālib. *Kanz al-ʿUmmāl* #26690; *Al-Ḥizb al-Aʿẓam*]

(155) [ʿAlī ibn Abī Ṭālib. *Kanz al-ʿUmmāl* #26692]
Ṣirāṭ means path and the path shown by Islam is the Straight Path (*aṣ-Ṣirāṭ al-Mustaqīm*). Ṣirāṭ is also the name of the bridge that will be laid over Hell in the Hereafter. The ease with which one will be →

بِسْمِ اللهِ الرَّحْمٰنِ الرَّحِيْمِ

﴿١٥١﴾ اَللّٰهُمَّ حَصِّنْ فَرْجِيْ وَيَسِّرْ لِيْ أَمْرِيْ۔

﴿١٥٢﴾ اَللّٰهُمَّ إِنِّيْ أَسْأَلُكَ تَمَامَ الْوُضُوْءِ، وَتَمَامَ الصَّلٰوةِ، وَتَمَامَ رِضْوَانِكَ، وَتَمَامَ مَغْفِرَتِكَ۔

﴿١٥٣﴾ اَللّٰهُمَّ أَعْطِنِيْ كِتَابِيْ بِيَمِيْنِيْ۔

﴿١٥٤﴾ اَللّٰهُمَّ غَشِّنِيْ بِرَحْمَتِكَ وَجَنِّبْنِيْ عَذَابَكَ۔

﴿١٥٥﴾ اَللّٰهُمَّ ثَبِّتْ قَدَمَيَّ عَلَى الصِّرَاطِ يَوْمَ تَزِلُّ فِيْهِ الْأَقْدَامُ۔

151. Allāhumma ḥaṣṣin farjī wa yassir lī amrī.

152. Allāhumma innī as'aluka tamāmal-wuḍū'(i), wa tamāmaṣ-ṣalā(ti), wa tamāma riḍwānik(a), wa tamāma maghfiratik.

153. Allāhumma aʿṭinī kitābī biyamīnī.

154. Allāhumma ghash-shinī biraḥmatika wa jannibnī ʿadhābak.

155. Allāhumma thabbit qadamayya ʿalaṣ-ṣirāṭi yawma tazillu fīhil-'aqdām.

---

able to cross this bridge will depend upon one's sincerity and firmness of faith and goodness of deeds. Virtuous believers will cross it easily and reach Paradise. The hypocrites will fall off from this bridge into Hell.

It has been a practice of some pious elders that they recited this duʿā' while washing their feet when performing wuḍū'.

(156) Oh Allah, make us successful.

(157) O Allah, open our hearts with Your remembrance, complete Your blessings on us through Your Grace, and make us from amongst Your pious servants.

(158) O Allah, give me the best of what You give to Your pious servants.

(159) O Allah, make me live as a Muslim and die as a Muslim.

(160) O Allah, punish the infidels, strike awe in their hearts, create dissension in their ranks, and bring down Your chastisement and punishment upon them. O Allah, punish the infidels—be they from the people of the Book or from the polytheists—who reject Your Signs, refute Your messengers, create roadblocks to Your Path, transgress the limits set by You, and call on other deities with You in worship. There is no god except You. Blessed are You and Exalted way

---

(156) [Muʿāwiyah ibn Abī Sufyān. *ʿAmal al-Yawm wal-Laylah (Ibn as-Sunnī)* #92]
This duʿā' should also be said when hearing "ḥayya ʿalal-falāḥ" in the adhān.

(157) [Anas ibn Mālik. *ʿAmal al-Yawm wal-Laylah (Ibn as-Sunnī)* #100]
This duʿā' should also be said at the time of the adhān.

(158) [Saʿd ibn Abī Waqqāṣ. *Mustadrak Ḥākim* #75/748]
Sayyidnā ʿAbdullāh ibn ʿAbbās ﵄ reports that a person said this as he reached the prayer row while Prophet ﷺ was leading. After the ṣalāt the Prophet ﷺ enquired who had said it and then told him: "Then, your horse will be hamstrung and you will be martyred in the path of Allah."

(159) [Samurah ibn Jundub. *Majmaʿ az-Zawā'id* #2615]

(160) [ʿUmar ibn al-Khaṭṭāb. *Al-Adhkār (Imām Nawawī)* #131; *Al-Ḥizb al-Aʿẓam*]
This is a rare example of a curse found in the vast collection of Islamic supplications. This one was said by Sayyidnā ʿUmar ﵁ in

﴿١٥٦﴾ اَللّٰهُمَّ اجْعَلْنَا مُفْلِحِيْنَ۔

﴿١٥٧﴾ اَللّٰهُمَّ افْتَحْ أَقْفَالَ قُلُوْبِنَا بِذِكْرِكَ، وَأَتْمِمْ عَلَيْنَا نِعْمَتَكَ مِنْ فَضْلِكَ، وَاجْعَلْنَا مِنْ عِبَادِكَ الصَّالِحِيْنَ۔

﴿١٥٨﴾ اَللّٰهُمَّ اٰتِنِيْ أَفْضَلَ مَا تُؤْتِيْ عِبَادَكَ الصَّالِحِيْنَ۔

﴿١٥٩﴾ اَللّٰهُمَّ أَحْيِنِيْ مُسْلِمًا وَّأَمِتْنِيْ مُسْلِمًا۔

﴿١٦٠﴾ اَللّٰهُمَّ عَذِّبِ الْكَفَرَةَ وَأَلْقِ فِيْ قُلُوْبِهِمُ الرُّعْبَ وَخَالِفْ بَيْنَ كَلِمَتِهِمْ وَأَنْزِلْ عَلَيْهِمْ رِجْزَكَ وَعَذَابَكَ. اَللّٰهُمَّ عَذِّبِ الْكَفَرَةَ أَهْلَ الْكِتَابِ وَالْمُشْرِكِيْنَ الَّذِيْنَ يَجْحَدُوْنَ اٰيَاتِكَ، وَيُكَذِّبُوْنَ رُسُلَكَ، وَيَصُدُّوْنَ عَنْ سَبِيْلِكَ، وَيَتَعَدُّوْنَ حُدُوْدَكَ، وَيَدْعُوْنَ مَعَكَ إِلٰهًا اٰخَرَ. لَا إِلٰهَ إِلَّا أَنْتَ تَبَارَكْتَ وَتَعَالَيْتَ

156. Allāhummaj-ʿalnā mufliḥīn.

157. Allāhummaf-taḥ aqfāla qulūbinā bidhikrik(a), wa atmim ʿalaynā niʿmataka min faḍlik(a), waj-ʿalnā min ʿibādikaṣ-ṣāliḥīn.

158. Allāhumma ātinī afḍala mā tu'tī ʿibādakaṣ-ṣāliḥīn.

159. Allāhumma aḥyinī musliman wa amitnī muslima.

160. Allāhumma ʿadh-dhibil-kafarata wa alqi fī qulūbihimur-ruʿba wa khālif bayna kalimatihim wa anzil ʿalayhim rijzaka wa ʿadhābak(a). Allāhumma ʿadh-dhibil-kafarata ahlal-kitābi wal-mushrikīnal-ladhīna yajḥadūna āyātik(a), wa yukadh-dhibūna rusulak(a), wa yaṣuddūna ʿan sabīlik(a), wa yataʿaddūna ḥudūdak(a), wa yadʿūna maʿaka ilāhan ākhar(a). Lā ilāha illā anta tabārakta wa taʿālayta ʿammā yaqūluẓ-ẓālimūna ʿuluwwan

above what these unjust people say.

O Allah, forgive me and the believing men and women, and the Muslim men and women. Set them aright and their mutual relationships, create mutual love in them, put faith and wisdom in their hearts, and make them firm on the religion of Your Messenger. Grant that they be grateful for Your blessings on them, and true to their pledge to You. Help them to victory over Your and their enemy, O True Lord.

(161) Glorified are You. There is no god besides You. Forgive my sins, and put my deeds in order. Indeed You forgive the sins of

---

the qunūt in Fajr. Imām Nawawī writes in his *al-Adhkār*: "Sayyidnā ʿUmar ؓ mentioned the People of the Book because at that time Muslims were facing their armies."

Its basis is in a similar qunūt from the Prophet ﷺ, which was said after the massacre at the Bi'r of Maʿūnah in 4 AH. A pagan tribal chief from Najd visited the Prophet ﷺ and requested him to send a group of Companions with him to his tribe as teachers. He offered his personal guarantee of protection for them, which was a time honored practice in the tribal society. A large number (forty according to one report and seventy according to another) of Companions were sent with him. But when they reached Bi'r Maʿūnah, they were ambushed in clear breach of the pledge of protection. All of them were massacred except one who came back to tell their story. This treachery and cold-blooded murder saddened the Prophet ﷺ deeply. For a month after that he prayed against them in the Fajr ṣalāt. When a helpless people are persecuted, they can pray against their oppressors.

However, it should also be noted that on numerous occasions Prophet Muḥammad ﷺ refused to invoke a curse against those who had hurt him personally. This includes his visit to Ṭā'if where he was not only insulted, but also injured by urchins pelting stones at him. When angels told him that those people could be punished for their gross transgression at his command, he refused to ask for it. See also duʿā' 112.

It should be obvious from this that invoking Allah's anger against →

عَمَّا يَقُوْلُ الظّٰلِمُوْنَ عُلُوًّا كَبِيْرًا. اَللّٰهُمَّ اغْفِرْ لِيْ وَلِلْمُؤْمِنِيْنَ وَالْمُؤْمِنَاتِ، وَالْمُسْلِمِيْنَ وَالْمُسْلِمَاتِ، وَأَصْلِحْهُمْ وَأَصْلِحْ ذَاتَ بَيْنِهِمْ وَأَلِّفْ بَيْنَ قُلُوْبِهِمْ، وَاجْعَلْ فِيْ قُلُوْبِهِمُ الْإِيْمَانَ وَالْحِكْمَةَ، وَثَبِّتْهُمْ عَلٰى مِلَّةِ رَسُوْلِكَ، وَأَوْزِعْهُمْ أَنْ يَّشْكُرُوْا نِعْمَتَكَ الَّتِيْ أَنْعَمْتَ عَلَيْهِمْ وَأَنْ يُّوْفُوْا بِعَهْدِكَ الَّذِيْ عَاهَدْتَّهُمْ عَلَيْهِ، وَانْصُرْهُمْ عَلٰى عَدُوِّكَ وَعَدُوِّهِمْ، إِلٰهَ الْحَقِّ.

﴿١٦١﴾ سُبْحَانَكَ لَا إِلٰهَ غَيْرُكَ، اغْفِرْ لِيْ ذَنْبِيْ وَأَصْلِحْ لِيْ عَمَلِيْ، إِنَّكَ تَغْفِرُ الذُّنُوْبَ لِمَنْ تَشَاءُ وَأَنْتَ الْغَفُوْرُ الرَّحِيْمُ. يَا

kabīra(n).

Allāhummagh-fir lī wa lil-mu'minīna wal-mu'mināt(i), wal-muslimīna wal-muslimāt(i), wa aṣliḥ-hum wa aṣliḥ dhāta baynihim wa allif bayna qulūbihim, waj-ʿal fī qulūbihimul-īmāna wal-ḥikma(ta), wa thabbit-hum ʿalā millati rasūlik(a), wa awziʿhum an yashkurū niʿmatakal-latī anʿamta ʿalayhim wa an yūfū biʿahdikal-ladhī ʿāhadttahum ʿalayh(i), wan-ṣurhum ʿalā ʿaduwwika wa ʿaduwwihim, Ilāhal-ḥaqq.

161. Subḥānaka lā ilāha ghayruk(a), igh-fir lī dhambī wa aṣliḥ lī ʿamalī, innaka taghfirudh-dhunūba liman tashā'u wa Antal-

---

enemies is an exception and not the rule in Islamic practice; it is limited to special and extenuating circumstances. This principle is clearly stated in the Qur'ān: "Allah loves not the utterance of harsh speech save by one who has been wronged. Allah is ever Hearer, Knower" (*An-Nisā'*, 4:148).

(161) [ʿAbdullāh ibn Masʿūd. *Majmaʿ az-Zawā'id* #2862]

whomever You will. And You are Very Forgiving, Most Merciful. O the Forgiver, forgive me. O the Grantor of pardons, accept my repentance. O the Most Compassionate, have mercy on me. O the Effacer of sins, efface my sins. O the Clement, have pity on me. O my Lord, enable me to be grateful for Your blessings on me. Give me energy to excel in Your worship. O Lord, I beg You for all good and I seek Your protection from all evil. Give me good from beginning to end. Give me longing to meet You without my facing a harmful affliction or a tribulation leading me astray. Protect me from evils. And whomever You protect from evils on that Day, You have really showed mercy to him. That is the supreme achievement.

(162) *O Allah, for You alone is all praise. For You alone is all gratitude. Yours alone is the entire dominion. To You alone belongs the entire creation. All good is in Your hands alone. And the disposal of all matters ultimately rests in You alone. I beg You for all good and seek protection in You from all evil.*

---

(162) [Abū Saʿīd al-Khudrī. *Kanz al-ʿUmmāl* #22551]

غَفَّارُ اغْفِرْ لِيْ، يَا تَوَّابُ تُبْ عَلَيَّ، يَا رَحْمٰنُ ارْحَمْنِيْ، يَا عَفُوُّ اعْفُ عَنِّيْ، يَا رَءُوْفُ ارْءُفْ بِيْ، يَا رَبِّ أَوْزِعْنِيْ أَنْ أَشْكُرَ نِعْمَتَكَ الَّتِيْ أَنْعَمْتَ عَلَيَّ وَطَوِّقْنِيْ حُسْنَ عِبَادَتِكَ. يَا رَبِّ أَسْئَلُكَ مِنَ الْخَيْرِ كُلِّهٖ، وَأَعُوذُ بِكَ مِنَ الشَّرِّ كُلِّهٖ. يَا رَبِّ افْتَحْ لِيْ بِخَيْرٍ وَّاخْتِمْ لِيْ بِخَيْرٍ، وَاٰتِنِيْ شَوْقًا إِلٰى لِقَائِكَ مِنْ غَيْرِ ضَرَّاءَ مُضِرَّةٍ وَّلَا فِتْنَةٍ مُّضِلَّةٍ، وَّقِنِي السَّيِّئَاتِ، وَمَنْ تَقِ السَّيِّئَاتِ يَوْمَئِذٍ فَقَدْ رَحِمْتَهٗ وَذٰلِكَ هُوَ الْفَوْزُ الْعَظِيْمُ۔

﴿١٦٢﴾ اَللّٰهُمَّ لَكَ الْحَمْدُ كُلُّهٗ، وَلَكَ الشُّكْرُ كُلُّهٗ، وَلَكَ الْمُلْكُ كُلُّهٗ، وَلَكَ الْخَلْقُ كُلُّهٗ، بِيَدِكَ الْخَيْرُ كُلُّهٗ، وَإِلَيْكَ يَرْجِعُ الْأَمْرُ كُلُّهٗ، أَسْأَلُكَ مِنَ الْخَيْرِ كُلِّهٖ، وَأَعُوْذُ بِكَ مِنَ الشَّرِّ كُلِّهٖ۔

Ghafūrur-Raḥīm(u). Yā Ghaffārugh-fir lī, yā Tawwābu tub ʿalayy(a), yā Raḥmānur-ḥamnī, yā ʿAfuwwuʿ-fu ʿannī, yā Raʾūfur-ʾuf bī, yā Rabbi awziʿnī an ashkura niʿmatakal-latī anʿamta ʿalayya wa ṭawwiqnī ḥusna ʿibādatik(a). Yā Rabbi as'aluka minal-khayri kullih(ī), wa aʿūdhu bika minash-sharri kullih(ī). Yā Rabbif-taḥ lī bikhayrin wakh-tim lī bikhayr(in), wa ātinī shawqan ilā liqāʾika min ghayri ḍarrāʾa muḍirratin wa lā fitnatim muḍilla(tin), wa qinis-sayyiʾāt(i), wa man taqis-sayyiʾāti yawmaʾidhin fa qad raḥimtahū wa dhālika huwal-fawzul-ʿaẓīm.

162. Allāhumma lakal-ḥamdu kulluh(ū), wa lakash-shukru kulluh(ū), wa lakal-mulku kulluh(ū), wa lakal-khalqu kulluh(ū), biyadikal-khayru kulluh(ū), wa ilayka yarjiʿul-ʾamru kulluh(ū), as'aluka minal-khayri kullih(ī), wa aʿūdhu bika minash-sharri kullih.

(163) In the name of Allah besides Whom there is no god and He is the Most Beneficent, Most Merciful. O Allah, relieve me of all worry and grief. O Allah, with Your praise I do move about and my faults I do confess.

(164) O Allah, my God and that of Ibrāhīm (Abraham), Is-ḥāq (Isaac), Ya'qūb (Jacob), and God of Jibrīl (Gabriel), Mīkā'īl (Michael), and Isrāfīl (Israpheel), I beseech You to accept my du'ā' as I am distressed, to guard me in my faith as I am hemmed in by trying circumstances, to extend Your mercy to me as I am delinquent, and to ward away poverty from me as I am destitute.

(165) O Allah, I beg of You in the name of the right that the beggars have upon You, for a beggar has a right upon You. That everyone of Your male or female servants from the land or sea whose supplication You have granted and to whose call You have readily responded, include us in their applicable supplications. And include them in our applicable supplications to You. And grant peace to us and to them.

---

(163) [Anas ibn Mālik. *Kanz al-'Ummāl* #17915; *Al-Ḥizb al-A'ẓam*. Second part only found in the Ḥizb.]
After every farḍ ṣalāt, one should touch his or her forehead with the right hand and make this du'ā' (بسم الله الذي لا إله غيره . . . الهم والحزن). This was the practice of the Prophet ﷺ.

(164) [Anas ibn Mālik. *'Amal al-Yawm wal-Laylah (Ibn as-Sunnī)* #138]
Prophet Muḥammad ﷺ said: "If after every ṣalāt a believer extends his hands and says this du'ā', it will be a right on Allah that He not turn him back empty-handed."

(165) [Abū Sa'īd al-Khudrī. *Kanz al-'Ummāl* #4977]
right that beggars have upon you: See commentary for du'ā' 94.

The Prophet ﷺ said: "Whoever makes a du'ā' using these words, Allah includes him in the du'ā's of the people of the land and the sea, while he is in his place."

﴿١٦٣﴾ بِسْمِ اللهِ الَّذِيْ لَا إِلٰهَ غَيْرُهُ الرَّحْمٰنُ الرَّحِيْمُ، اَللّٰهُمَّ أَذْهِبْ عَنِّي الْهَمَّ وَالْحُزْنَ. اَللّٰهُمَّ بِحَمْدِكَ انْصَرَفْتُ وَبِذَنْبِي اعْتَرَفْتُ.

﴿١٦٤﴾ اَللّٰهُمَّ إِلٰهِيْ وَإِلٰهَ إِبْرَاهِيْمَ وَإِسْحَاقَ وَيَعْقُوْبَ، وَإِلٰهَ جِبْرِيْلَ وَمِيْكَائِيْلَ وَإِسْرَافِيْلَ، أَسْأَلُكَ أَنْ تَسْتَجِيْبَ دَعْوَتِيْ فَإِنِّيْ مُضْطَرٌّ، وَتَعْصِمَنِيْ فِيْ دِيْنِيْ فَإِنِّيْ مُبْتَلًى، وَتَنَالَنِيْ بِرَحْمَتِكَ فَإِنِّيْ مُذْنِبٌ، وَتَنْفِيَ عَنِّي الْفَقْرَ فَإِنِّيْ مُتَمَسْكِنٌ.

﴿١٦٥﴾ اَللّٰهُمَّ إِنِّيْ أَسْأَلُكَ بِحَقِّ السَّائِلِيْنَ عَلَيْكَ، فَإِنَّ لِلسَّائِلِ عَلَيْكَ حَقًّا، أَيُّمَا عَبْدٍ أَوْ أَمَةٍ مِّنْ أَهْلِ الْبَرِّ وَالْبَحْرِ تَقَبَّلْتَ دَعْوَتَهُمْ وَاسْتَجَبْتَ دُعَاءَهُمْ، أَنْ تُشْرِكَنَا فِيْ صَالِحِ مَا يَدْعُوْنَكَ، وَأَنْ تُشْرِكَهُمْ فِيْ صَالِحِ مَا نَدْعُوْكَ، وَأَنْ تُعَافِيَنَا

163. Bismillāhil-ladhī lā ilāha ghayruhur-Raḥmānur-Raḥīm(u), Allāhumma adh-hib ʿannil-hamma wal-ḥuzn(a). Allāhumma biḥamdikan-ṣaraftu wa bidhambiʿ-taraft.

164. Allāhumma Ilāhī wa Ilāha Ibrāhīma wa Isḥāqa wa Yaʿqūb(a), wa Ilāha Jibrīla wa Mīkā'īla wa Isrāfīl(a), as'aluka an tastajība daʿwatī fa innī muḍṭarr(un), wa taʿṣimanī fī dīnī fa innī mubtal(an), wa tanālanī biraḥmatika fa innī mudhnib(un), wa tanfiya ʿannil-faqra fa innī mutamaskin.

165. Allāhumma innī as'aluka biḥaqqis-sā'ilīna ʿalayk(a), fa inna lis-sa'ili ʿalayka ḥaqqa(n), ayyamā ʿabdin aw amatim min ahlil-barri wal-baḥri taqabbalta daʿwatahum was-tajabta duʿā'ahum, an tushrikanā fī ṣāliḥi mā yadʿūnak(a), wa an tushrikahum fī ṣāliḥi

Accept our du'ā's and theirs. And ignore our faults and theirs. For we believed in what You revealed, and followed the Messenger. So list us among the witnesses (of truth).

(166) O Allah, grant Muḥammad ﷺ the wasīlah, instill in the hearts of the chosen ones his love, and grant him his position among those of the highest rank and his remembrance among those close to You.

(167) O Allah, grant me Your special guidance, confer upon me Your grace, bestow amply on me Your mercy, and send down upon me Your blessings.

(168) O Allah, forgive me, have mercy on me, and accept my repentance; verily You are the Grantor of pardons and the Most Merciful.

(169) O Allah, I beseech You for the inspiration of the guided, the deeds of the firm believers, the sincerity of the repenters, the deter-

---

(166) [Abū Umāmah al-Bāhilī. *Kanz al-'Ummāl* #3479]
Al-Wasīlah is the station of intercession in the Hereafter. According to aḥādīth a person reciting this du'ā' after every ṣalāt or adhān will, inshā Allah, receive the intercession of the Prophet ﷺ on the Day of Judgment.

(167) ['Abdullāh ibn 'Abbās. *'Amal al-Yawm wal-Laylah (Ibn as-Sunnī)* #133]
According to a report by Sayyidnā 'Abdullāh ibn 'Abbās رضي الله عنهما a maternal uncle of the Prophet ﷺ, named Qubaysah, came to him. He was very old and weak and requested the Prophet ﷺ to teach him some brief du'ā' that would benefit him in this world and the Hereafter. The Prophet ﷺ told him, "For this world, say سبحان الله العظيم وبحمده ولا حول ولا قوة إلا بالله three times after every Fajr ṣalāt. This will protect you from four calamities: leprosy, dementia, blindness, and paralysis." And for the Hereafter he taught him the du'ā' mentioned here, also to be repeated three times after Fajr. Then the Prophet ﷺ said to those around him, "By the One in whose Hand is my life, if he brings these [words] on the Day of Judgment, having never missed saying them, then four doors of

وَإِيَّاهُمْ، وَأَنْ تَقْبَلَ مِنَّا وَمِنْهُمْ، وَأَنْ تَجَاوَزَ عَنَّا وَعَنْهُمْ، فَإِنَّا
اٰمَنَّا بِمَا أَنْزَلْتَ وَاتَّبَعْنَا الرَّسُوْلَ، فَاكْتُبْنَا مَعَ الشَّاهِدِيْنَ۔

﴿١٦٦﴾ اَللّٰهُمَّ أَعْطِ مُحَمَّدَ نِ الْوَسِيْلَةَ، وَاجْعَلْ فِي الْمُصْطَفَيْنَ
مَحَبَّتَهٗ، وَفِي الْأَعْلَيْنَ دَرَجَتَهٗ، وَفِي الْمُقَرَّبِيْنَ ذِكْرَهٗ۔

﴿١٦٧﴾ اَللّٰهُمَّ اهْدِنِيْ مِنْ عِنْدِكَ، وَأَفِضْ عَلَيَّ مِنْ فَضْلِكَ،
وَانْشُرْ عَلَيَّ مِنْ رَّحْمَتِكَ، وَأَنْزِلْ عَلَيَّ مِنْ بَرَكَاتِكَ۔

﴿١٦٨﴾ اَللّٰهُمَّ اغْفِرْ لِيْ، وَارْحَمْنِيْ، وَتُبْ عَلَيَّ، إِنَّكَ أَنْتَ
التَّوَّابُ الرَّحِيْمُ۔

﴿١٦٩﴾ اَللّٰهُمَّ إِنِّيْ أَسْأَلُكَ تَوْفِيْقَ أَهْلِ الْهُدٰى، وَأَعْمَالَ أَهْلِ
الْيَقِيْنِ، وَمُنَاصَحَةَ أَهْلِ التَّوْبَةِ، وَعَزْمَ أَهْلِ الصَّبْرِ، وَجِدَّ أَهْلِ

mā nadʿūk(a), wa an tuʿāfiyanā wa iyyāhum, wa an taqbala minnā wa minhum, wa an tajāwaza ʿannā wa ʿanhum, fa innā āmannā bimā anzalta wat-tabaʿnar-Rasūl(a), fak-tubnā maʿash-shāhidīn.

166. Allāhumma aʿṭi Muḥammadanil-wasīla(ta), waj-ʿal fil-muṣṭafayna maḥabbatah(ū), wa fil-ʾaʿalayna darajatah(ū), wa fil-muqarrabīna dhikrah.

167. Allāhummah-dinī min ʿindik(a), wa afiḍ ʿalayya min faḍlik(a), wan-shur ʿalayya min raḥmatik(a), wa anzil ʿalayya mim barakātik.

168. Allāhummagh-fir lī, war-ḥamnī, wa tub ʿalayy(a), innaka antat-Tawwābur-Raḥīm.

169. Allāhumma innī asʾaluka tawfīqa ahlil-hudā, wa aʿmāla ahlil-yaqīn(i), wa munāṣaḥata ahlit-tawba(ti), wa ʿazma ahliṣ-

mination of the patient, the effort of the God-fearing, the aspirations of the enthusiasts, the devoutness of the pious, and the cognition of the knowledgeable—so that I fear You. O Allah, I beg You for such fear that will restrain me from Your disobedience so that I may act in obedience to You earning Your pleasure. And so that I may repent sincerely out of Your fear. And so that I may achieve sincerity to You to avoid embarrassment before You. And so that I may put my trust totally in You. (And I beg You for having) the best expectations from You, O the Glorified, the Creator of light.

(170) O Allah, do not cause us to suffer sudden destruction, nor seize us by surprise, nor hasten us (to death) out of rights and wills.

(171) O Allah, comfort me in my desolation in the grave. O Allah, have mercy on me by dint of the Great Qur'ān and make it my leader, light, guidance, and mercy. O Allah, make me remember

---

Paradise will be opened for him and he will be able to enter through whichever one he wishes."

(168) ['Abdullāh ibn 'Umar. *Musnad Aḥmad* #5100]

(169) ['Abdullāh ibn 'Abbās. *Kanz al-'Ummāl* #21549; Ibid. *Majma' az-Zawā'id* #3679]

(170) ['Abdullāh ibn Mas'ūd. *Majma' az-Zawā'id* #3226]
hasten us (to death): Do not give us death before we can discharge all others' rights over us and write our will.

(171) [Composite: Abū Umāmah al-Bāhilī. Kanz al-'Ummāl #2784; Abū Manṣūr al-Muẓaffar's *Faḍā'il al-Qur'ān* as reported by Ḥafiẓ 'Iraqī in *Takhrīj Aḥādith al-Iḥyā'*]
This du'ā' should also be made at a completion of the recitation of the entire Qur'ān.

الْخَشْيَةِ، وَطَلَبَ أَهْلِ الرَّغْبَةِ، وَتَعَبُّدَ أَهْلِ الْوَرَعِ، وَعِرْفَانَ أَهْلِ الْعِلْمِ حَتّٰى أَخَافَكَ. اَللّٰهُمَّ إِنِّيْ أَسْأَلُكَ مَخَافَةً تَحْجُزُنِيْ عَنْ مَّعَاصِيْكَ، حَتّٰى أَعْمَلَ بِطَاعَتِكَ عَمَلًا أَسْتَحِقُّ بِهٖ رِضَاكَ، وَحَتّٰى أُنَاصِحَكَ بِالتَّوْبَةِ خَوْفًا مِّنْكَ، وَحَتّٰى أُخْلِصَ لَكَ النَّصِيْحَةَ حَيَاءً مِّنْكَ، وَحَتّٰى أَتَوَكَّلَ عَلَيْكَ فِي الْأُمُوْرِ كُلِّهَا، وَحُسْنَ الظَّنِّ بِكَ، سُبْحَانَ خَالِقِ النُّوْرِ۔

﴿١٧٠﴾ اَللّٰهُمَّ لَا تُهْلِكْنَا فُجَاءَةً، وَّلَا تَأْخُذْنَا بَغْتَةً، وَّلَا تُعْجِلْنَا عَنْ حَقٍّ وَّلَا وَصِيَّةٍ۔

﴿١٧١﴾ اَللّٰهُمَّ اٰنِسْ وَحْشَتِيْ فِيْ قَبْرِيْ۔ اَللّٰهُمَّ ارْحَمْنِيْ بِالْقُرْاٰنِ الْعَظِيْمِ، وَاجْعَلْهُ لِيْ إِمَامًا وَّنُوْرًا وَّهُدًى وَّرَحْمَةً. اَللّٰهُمَّ ذَكِّرْنِيْ

ṣabr(i), wa jidda ahlil-khashya(ti), wa ṭalaba ahlir-raghba(ti), wa taʿabbuda ahlil-waraʿ(i), wa ʿirfāna ahlil-ʿilmi ḥattā akhāfak(a). Allāhumma innī as'aluka makhāfatan taḥjuzunī ʿam maʿāṣīk(a), ḥattā aʿmala biṭāʿatika ʿamalan astaḥiqqu bihī riḍāk(a), wa ḥattā unāṣiḥaka bit-tawbati khawfam mink(a), wa ḥattā ukhliṣa lakan-naṣīḥata ḥayā'am mink(a), wa ḥattā atawakkala ʿalayka fil-'umūri kullihā, wa ḥusnaẓ-ẓanni bik(a), subḥāna Khāliqin-nūr.

170. Allāhumma lā tuhliknā fujā'a(tan), wa lā ta'khudhnā baghta(tan), wa lā tuʿjilnā ʿan ḥaqqin wa lā waṣiyyah.

171. Allāhumma ānis waḥshatī fī qabrī. Allāhummar-ḥamnī bil-Qur'ānil-ʿaẓīm(i), waj-ʿalhu lī imāman wa nūran wa hudan wa raḥma(tan). Allāhumma dhakkirnī minhu mā nasīt(u), wa

whatever I forget from it. Teach me whatever part of it I do not understand. Endow me with its recitation during the hours of the day and the night. And make it an evidence for me, O Lord of the worlds.

(172) O Allah, I am Your servant, son of Your male servant, and son of Your female servant. My forehead is in Your hands. I move around under Your control. I testify to the meeting with You. I believe in Your promise. You commanded me but I disobeyed. You forbade me but I committed. This is the place of the seekers of protection from You against the Fire. There is no god except You. Glorified are You. I have wronged my soul so forgive me. Indeed no one can forgive sins except You.

(173) O Allah, all praise is for You. Complaints are submitted to You. Cries for help are made to You. Help is sought from You. There is no power or strength except through the help of Allah.

(174) O Allah, I seek protection in Your pleasure from Your anger,

---

(172) [*Al-Ḥizb al-Aʿẓam*]
This duʿā' is to be recited while making ṭawāf. Variations of this duʿā' can be found in *Al-Adkār* of Imām Nawawī as well as books of *fiqh* in the sections on Ḥajj and ʿUmrah. The word "maqām" here refers to *Maqām Ibrahīm* in the Ḥaram. Probably it was included in the collection for daily reading as a reminder of the Sacred Pilgrimage. And Allah ﷻ knows best.

In the beginning part, a woman should say here as well as in duʿā' 109: اَللّٰهُمَّ أَنَا أَمَتُكَ وَبِنْتُ عَبْدِكَ وَبِنْتُ أَمَتِكَ ("O Allah, I am Your female servant, daughter of your male servant, and daughter of your female servant").

(173) [ʿAbdullāh ibn Masʿūd. *Al-Firdaws al-Akhbār* (Daylamī) #1812]
power or strength: That is power to turn away from sin or strength to perform an act of virtue.

This is the duʿā' that Sayyidnā Mūsā عليه السلام made when crossing the sea with Banī Isrā'īl.

مِنْهُ مَا نَسِيْتُ، وَعَلِّمْنِي مِنْهُ مَا جَهِلْتُ، وَارْزُقْنِي تِلَاوَتَهُ اٰنَاءَ اللَّيْلِ وَأَطْرَافَ النَّهَارِ، وَاجْعَلْهُ لِيْ حُجَّةً يَا رَبَّ الْعٰلَمِيْنَ۔

﴿١٧٢﴾ اَللّٰهُمَّ أَنَا عَبْدُكَ وَابْنُ عَبْدِكَ وَابْنُ أَمَتِكَ، نَاصِيَتِيْ بِيَدِكَ، أَتَقَلَّبُ فِيْ قَبْضَتِكَ، وَأُصَدِّقُ بِلِقَائِكَ، وَاُوْمِنُ بِوَعْدِكَ. أَمَرْتَنِيْ فَعَصَيْتُ، وَنَهَيْتَنِيْ فَأَتَيْتُ، هٰذَا مَقَامُ الْعَائِذِ بِكَ مِنَ النَّارِ، لَا إِلٰهَ إِلَّا أَنْتَ سُبْحَانَكَ ظَلَمْتُ نَفْسِيْ فَاغْفِرْ لِيْ، إِنَّهُ لَا يَغْفِرُ الذُّنُوْبَ إِلَّا أَنْتَ۔

﴿١٧٣﴾ اَللّٰهُمَّ لَكَ الْحَمْدُ، وَإِلَيْكَ الْمُشْتَكٰى، وَبِكَ الْمُسْتَغَاثُ، وَأَنْتَ الْمُسْتَعَانُ، وَلَا حَوْلَ وَلَا قُوَّةَ إِلَّا بِاللهِ۔

﴿١٧٤﴾ اَللّٰهُمَّ إِنِّيْ أَعُوْذُ بِرِضَاكَ مِنْ سَخَطِكَ، وَبِمُعَافَاتِكَ

ʿallimnī minhu mā jahilt(u), war-zuqnī tilāwatahū ānā'al-layli wa aṭrāfan-nahār(i), waj-ʿalhu lī ḥujjatan yā Rabbal-ʿālamīn.

172. Allāhumma ana ʿabduka wab-nu ʿabdika wab-nu amatik(a), nāṣiyatī biyadik(a), ataqallabu fī qabḍatik(a), wa uṣaddiqu biliqā'ik(a), wa ūminu biwaʿdik(a). Amartanī fa ʿaṣayt(u), wa nahaytanī fa atayt(u), hādhā makānul-ʿā'idhi bika minan-nār(i), lā ilāha illā Anta subḥānaka ẓalamtu nafsī fagh-fir lī, innahū lā yaghfirudh-dhunūba illā Ant.

173. Allāhumma lakal-ḥamd(u), wa ilaykal-mushtakā, wa bikal-mustaghāth(u), wa Antal-mustaʿān(u), wa lā ḥawla wa lā quwwata illā bilLāh.

174. Allāhumma innī aʿūdhu biriḍāka min sakhaṭik(a), wa bimuʿāfātika min ʿuqūbatik(a), wa aʿūdhu bika minka lā uḥṣī

and in Your forgiveness from Your punishment. I seek protection in You from You. I cannot fully praise You. You are the way You have praised Yourself. O Allah, we seek Your protection from erring; from misleading others; from doing injustice to others or receiving injustices from them; from treating others with ignorance or being treated with ignorance; from misleading others or being misled by them. I seek protection in the Light of Your Countenance—which has illuminated the heavens and lighted the darknesses and which sets aright all affairs of this world and the Hereafter—from that You should allow Your anger and bring down Your displeasure on me. Your good will is to be constantly sought until You are pleased. There is no power or strength except through You. O Allah, I seek protection the way You protect a little baby. O Allah, I seek Your protection from the two blind forces: flood and attacking (mad) camel.

---

(174) [Composite: ʿĀ'ishah. *Ṣaḥīḥ Muslim* #751; Um Salamah. *Sunan at-Tirmidhī* #3349; ʿAbdullāh ibn Jaʿfar. *Kanz al-ʿUmmāl* #3613; ʿAbdullāh ibn ʿUmar. *Kanz al-ʿUmmāl* #3678; ʿĀ'ishah bint Qudāmah. *Kanz al-ʿUmmāl* #3649]

I seek protection in You from You: There is no protection from Allah's wrath but in Allah's mercy.

from misleading others or being misled by them: It was the practice of the Prophet ﷺ to say the following duʿā' before leaving home:

(اَللّٰهُمَّ إِنَّا نَعُوْذُ بِكَ مِنْ أَنْ نَزِلَّ أَوْ نُضِلَّ، أَوْ نَظْلِمَ أَوْ نُظْلَمَ، أَوْ نَجْهَلَ أَوْ يُجْهَلَ عَلَيْنَا)

By saying it at that time we will renew our commitment to save others from our wrongful actions and seek Allah's help against theirs.

little baby: It has been said that the "little baby" refers to Sayyidnā Mūsā عليه السلام, who was protected as a child by Allah (*Fayḍ al-Qadīr*).

two blind forces: Flash floods are a devastating phenomenon in desert areas. A flash flood is a rapidly rising local flood that comes without warning and that can reach full peak in only a few minutes. Desert lands cannot hold much rain due to the lack of vegetation and soil, resulting in flash floods after a heavy downpour. Similarly a mad camel can bring out deadly force against human beings. →

مِنْ عُقُوْبَتِكَ، وَأَعُوْذُ بِكَ مِنْكَ لَا أُحْصِيْ ثَنَاءً عَلَيْكَ، أَنْتَ كَمَا أَثْنَيْتَ عَلٰى نَفْسِكَ۔ اَللّٰهُمَّ إِنَّا نَعُوْذُ بِكَ مِنْ أَنْ نَزِلَّ، أَوْ نُضِلَّ، أَوْ نَظْلِمَ أَوْ نُظْلَمَ، أَوْ نَجْهَلَ أَوْ يُجْهَلَ عَلَيْنَا، أَوْ أَضِلَّ أَوْ أُضَلَّ۔ أَعُوْذُ بِنُوْرِ وَجْهِكَ الْكَرِيْمِ الَّذِيْ أَضَاءَتْ لَهُ السَّمٰوٰتُ، وَأَشْرَقَتْ لَهُ الظُّلُمَاتُ، وَصَلُحَ عَلَيْهِ أَمْرُ الدُّنْيَا وَالْاٰخِرَةِ، أَنْ تُحِلَّ عَلَيَّ غَضَبَكَ، أَوْ تُنْزِلَ عَلَيَّ سَخَطَكَ، وَلَكَ الْعُتْبٰى حَتّٰى تَرْضٰى، وَلَا حَوْلَ وَلَا قُوَّةَ إِلَّا بِكَ۔ اَللّٰهُمَّ وَاقِيَةً كَوَاقِيَةِ الْوَلِيْدِ۔ اَللّٰهُمَّ إِنِّيْ أَعُوْذُ بِكَ مِنْ شَرِّ الْأَعْمَيَيْنِ: السَّيْلِ وَالْبَعِيْرِ الصَّئُوْلِ۔

thanā'an ʿalayka Anta kamā athnayta ʿalā nafsik(a). Allāhumma innā naʿūdhu bika min an nazilla aw nuḍill(a), aw naẓlima aw nuẓlam(a), aw najhala aw yujhala ʿalaynā, aw aḍilla aw uḍall(a). Aʿūdhu binūri Wajhikal-karīmil-ladhī aḍā'at lahus-samāwāt(u), wa ashraqat lahuẓ-ẓulumāt(u), wa ṣaluḥa ʿalayhi amrud-dunyā wal-ākhira(ti), an tuḥilla ʿalayya ghaḍabak(a), aw tunzila ʿalayya sakhaṭak(a), wa lakal-ʿutbā ḥattā tarḍā, wa lā ḥawla wa lā quwwata illā bik(a). Allāhumma wāqiyatan kawāqiyatil-walīd(i). Allāhumma innī aʿūdhu bika min sharril-'aʿmayaynis-sayli wal-baʿīriṣ-ṣa'ūl.

Prophet Muḥammad ﷺ made this duʿā' during sajdah (prostration) in a nafl ṣalāt at night.

THURSDAY

In the Name of Allah, the Most Compassionate, the Most Merciful

(175) O Allah, I beg You in the name of Muḥammad—Your Prophet; Ibrāhīm (Abraham) —Your friend; Mūsā (Moses)—Your confidant; and ʿĪsā (Jesus)—(created by) Your Breath and Your Word; I beg You in the name of the Tawrāt (Torah) of Mūsā, Injīl (Gospel) of Isa, Zabūr (Psalms) of Dāwūd (David), and the Furqān (Criterion, i.e. the Noble Qur'ān) of Muḥammad ﷺ—may Allah's blessings and peace be on all of them; I beg You in the name of all the revelations You sent, or judgments You made. (I beg You to grant me) by virtue of every beggar whom You gave, every rich man You made poor, every poor man You made rich, and every misguided person whom You guided; I beg You in that name of Yours that You applied to the earth and it became steady and to the heavens which were thus held up and to the mountains which thus got firmly embedded; and I beg You in that name of Yours by which Your Throne (ʿArsh) was made stationary and in the pure and holy name of Yours which You revealed in Your Book from Your presence; and in that name of Yours which, when You applied to the day it brightened and when You applied to the night it darkened; and in the name of Your greatness, glory, and the light of Your Countenance, (I beg You) that with

---

(175) [Composite: Abū Bakr. *Takhrīj Aḥādith al-Iḥyā'* (Ḥafiẓ ʿIraqī); *Al-Ḥizb al-Aʿẓam*; ʿAbdullāh ibn ʿAbbās. *Kanz al-ʿUmmāl* #41326]

بِسْمِ اللهِ الرَّحْمٰنِ الرَّحِيمِ

﴿١٧٥﴾ اَللّٰهُمَّ إِنِّيْ أَسْأَلُكَ بِمُحَمَّدٍ نَّبِيِّكَ وَإِبْرَاهِيْمَ خَلِيْلِكَ
وَمُوْسٰى نَجِيِّكَ وَعِيْسٰى رُوْحِكَ وَكَلِمَتِكَ، وَبِتَوْرَاةِ مُوْسٰى
وَإِنْجِيْلِ عِيْسٰى وَزَبُوْرِ دَاوُدَ وَفُرْقَانِ مُحَمَّدٍ صَلَّى اللهُ عَلَيْهِ
وَسَلَّمَ وَعَلَيْهِمْ أَجْمَعِيْنَ، وَبِكُلِّ وَحْيٍ أَوْحَيْتَهُ، أَوْ قَضَاءٍ
قَضَيْتَهُ، أَوْ سَائِلٍ أَعْطَيْتَهُ، أَوْ غَنِيٍّ أَفْقَرْتَهُ، أَوْ فَقِيْرٍ أَغْنَيْتَهُ، أَوْ
ضَالٍّ هَدَيْتَهُ، وَأَسْأَلُكَ بِاسْمِكَ الَّذِيْ وَضَعْتَهُ عَلَى الْأَرْضِ
فَاسْتَقَرَّتْ، وَعَلَى السَّمٰوٰتِ فَاسْتَقَلَّتْ، وَعَلَى الْجِبَالِ فَرَسَتْ،
وَأَسْأَلُكَ بِاسْمِكَ الَّذِيْ اسْتَقَرَّ بِهٖ عَرْشُكَ، وَأَسْأَلُكَ بِاسْمِكَ
الطَّاهِرِ الْمُطَهَّرِ الْمُنَزَّلِ فِيْ كِتَابِكَ مِنْ لَّدُنْكَ، وَبِاسْمِكَ الَّذِيْ
وَضَعْتَهُ عَلَى النَّهَارِ فَاسْتَنَارَ وَعَلَى اللَّيْلِ فَأَظْلَمَ، وَبِعَظَمَتِكَ

175. Allāhumma innī as'aluka biMuḥammadin nabiyyika wa Ibrāhīma khalīlika wa Mūsā najiyyika wa ʿĪsā rūḥika wa kalimatik(a), wa biTawrāti Mūsā wa Injīli ʿĪsā wa Zabūri Dāwūda wa Furqāni Muḥammadin ṣallAllāhu ʿalayhi wa sallama wa ʿalayhim ajmaʿīn(a), wa bikulli waḥyin awḥaytah(ū), aw qaḍā'in qaḍaytah(ū), aw sā'ilin aʿṭaytah(ū), aw ghaniyyin afqartah(ū), aw faqīrin aghnaytah(ū), aw ḍāllin hadaytah(ū), wa as'aluka bismikal-ladhī waḍaʿtahū ʿalal-'arḍ(i), fas-taqarrat wa ʿalas-samāwāti fas-taqallat, wa ʿalal-jibāli fa rasat, wa as'aluka bismikal-ladhis-taqarra bihī ʿArshuk(a), wa as'aluka bismikaṭ-ṭāhiril-muṭahharil-munazzali fī kitābika min ladunk(a), wa bismikal-ladhī waḍaʿtahū ʿalan-nahāri fas-tanāra wa ʿalal-layli fa aẓlam(a), wa biʿaẓamatika

Your power and strength You endow me with the Great Qur'ān and make it permeate my flesh, blood, ears, and eyes and make my body its practitioner. For indeed there is no power or strength without You. O Allah, do not let us become carefree about Your secret grip, or forget Your remembrance. Do not lift Your cover from us and do not let us become one of the negligent.

(176) O Allah, I beg You for hastening of good health from You, patience over Your trials, and exit from this world into Your mercy. O the One Who is sufficient against all and none is sufficient against Him. O the One for the person who has no one. O the Support of the one who has no support. There are no hopes except in You. Liberate me from the state I am in, and help me against what I currently face from that which has befallen me, in the name of Your Gracious Self and by virtue of the right of Muḥammad ﷺ on You. Āmīn.

---

(176) [Composite: ʿĀ'ishah. *Kanz al-ʿUmmāl* #3698; ʿUmar ibn al-Khaṭṭāb and ʿAlī ibn Abī Ṭālib. *Al-Firdaws al-Akhbār* (Daylamī) #1290]

. . . exit from this world into Your mercy: According to a ḥadīth, angel Jibrīl came to the Prophet ﷺ and said, Allah has commanded you to supplicate with these words (اللهم إني أسألك تعجيل عافيتك، وصبرا على بليتك، وخروجا من الدنيا إلى رحمتك) so He will grant you one of the three mentioned things.

O the One Who is sufficient . . . Āmīn: According to a ḥadīth, this duʿā' (يا من يكفي عن كل أحد . . . وبحق محمد عليك آمين) should be said when one is worried about the machinations of a ruler or shayṭān.

وَكِبْرِيَائِكَ، وَبِنُوْرِ وَجْهِكَ أَنْ تَرْزُقَنِيَ الْقُرْاٰنَ العَظِيْمَ وَتُخَلِّطَهٗ بِلَحْمِيْ وَدَمِيْ وَسَمْعِيْ وَبَصَرِيْ، وَتَسْتَعْمِلَ بِهٖ جَسَدِيْ، بِحَوْلِكَ وَقُوَّتِكَ فَإِنَّهٗ لَا حَوْلَ وَلَا قُوَّةَ إِلَّا بِكَ. اَللّٰهُمَّ لَا تُؤْمِنَّا مَكْرَكَ، وَلَا تُنْسِنَا ذِكْرَكَ، وَلَا تَهْتِكْ عَنَّا سِتْرَكَ، وَلَا تَجْعَلْنَا مِنَ الْغَافِلِيْنَ.

﴿١٧٦﴾ اَللّٰهُمَّ إِنِّيْ أَسْأَلُكَ تَعْجِيْلَ عَافِيَتِكَ، وَصَبْرًا عَلٰى بَلِيَّتِكَ، وَخُرُوْجًا مِّنَ الدُّنْيَا إِلٰى رَحْمَتِكَ. يَا مَنْ يَّكْفِيْ عَنْ كُلِّ أَحَدٍ وَّلَا يَكْفِيْ مِنْهُ أَحَدٌ، يَّا أَحَدَ مَنْ لَّا أَحَدَ لَهٗ، وَيَا سَنَدَ مَنْ لَّا سَنَدَ لَهٗ، انْقَطَعَ الرَّجَاءُ إِلَّا مِنْكَ، نَجِّنِيْ مِمَّا أَنَا فِيْهِ وَأَعِنِّيْ عَلٰى مَا أَنَا عَلَيْهِ مِمَّا نَزَلَ بِيْ، بِجَاهِ وَجْهِكَ الْكَرِيْمِ، وَبِحَقِّ مُحَمَّدٍ عَلَيْكَ، اٰمِيْنَ.

wa kibriyā'ik(a), wa binūri Wajhika an tarzuqaniyal-Qur'ānal-ʿaẓīma wa tukhalliṭahū bilaḥmī wa damī wa samʿī wa baṣarī, wa tastaʿmila bihī jasadī, biḥawlika wa quwwatika fa innahū lā ḥawla wa lā quwwata illā bik(a). Allāhumma lā tu'minnā makrak(a), wa lā tunsinā dhikrak(a), wa lā tahtik ʿannā sitrak(a), wa lā tajʿalnā minal-ghāfilīn.

176. Allāhumma innī as'aluka taʿjīla ʿāfiyatik(a), wa ṣabran ʿalā baliyyatik(a), wa khurūjam minad-dunyā ilā raḥmatik(a). Yā man yakfī ʿan kulli aḥadin wa lā yakfī minhu aḥad(un), yā Aḥada man lā aḥada lah(ū), wa yā Sanada man lā sanada lah(u), in-qaṭaʿar-rajā'u illā mink(a), najjinī mimmā ana fīhi wa aʿinnī ʿalā mā ana ʿalayhi mimmā nazala bī, bijāhi Wajhikal-karīm(i), wa biḥaqqi Muḥammadin ʿalayka, Āmīn.

(177) O Allah, watch over me with Your Eye that never sleeps, protect me with Your unassailable patronage, and forgive me by virtue of Your power over me so that I may not perish. You are my Hope. How many a bounty there is with which You have favored me; yet little has been my gratitude for that. And how many a trial have You tested me with; yet little has been my patience with that. O the One for Whose bounties my gratitude has been little, yet He did not deprive me. O the One against Whose trial I showed little patience, yet He did not abandon me. O the One Who saw me committing mistakes yet He did not disgrace me.

(178) O the Dispenser of good that will never end, and O the Dispenser of favors that can never be counted, I beseech You to shower blessings on Muḥammad ﷺ and on his family. It is with Your strength alone that I face enemies and oppressors.

(179) O Allah, help me in my religion through my worldly affairs and in my Hereafter through my piety. Look after for me in things

---

(177) [ʿAlī ibn Abī Ṭālib. *Kanz al-ʿUmmāl* #3441; ʿAlī ibn al-Ḥusayn. *Kanz al-ʿUmmāl* #5014]

This beautiful duʿā', combined with the next, was taught by the Prophet ﷺ to Sayyidnā ʿAlī رضي الله عنه to say when facing major hardships and worries. He taught it to his family and his great-great-grandson Jaʿfar ibn Muḥammad used a version of this duʿā' when summoned by an angry Al-Manṣūr.

According to a report, when the Abbasid Khalīfah came to Madīnah some people incited him against Jaʿfar, saying that the latter did not approve of praying behind him or greeting him with salām. Al-Manṣūr was so angry that he ordered Jaʿfar to be brought to him and vowed to kill him. But when Jaʿfar came and talked to Al-Manṣūr his anger subsided. As he was leaving, he was asked about the words he had whispered before entering upon Al-Manṣūr. He replied with this duʿā':

اَللّٰهُمَّ احْرُسْنِيْ بِعَيْنِكَ الَّتِيْ لَا تَنَامُ، وَاكْنُفْنِيْ بِكَنَفِكَ الَّذِيْ لَا يُرَامُ، وَاغْفِرْ
لِيْ بِقُدْرَتِكَ عَلَيَّ، وَإِلَّا هَلَكْتُ وَأَنْتَ رَجَائِيْ، فَكَمْ مِّنْ نِّعْمَةٍ قَدْ أَنْعَمْتَ بِهَا

﴿١٧٧﴾ اَللّٰهُمَّ احْرُسْنِي بِعَيْنِكَ الَّتِيْ لَا تَنَامُ، وَاكْنُفْنِي بِكَنَفِكَ الَّذِيْ لَا يُرَامُ، وَاغْفِرْ لِيْ بِقُدْرَتِكَ عَلَيَّ فَلَا أَهْلِكُ، وَأَنْتَ رَجَائِيْ. فَكَمْ مِّنْ نِّعْمَةٍ أَنْعَمْتَ بِهَا عَلَيَّ قَلَّ لَكَ عِنْدَهَا شُكْرِيْ، وَكَمْ مِّنْ بَلِيَّةٍ اِبْتَلَيْتَنِي بِهَا قَلَّ لَكَ عِنْدَهَا صَبْرِيْ. فَيَا مَنْ قَلَّ عِنْدَ نِعْمَتِهٖ شُكْرِيْ فَلَمْ يَحْرِمْنِيْ، وَيَا مَنْ قَلَّ عِنْدَ بَلِيَّتِهٖ صَبْرِيْ فَلَمْ يَخْذُلْنِيْ، وَيَا مَنْ رَّاٰنِي عَلَى الْخَطَايَا فَلَمْ يَفْضَحْنِيْ-

﴿١٧٨﴾ يَا ذَا الْمَعْرُوْفِ الَّذِيْ لَا يَنْقَضِيْ أَبَدًا، وَّيَا ذَا النَّعْمَاءِ الَّتِيْ لَا تُحْصٰى أَبَدًا، أَسْأَلُكَ أَنْ تُصَلِّيَ عَلٰى مُحَمَّدٍ، وَعَلٰى اٰلِ مُحَمَّدٍ، وَّبِكَ أَدْرَأُ فِيْ نُحُوْرِ الْأَعْدَاءِ وَالْجَبَّارِيْنَ-

﴿١٧٩﴾ اَللّٰهُمَّ أَعِنِّيْ عَلٰى دِيْنِيْ بِدُنْيَايَ، وَعَلٰى اٰخِرَتِيْ بِتَقْوَايَ-

177. Allāhummaḥ-rusnī biʿaynikal-latī lā tanām(u), wak-nufnī bikanafikal-ladhī lā yurām(u), wagh-fir lī biqudratika ʿalayya fa lā ahlik(u), wa anta rajāʾī. Fa kam min niʿmatin anʿamta bihā ʿalayya qalla laka ʿindahā shukrī, wa kam mim baliyyatinib-talaytanī bihā qalla laka ʿindahā ṣabrī. Fa yā man qalla ʿinda niʿmatihī shukrī fa lam yaḥrimnī, wa yā man qalla ʿinda baliyyatihī ṣabrī fa lam yakhdhulnī, wa yā man raʾānī ʿalal-khaṭāyā fa lam yafḍaḥnī.

178. Yā Dhal-maʿrūfil-ladhī lā yanqaḍī abada(n) wa yā Dhan-naʿmāʾil-latī lā tuḥṣā abada(n), asʾaluka an tuṣalliya ʿalā Muḥammad(in), wa ʿalā āli Muḥammad(in), wa bika adraʾu fī nuḥūril-ʾaʿdāʾi wal-jabbārīn.

179. Allāhumma aʿinnī ʿalā dīnī bidunyāy(a), wa ʿalā ākhiratī

that are out of my sight, and do not let me rely upon myself in dealing with those that are before me; O the One Whom sins cannot harm and forgiveness cannot cause any loss, grant me what does not cause you any loss and forgive me what does not harm You. Verily, You are the Generous Giver. O Allah, I beg You for quick relief, noble patience, ample sustenance, and safety from all trials; and I beg You for full and lasting protection, gratitude for protection, and freedom from need towards others; there is no turning (away from sin) or strength (to worship) in us except with the help of Allah, Most High and Great.

(180) O Allah, make my inner self better than my public appearance and make my public appearance righteous. O Allah, I beg You for the good of what You bestow upon people—wealth, family, and children—that they should neither be misled nor misleading.

عَلَيَّ قَلَّ لَكَ عِنْدَهَا شُكْرِيْ، وَكَمْ مِّنْ بَلِيَّةٍ قَدِ ابْتَلَيْتَنِيْ بِهَا قَلَّ لَكَ عِنْدَهَا
صَبْرِيْ. يَا مَنْ قَلَّ عِنْدَ نِعْمَتِهٖ شُكْرِيْ فَلَمْ يَحْرِمْنِيْ، وَيَا مَنْ قَلَّ عِنْدَ بَلِيَّتِهٖ
صَبْرِيْ فَلَمْ يَخْذُلْنِيْ، وَيَا مَنْ رَّاٰنِي عَلَى الْخَطَايَا فَلَمْ يَفْضَحْنِيْ وَيَا ذَا النَّعْمَاءِ
الَّتِيْ لَا تُحْصٰى وَيَا ذَا الْأَيَادِي الَّتِيْ لَا تَنْقَضِيْ، أَسْتَدْفِعُ مَكْرُوْهَ مَا أَنَا فِيْهِ،
وَأَعُوْذُ بِكَ مِنْ شَرِّهٖ يَا أَرْحَمَ الرَّاحِمِيْنَ

(178) ['Alī ibn Abī Ṭālib. *Kanz al-'Ummāl* #3441]

(179) [Composite: Jābir ibn 'Abdillāh. *Kanz al-'Ummāl* #5110; *Al-Ḥizb al-A'ẓam*; 'Alī ibn Abī Ṭālib. *Kanz al-'Ummāl* #5055]

(180) ['Umar ibn al-Khaṭṭāb. *Sunan at-Tirmidhī* #3510]
This should remove a rather common misunderstanding that a good inner self may coexist with a sinful public conduct.

وَاحْفَظْنِيْ فِيْمَا غِبْتُ عَنْهُ، وَلَا تَكِلْنِيْ إِلىٰ نَفْسِيْ فِيْمَا حَضَرْتُهُ، يَا مَنْ لَّا تَضُرُّهُ الذُّنُوْبُ وَلَا تَنْقُصُهُ الْمَغْفِرَةُ، هَبْ لِيْ مَا لَا يَنْقُصُكَ وَاغْفِرْلِيْ مَا لَا يَضُرُّكَ، إِنَّكَ أَنْتَ الْوَهَّابُ. أَسْأَلُكَ فَرَجًا قَرِيْبًا، وَّصَبْرًا جَمِيْلًا، وَّرِزْقًا وَّاسِعًا، وَّالْعَافِيَةِ مِنْ جَمِيْعِ الْبَلَاءِ. وَأَسْأَلُكَ تَمَامَ الْعَافِيَةِ، وَأَسْأَلُكَ دَوَامَ الْعَافِيَةِ، وَأَسْأَلُكَ الشُّكْرَ عَلَى الْعَافِيَةِ، وَأَسْأَلُكَ الْغِنٰى عَنِ النَّاسِ، وَلَا حَوْلَ وَلَا قُوَّةَ إِلَّا بِاللهِ الْعَلِيِّ الْعَظِيْمِ.

﴿١٨٠﴾ اَللّٰهُمَّ اجْعَلْ سَرِيْرَتِيْ خَيْرًا مِّنْ عَلَانِيَتِيْ، وَاجْعَلْ عَلَانِيَتِيْ صَالِحَةً. اَللّٰهُمَّ إِنِّيْ أَسْأَلُكَ مِنْ صَالِحِ مَا تُؤْتِي النَّاسَ مِنَ الْمَالِ وَالْأَهْلِ وَالْوَلَدِ، غَيْرِ الضَّالِّ وَلَا الْمُضِلِّ.

bitaqwāy(a). Waḥ-faẓnī fīmā ghibtu ʿanh(u), wa lā takilnī ilā nafsī fīmā ḥaḍartuh(ū), yā man lā taḍurruhudh-dhunūbu wa lā tanquṣuhul-maghfira(tu), hab lī mā lā yanquṣuka wagh-firlī mā lā yaḍurruk(a), innaka Antal-Wahhāb(u). As'aluka farajan qarība(n), wa ṣabran jamīla(n), wa rizqan wāsiʿa(n), wal-ʿāfiyati min jamīʿil-balā'(i). Wa as'aluka tamāmal-ʿāfiya(ti), wa as'aluka dawāmal-ʿāfiya(ti), wa as'alukash-shukra ʿalal-ʿāfiya(ti), wa as'alukal-ghinā ʿanin-nās(i), wa lā ḥawla wa lā quwwata illā bilLāhil-ʿAliyyil-ʿAẓīm.

180. Allāhummaj-ʿal sarīratī khayram min ʿalāniyatī, waj-ʿal ʿalāniyatī ṣāliḥa(tan). Allāhumma innī as'aluka min ṣāliḥi mā tu'tin-nāsa minal-māli wal-'ahli wal-walad(i), ghayriḍ-ḍālli wa lal-muḍill.

(181) O Allah, make us from among Your chosen servants, with bright faces, arms, and feet, who will be the welcome guests. O Allah, I beg of You a soul satisfied with You—one that believes in meeting with You, is pleased with Your decree, and is content with Your gifts.

(182) O Allah, all praise is due to You, the praise everlasting with Your Eternity. All praise is due to You, the praise which has no end outside Your Will. All praise is due to You, the praise the giver of which seeks but Your pleasure. All praise is due to You, the long lasting praise which is offered with every blink of the eye and with every breath.

O Allah, turn my heart to Your religion and protect us from all around with Your mercy.

O Allah, make me steadfast, lest I slip, and guide me lest I go astray.

---

(181) [Composite: Wafd ʿAbd al-Qays. *Musnad Aḥmad* #17163; Abū Umāmah al-Bāhilī. *Muʿjam al-Kabīr (Ṭabarānī)*]

chosen servants . . . welcome guests: According to the report in *Musnad Aḥmad*, the delegation of ʿAbdul-Qays heard the Prophet ﷺ make this duʿā'. They asked, who were the chosen servants. He replied: "Allah's pious servants." Then they asked who were the people with the bright faces, arms, and feet. He replied: "The people whose limbs will become bright due to wuḍū'." Then they asked who were the honored guests. He replied: "They will be the delegation from this ummah that will accompany their Prophet to meet their Lord, Blessed and Most High."

soul satisfied: satisfied with the belief in *Tawḥīd* (Islamic monotheism) and the truth of all the teachings of the Prophet ﷺ.

pleased with Your decree: one that completely and wholeheartedly submits to the Will of Allah.

This duʿā' defines the "contented soul." May Allah سُبْحَانَهُ وَتَعَالَىٰ grant us this soul.

→

﴿١٨١﴾ اَللّٰهُمَّ اجْعَلْنَا مِنْ عِبَادِكَ الْمُنْتَخَبِيْنَ الْغُرِّ الْمُحَجَّلِيْنَ الْوَفْدِ الْمُتَقَبَّلِيْنَ۔ اَللّٰهُمَّ إِنِّيْ أَسْأَلُكَ نَفْسًا بِكَ مُطْمَئِنَّةً تُؤْمِنُ بِلِقَائِكَ، وَتَرْضٰى بِقَضَائِكَ، وَتَقْنَعُ بِعَطَائِكَ۔

﴿١٨٢﴾ اَللّٰهُمَّ لَكَ الْحَمْدُ حَمْدًا دَائِمًا مَّعَ خُلُوْدِكَ، وَلَكَ الْحَمْدُ حَمْدًا لَّا مُنْتَهٰى لَهٗ دُوْنَ مَشِيَّتِكَ، وَلَكَ الْحَمْدُ حَمْدًا لَّا يُرِيْدُ قَائِلُهٗ إِلَّا رِضَاكَ، وَلَكَ الْحَمْدُ حَمْدًا مَّلِيًّا عِنْدَ كُلِّ طَرْفَةِ عَيْنٍ وَّتَنَفُّسِ نَفْسٍ۔ اَللّٰهُمَّ أَقْبِلْ بِقَلْبِيْ إِلٰى دِيْنِكَ، وَاحْفَظْ مِنْ وَّرَائِنَا بِرَحْمَتِكَ۔ اَللّٰهُمَّ ثَبِّتْنِيْ أَنْ أَزِلَّ، وَاهْدِنِيْ أَنْ أَضِلَّ۔

181. Allāhummaj-ʿalnā min ʿibādikal-muntakhabīnal-ghurril-muḥajjalīnal-wafdil-mutaqabbalīn(a). Allāhumma innī as'aluka nafsam bika muṭma'innatan tu'minu biliqā'ik(a), wa tarḍā biqaḍā'ik(a), wa taqnaʿu biʿaṭā'ik.

182. Allāhumma lakal-ḥamdu ḥamdan dā'imam maʿa khulūdik(a), wa lakal-ḥamdu ḥamdan lā muntahā lahū dūna mashiyyatik(a), wa lakal-ḥamdu ḥamdan lā yurīdu qā'iluhū illā riḍāk(a), wa lakal-ḥamdu ḥamdam maliyyan ʿinda kulli ṭarfati ʿaynin wa tanaffusi nafs(in). Allāhumma aqbil biqalbī ilā dīnik(a), waḥ-faẓ min wa rā'inā biraḥmatik(a). Allāhumma thabbitnī an azill(a), wah-dinī an aḍill.

---

(182) [Composite: ʿAlī ibn Abī Ṭālib. *Kanz al-ʿUmmāl* #3857; Anas ibn Mālik. *Majmaʿ az-Zawā'id* #17383; *Al-Ḥizb al-Aʿẓam*]

Angel Jibrīl ﷺ taught this duʿā' (اللهم لك الحمد حمدا...وتنفس نفس) to the Prophet ﷺ saying: "If it pleases you to worship Allah ﷻ all day or night the way He should be worshipped, then say these words" (*Kanz al-ʿUmmāl*).

(183) O Allah, just as You come between me and my heart, so come between me and the Shayṭān and his machinations. O Allah, endow us with Your bounty, deprive us not of Your sustenance, bless us in what You have bestowed upon us, make our heart free of wants, and put in us the desire for that which is with You.

(184) O Allah, make me from those who put their trust in You and You became sufficient for them, who sought guidance from You and You guided them, and who sought help from You and You helped them.

(185) O Allah, turn the stray thoughts of my heart into Your fear and remembrance. Turn my aspirations and desires toward things of Your liking and pleasure. And when You try me with ease or discomforts, then make me stick to the path of truth and the Sharīʿah of Islam.

(186) O Allah, I beg You for the completion of Your blessings in all things and gratitude to You over those until You are pleased and

---

(183) [Composite: *Al-Ḥizb al-Aʿẓam;* ʿAbdullāh ibn ʿAbbās. *Kanz al-ʿUmmāl* #3801]

(184) [Anas ibn Mālik. *Kanz al-ʿUmmāl* #5106]

(185) [*Al-Ḥizb al-Aʿẓam*]

(186) [Abū Bakr. *Kanz al-ʿUmmāl* #5034]

﴿١٨٣﴾ اَللّٰهُمَّ كَمَا حُلْتَ بَيْنِي وَبَيْنَ قَلْبِي فَحُلْ بَيْنِي وَبَيْنَ الشَّيْطَانِ وَعَمَلِهٖ۔ اَللّٰهُمَّ ارْزُقْنَا مِنْ فَضْلِكَ، وَلَا تَحْرِمْنَا رِزْقَكَ، وَبَارِكْ لَنَا فِيْمَا رَزَقْتَنَا، وَاجْعَلْ غِنَانَا فِيْ أَنْفُسِنَا، وَاجْعَلْ رَغْبَتَنَا فِيْمَا عِنْدَكَ۔

﴿١٨٤﴾ اَللّٰهُمَّ اجْعَلْنِيْ مِمَّنْ تَوَكَّلَ عَلَيْكَ فَكَفَيْتَهٗ، وَاسْتَهْدَاكَ فَهَدَيْتَهٗ، وَاسْتَنْصَرَكَ فَنَصَرْتَهٗ۔

﴿١٨٥﴾ اَللّٰهُمَّ اجْعَلْ وَسَاوِسَ قَلْبِيْ خَشْيَتَكَ وَذِكْرَكَ، وَاجْعَلْ هِمَّتِيْ وَهَوَايَ فِيْمَا تُحِبُّ وَتَرْضٰى. اَللّٰهُمَّ وَمَا ابْتَلَيْتَنِيْ بِهٖ مِنْ رَّخَاءٍ وَّشِدَّةٍ فَمَسِّكْنِيْ بِسُنَّةِ الْحَقِّ وَشَرِيْعَةِ الْإِسْلَامِ۔

﴿١٨٦﴾ اَللّٰهُمَّ إِنِّيْ أَسْأَلُكَ تَمَامَ النِّعْمَةِ فِي الْأَشْيَاءِ كُلِّهَا،

183. Allāhumma kamā ḥulta baynī wa bayna qalbī fa ḥul baynī wa baynash-shayṭāni wa ʿamalih(ī). Allāhummar-zuqnā min faḍlik(a), wa lā taḥrimnā rizqak(a), wa bārik lanā fīmā razaqtanā, waj-ʿal ghinānā fī anfusinā, waj-ʿal raghbatanā fīmā ʿindak.

184. Allāhummaj-ʿalnī mimman tawakkala ʿalayka fa kafaytah(ū), was-tahdāka fa hadaytah(ū), was-tanṣaraka fa naṣartah.

185. Allāhummaj-ʿal wasāwisa qalbī khashyataka wa dhikrak(a), waj-ʿal himmatī wa hawāya fīmā tuḥibbu wa tarḍā. Allāhumma wa mab-talaytanī bihī min rakhā'in wa shiddatin fa massiknī bisunnatil-ḥaqqi wa sharīʿatil-'Islām.

186. Allāhumma innī as'aluka tamāman-niʿmati fil-'ashyā'i

even after Your pleasure. (I beg that) You choose for me in all matters in which there is choice. And make easy choices, not the hard ones for me, O the Generous One.

(187) O Allah, the One Who breaks the dawn and turns the night into an occasion for rest and Who makes the (movement of) the sun and moon a means of keeping time, grant me the strength for jihād in Your way.

(188) O Allah, all praise is due to You for the tribulations and actions You direct toward Your creations. All praise is due to You for the tribulations and actions You direct toward our families. All praise is due to You for the tribulations and actions You direct specially toward us. All praise is due to You for guiding us. All praise is due to You for granting us honor. All praise is due to You for covering our faults. All praise is due to You for the Qur'ān. All praise is due to You for our family, property, and grant of safety. Praise is due to You until You are pleased and praise is due to You when You

---

(187) [Abū Sa'īd al-Khudrī. *Al-Firdaws al-Akhbār* (Daylamī) (as reported by Ḥāfiẓ al-'Irāqī in *Takhrīj Aḥādīth al-Iḥyā'*)]

(188) [Anas ibn Mālik. *Kanz al-'Ummāl* #5100]

وَالشُّكْرَ لَكَ عَلَيْهَا حَتّٰى تَرْضٰى وَبَعْدَ الرِّضٰى، وَالْخِيَرَةَ فِيْ جَمِيْعِ مَا يَكُوْنُ فِيْهِ الْخِيَرَةُ، بِجَمِيْعِ مَيْسُوْرِ الْأُمُوْرِ كُلِّهَا لَا بِمَعْسُوْرِهَا يَا كَرِيْمُ۔

﴿١٨٧﴾ اَللّٰهُمَّ فَالِقَ الْإِصْبَاحِ وَجَاعِلَ اللَّيْلِ سَكَنًا وَّالشَّمْسِ وَالْقَمَرِ حُسْبَانًا قَوِّنِيْ عَلَى الْجِهَادِ فِيْ سَبِيْلِكَ۔

﴿١٨٨﴾ اَللّٰهُمَّ لَكَ الْحَمْدُ فِيْ بَلَائِكَ وَصَنِيْعِكَ إِلٰى خَلْقِكَ، وَلَكَ الْحَمْدُ فِيْ بَلَائِكَ وَصَنِيْعِكَ إِلٰى أَهْلِ بُيُوْتِنَا، وَلَكَ الْحَمْدُ فِيْ بَلَائِكَ وَصَنِيْعِكَ إِلٰى أَنْفُسِنَا خَاصَّةً، وَّلَكَ الْحَمْدُ بِمَا هَدَيْتَنَا، وَلَكَ الْحَمْدُ بِمَا أَكْرَمْتَنَا، وَلَكَ الْحَمْدُ بِمَا سَتَرْتَنَا، وَلَكَ الْحَمْدُ بِالْقُرْاٰنِ، وَلَكَ الْحَمْدُ بِالْأَهْلِ وَالْمَالِ، وَلَكَ الْحَمْدُ بِالْمُعَافَاةِ، وَلَكَ الْحَمْدُ حَتّٰى تَرْضٰى، وَلَكَ الْحَمْدُ إِذَا رَضِيْتَ، يَا أَهْلَ

kullihā, wash-shukra laka ʿalayhā ḥattā tarḍā wa baʿdar-riḍā, wal-khiyarata fī jamīʿi mā yakūnu fīhil-khiyara(tu), bijamīʿi maysūril-ʾumūri kullihā lā bimaʿsūrihā yā Karīm.

187. Allāhumma Fāliqal-ʾiṣbāḥi wa Jāʿilal-layli sakanan wash-shamsi wal-qamari ḥusbānan qawwinī ʿalal-jihādi fī sabīlik.

188. Allāhumma lakal-ḥamdu fī balāʾika wa ṣanīʿika ilā khalqik(a), wa lakal-ḥamdu fī balāʾika wa ṣanīʿika ilā ahli buyūtinā, wa lakal-ḥamdu fī balāʾika wa ṣanīʿika ilā anfusinā khāṣṣa(tan), wa lakal-ḥamdu bimā hadaytanā, wa lakal-ḥamdu bimā akramtanā, wa lakal-ḥamdu bimā satartanā, wa lakal-ḥamdu bil-Qurʾān(i), wa lakal-ḥamdu bil-ʾahli wal-māl(i), wa lakal-ḥamdu bil-muʿāfā(ti), wa lakal-ḥamdu ḥattā tarḍā, wa lakal-ḥamdu idhā raḍīt(a), yā

become pleased. O the One Who alone is deserving to be feared. O the One Who alone is capable of forgiving sins.

(189) O Allah, direct me toward what You like and approve of in my words, actions, deeds, intentions, and courses of action. Indeed You are powerful over all things.

(190) O Allah, I seek Your protection from a cunning friend whose eyes are turned to me (with apparent affection) but his heart keeps a watch on me (to find faults); if he sees good, he buries it, and if he sees something bad he announces it. O Allah, I seek Your protection from wretchedness and display of poverty. O Allah, I seek Your

---

(189) [ʿAbdullāh ibn ʿUmar. *Kanz al-ʿUmmāl* #3797]

(190) [Composite: Saʿīd al-Maqburī (Mursal). *Kanz al-ʿUmmāl* #3666; Abū Umāmah al-Bāhilī. *ʿAmal al-Yawm wal-Laylah (Ibn as-Sunnī)* #155; Saʿd ibn Abī Waqqāṣ. *Kanz al-ʿUmmāl* #3687; Samurah ibn Jundub. *Majmaʿ az-Zawāʾid* #2615; Anas ibn Mālik. *ʿAmal al-Yawm wal-Laylah (Ibn as-Sunnī)* #120; Abū Hurayrah. *Kanz al-ʿUmmāl* #3775; *Al-Ḥizb al-Aʿẓam*]

cunning friend: This is referring to an enemy that poses to be a friend. It is said that an enemy giving a friendly smile is like the *ḥanẓalah* plant (colocynth). Its leaves look green and refreshing. But tasting it causes great pain and can lead to death.

if he sees good, he buries it, and if he sees something bad he announces it: One wonders at how accurately this description fits the mainstream media and their coverage of Islam and Muslims.

wretchedness and display of poverty: (اَلْبُؤْسِ وَالتَّبَاؤُس) : These words imply a display of one's real or feigned sorry state to attract pity. This has been condemned in aḥādith. According to a ḥadīth, the Prophet ﷺ said,

> إذا آتاك الله مالا فلير عليك، فإن الله يحب أن يرى أثره على عبده حسنا، ولا يحب البؤس ولا التباؤس (البخاري في التاريخ والطبراني في الكبير عن زهير بن أبي علقمة)
>
> When Allah gives you wealth, then it should be seen on you, because indeed Allah loves to see its signs on His servant in a →

التَّقْوٰى، وَيَا أَهْلَ الْمَغْفِرَةِ۔

﴿١٨٩﴾ اَللّٰهُمَّ وَفِّقْنِيْ لِمَا تُحِبُّ وَتَرْضٰى مِنَ الْقَوْلِ وَالْعَمَلِ وَالْفِعْلِ وَالنِّيَّةِ وَالْهَدْيِ، إِنَّكَ عَلٰى كُلِّ شَيْءٍ قَدِيْرٌ۔

﴿١٩٠﴾ اَللّٰهُمَّ إِنِّيْ أَعُوْذُ بِكَ مِنْ خَلِيْلٍ مَّاكِرٍ عَيْنَاهُ تَرَيَانِيْ وَقَلْبُهٗ يَرْعَانِيْ، إِنْ رَّاٰى حَسَنَةً دَفَنَهَا وَإِنْ رَّاٰى سَيِّئَةً أَذَاعَهَا۔ اَللّٰهُمَّ إِنِّيْ أَعُوْذُ بِكَ مِنَ الْبُؤْسِ وَالتَّبَاؤُسِ۔ اَللّٰهُمَّ إِنِّيْ أَعُوْذُ

Ahlat-taqwā, wa yā Ahlal-maghfirah.

189. Allāhumma waffiqnī limā tuḥibbu wa tarḍā minal-qawli wal-ʿamali wal-fiʿli wan-niyyati wal-hady(i), innaka ʿalā kulli shay'in qadīr.

190. Allāhumma innī aʿūdhu bika min khalīlim mākirin ʿaynāhu tarayānī wa qalbuhū yarʿānī, in ra'ā ḥasanatan dafanahā wa in ra'ā sayyi'atan adhāʿahā. Allāhumma innī aʿūdhu bika minal-bu'si wat-tabā'us(i). Allāhumma innī aʿūdhu bika min iblīsa wa

---

beautiful manner, and He dislikes wretchedness and display of poverty.

When Allah blesses us, we use His blessings with thanks. When He tests us with difficult conditions, we turn solely to Him, instead of begging before other human beings. This should give us a lot to reflect on the practice of engaging in disaster pornography, which has become a preferred tool for eliciting charity in the media age.

protection from the devil and his army. O Allah, I seek Your protection from the sedition of women. O Allah, I seek Your protection from that You should turn Your Face away from me on the Day of Judgment. O Allah, I seek Your protection from actions that would humiliate me, companions who would ruin me, wishes that would distract me, poverty that would make me forget everything, and affluence that would lead me to exorbitance. O Allah, I seek Your protection from a worrisome death and I seek Your protection from a sorrowful death.

I seek Your protection from the devil and his army: According to a ḥadīth, this du'ā' (اَللّٰهُمَّ إِنِّيْ أَعُوْذُ بِكَ مِنْ إِبْلِيْسَ وَجُنُوْدِهٖ) should be said when leaving the masjid.

بِكَ مِنْ إِبْلِيْسَ وَجُنُوْدِهٖ۔ اَللّٰهُمَّ إِنِّيْ أَعُوْذُ بِكَ مِنْ فِتْنَةِ النِّسَاءِ۔
اَللّٰهُمَّ إِنِّيْ أَعُوْذُ بِكَ مِنْ أَنْ تَصُدَّ عَنِّيْ وَجْهَكَ يَوْمَ الْقِيَامَةِ۔
اَللّٰهُمَّ إِنِّيْ أَعُوْذُ بِكَ مِنْ كُلِّ عَمَلٍ يُّخْزِيْنِيْ، وَأَعُوْذُ بِكَ مِنْ كُلِّ
صَاحِبٍ يُّرْدِيْنِيْ، وَأَعُوْذُ بِكَ مِنْ كُلِّ أَمَلٍ يُّلْهِيْنِيْ، وَأَعُوْذُ بِكَ
مِنْ كُلِّ فَقْرٍ يُّنْسِيْنِيْ، وَأَعُوْذُ بِكَ مِنْ كُلِّ غِنًى يُّطْغِيْنِيْ۔ اَللّٰهُمَّ
إِنِّيْ أَعُوْذُ بِكَ مِنْ مَّوْتِ الْهَمِّ، وَأَعُوْذُ بِكَ مِنْ مَّوْتِ الْغَمِّ۔

junūdih(ī). Allāhumma innī aʿūdhu bika min fitnatin-nisā'(i). Allāhumma innī aʿūdhu bika min an taṣudda ʿannī Wajhaka yawmal-qiyāma(ti). Allāhumma innī aʿūdhu bika min kulli ʿamalin yukhzīnī, wa aʿūdhu bika min kulli ṣāḥibin yurdīnī, wa aʿūdhu bika min kulli amalin yulhīnī, wa aʿūdhu bika min kulli faqrin yunsīnī, wa aʿūdhu bika min kulli ghinan yuṭghīnī. Allāhumma innī aʿūdhu bika mim mawtil-hamm(i), wa aʿūdhu bika mim mawtil-ghamm.

FRIDAY

In the Name of Allah, the Most Compassionate, the Most Merciful

(191) O Lord, O Lord, O Lord. O Allah, O the Greatest, O the Hearer and Seer of all things, O He Who has no partner or assistant, O the Creator of the sun and the luminous moon, O the Refuge of a fear-stricken destitute, O the Nourisher of the little baby, O the Healer of a fractured bone, I cry unto You like the crying of a poor beggar or that of a helpless blind or emaciated man. I beg of You that You make the Qur'ān the springtime for my heart and a remedy for my grief.

(192) O Lord, give us in this world such and such ___ (here mention your needs); O the Comforter of every lonely person; O the Companion of every person who is alone; O the One Who is near and not remote; O the One Who is present and not away; O the One Who overcomes all and is not overcome; O the Living, the Eternal, the Majestic, and the Benevolent. O the Light of the heavens and the earth. O the Adornment of the heavens and the earth. O the

---

(191) [*Al-Ḥizb al-Aʿẓam*]

the Healer of a fractured bone: Only Allah سُبْحَانَهُ وَتَعَالَىٰ can heal a fractured bone. All a physician can do is to put the fractured parts together and hold them in place through casts (external fixation) or wires, plates, and screws, etc. (internal fixation). After that, they wait until the fracture is healed.

(192) [Composite: *Al-Ḥizb al-Aʿẓam*; Anas ibn Mālik. *Kanz al-ʿUmmāl* #5103; Ḥudhayfah ibn al-Yamān. *Majmaʿ az-Zawā'id* #17396]

بِسْمِ اللّٰهِ الرَّحْمٰنِ الرَّحِيْمِ

﴿١٩١﴾ يَا رَبِّ يَا رَبِّ يَا رَبِّ، اَللّٰهُمَّ يَا كَبِيْرُ يَا سَمِيْعُ يَا بَصِيْرُ، يَا مَنْ لَّا شَرِيْكَ لَهٗ وَلَا وَزِيْرَ لَهٗ، وَيَا خَالِقَ الشَّمْسِ وَالْقَمَرِ الْمُنِيْرِ، وَيَا عِصْمَةَ الْبَائِسِ الْخَائِفِ الْمُسْتَجِيْرِ، وَيَا رَازِقَ الطِّفْلِ الصَّغِيْرِ، وَيَا جَابِرَ الْعَظْمِ الْكَسِيْرِ، أَدْعُوْكَ دُعَاءَ الْبَائِسِ الْفَقِيْرِ كَدُعَاءِ الْمُضْطَرِّ الضَّرِيْرِ. أَسْأَلُكَ أَنْ تَجْعَلَ الْقُرْاٰنَ رَبِيْعَ قَلْبِيْ وَجَلَاءَ حُزْنِيْ۔

﴿١٩٢﴾ رَبَّنَا اٰتِنَا فِي الدُّنْيَا (كَذَا وَكَذَا) يَا مُؤْنِسَ كُلِّ وَحِيْدٍ، وَّيَا صَاحِبَ كُلِّ فَرِيْدٍ، وَّيَا قَرِيْبًا غَيْرَ بَعِيْدٍ، وَّيَا شَاهِدًا غَيْرَ غَائِبٍ، وَّيَا غَالِبًا غَيْرَ مَغْلُوْبٍ، يَّا حَيُّ يَا قَيُّوْمُ، يَا ذَا الْجَلَالِ وَالْإِكْرَامِ۔ يَا نُوْرَ السَّمٰوٰتِ وَالْأَرْضِ، يَا زَيْنَ السَّمٰوٰتِ

191. Yā Rabbi yā Rabbi yā Rabb(i), Allāhumma yā Kabīru yā Samīʿu yā Baṣīr(u), yā man lā sharīka lahū wa lā wa zīra lah(ū), wa yā Khāliqash-shamsi wal-qamaril-munīr(i), wa yā ʿIṣmatal-bā'isil-khā'ifil-mustajīr(i), wa yā Rāziqaṭ-ṭifliṣ-ṣaghīr(i), wa yā Jābiral-ʿaẓmil-kasīr(i), adʿūka duʿā'al-bā'isil-faqīri kaduʿā'il-muḍṭarriḍ-ḍarīr(i). As'aluka an tajʿalal-Qur'āna rabīʿa qalbī wa jalā'a ḥuznī.

192. Rabbanā ātinā fid-dunyā kadhā wa kadha yā Mu'nisa kulli waḥīd(in), wa yā Ṣāḥiba kulli farīd(in), wa yā Qarīban ghayra baʿīd(in), wa yā Shāhidan ghayra ghā'ib(in), wa yā Ghāliban ghayra maghlūb(in), yā Ḥayyu yā Qayyūm(u), yā Dhal-Jalāli wal-'ikrām(i). Yā Nūras-samāwāti wal-'arḍ(i), yā Zaynas-samāwāti

Mighty Sovereign of the heavens and the earth. O the Sole Support of the heavens and the earth. O the Originator of the heavens and the earth. O the Sustainer of the heavens and the earth. O the Majestic and Benevolent. O the Succorer of those crying for help. O the Last Resort of seekers of protection. O the Reliever of the pain of the people in anguish. O the Soother of the grieved ones. O the Acceptor of the du'ā' of desperate supplicants. O the Remover of all pains. O Lord of all the worlds. O the Most Merciful of those who show mercy, we humbly place our needs before You.

(193) O Allah, indeed You are the Mighty Creator of everything. You are the All-Hearing, All-Knowing. You are the Forgiving, the Merciful. You are the Lord of the Great Throne. O Allah, You are the Most Gracious, the Most Generous, the Benevolent. Forgive me. Have mercy on me. Protect me. Provide me with sustenance. Conceal my faults. Support me. Uplift and elevate me. Guide me aright. Do not let me go astray. And admit me to Paradise through Your

---

(193) [Composite: Jābir ibn ʿAbdillāh. *Al-Firdaws al-Akhbār* (Daylamī) #1805; Ibid. *Kanz al-ʿUmmāl* #5111; ʿAbdullāh ibn Masʿūd. *Kanz al-ʿUmmāl* #5087; Abū Hurayrah. *Al-Jāmiʿ aṣ-Ṣaghīr* #1459]

وَالْأَرْضِ، يَا جَبَّارَ السَّمٰوٰتِ وَالْأَرْضِ، يَا عِمَادَ السَّمٰوٰتِ وَالْأَرْضِ، يَا بَدِيْعَ السَّمٰوٰتِ وَالْأَرْضِ، يَا قَيَّامَ السَّمٰوٰتِ وَالْأَرْضِ، يَا ذَا الْجَلَالِ وَالْإِكْرَامِ، يَا صَرِيْخَ الْمُسْتَصْرِخِيْنَ، وَمُنْتَهَى الْعَائِذِيْنَ، وَالْمُفَرِّجُ عَنِ الْمَكْرُوْبِيْنَ، وَالْمُرَوِّحُ عَنِ الْمَغْمُوْمِيْنَ، وَمُجِيْبَ دُعَاءِ الْمُضْطَرِّيْنَ، وَيَا كَاشِفَ الْكَرْبِ، يَا إِلٰهَ الْعٰلَمِيْنَ وَيَا أَرْحَمَ الرَّاحِمِيْنَ، مَنْزُوْلٌ بِكَ كُلُّ حَاجَةٍ۔

﴿١٩٣﴾ اَللّٰهُمَّ إِنَّكَ خَلَّاقٌ عَظِيْمٌ، إِنَّكَ سَمِيْعٌ عَلِيْمٌ، إِنَّكَ غَفُوْرٌ رَّحِيْمٌ، إِنَّكَ رَبُّ الْعَرْشِ الْعَظِيْمِ. اَللّٰهُمَّ إِنَّكَ الْبَرُّ الْجَوَادُ الْكَرِيْمُ، اغْفِرْلِيْ، وَارْحَمْنِيْ، وَعَافِنِيْ، وَارْزُقْنِيْ، وَاسْتُرْنِيْ، وَاجْبُرْنِيْ، وَارْفَعْنِيْ، وَاهْدِنِيْ، وَلَا تُضِلَّنِيْ، وَأَدْخِلْنِي الْجَنَّةَ،

wal-'arḍ(i), yā Jabbāras-samāwāti wal-'arḍ(i), yā ʿImādas-samāwāti wal-'arḍ(i), yā Badīʿas-samāwāti wal-'arḍ(i), yā Qayyāmas-samāwāti wal-'arḍ(i), yā Dhal-jalāli wal-'ikrām(i), yā Ṣarīkhal-mustaṣrikhīn(a), wa Muntahal-ʿā'idhīn(a), wal-Mufarriju ʿanil-makrūbīn(a), wal-Murawwiḥu ʿanil-maghmūmīn(a), wa Mujība duʿā'il-muḍṭarrīn(a), wa yā Kāshifal-karb(i), yā Ilāhal-ʿālamīna wa yā Arḥamar-rāḥimīn(a), manzūlum bika kullu ḥājah.

193. Allāhumma innaka Khallāqun ʿAẓīm(un), innaka Samīʿun ʿAlīm(un), innaka Ghafūrun Raḥīm(un), innaka Rabbul-ʿarshil-ʿaẓīm(i). Allāhumma innakal-Barrul-Jawādul-Karīm(u), igh-firlī, war-ḥamnī, wa ʿāfinī, war-zuqnī, was-turnī, waj-burnī, war-faʿnī, wah-dinī, wa lā tuḍillanī, wa adkhilnil-Janna(ta), biraḥmatika yā

mercy, O the Most Merciful of those who show mercy. O my Lord, in Your Sight make me dear, in my heart make me humble before You, and in the eyes of other people make me honorable. Protect me from bad manners and morals. O Allah, You asked from us that which we do not control except with Your help. So grant us from it that which will make You be pleased with us.

(194) O Allah, I beseech You for abiding faith, a fearful heart, beneficial knowledge, true belief, and the right religion. I beg of You safety from all mishaps, full and lasting protection, and gratitude for that protection. I seek from You freedom from dependence on other people.

(195) O Allah, I beg forgiveness for sins which I have repeated after having repented from them before You. I beg forgiveness for all the promises which I have made to You on my behalf and then did not

---

(194) [ʿAlī ibn Abī Ṭālib. *Kanz al-ʿUmmāl* #5055]
This was the duʿā' of Sayyidnā Abū Dharr al-Ghifārī رضي الله عنه. According to a ḥadīth, angel Jibrīl عليه السلام said that Abū Dharr رضي الله عنه was more well-known among the angels than he was among the people of the world because of this duʿā'. He further said, whoever makes this duʿā' twice a day, all of his sins will be forgiven and he will be called to enter the Paradise through whichever door he wished.

(195) [ʿAbdullāh ibn ʿUmar. *Kanz al-ʿUmmāl* #5126]
According to Sayyidnā ʿAbdullāh ibn ʿUmar رضي الله عنهما, Prophet Muḥammad صلى الله عليه وسلم, frequently used to remind his Companions to say these words of Sayyidnā Khiḍr عليه السلام, which would wipe out sins.

بِرَحْمَتِكَ يَا أَرْحَمَ الرَّاحِمِيْنَ۔ إِلَيْكَ رَبِّيْ فَحَبِّبْنِيْ، وَفِيْ نَفْسِيْ لَكَ رَبِّيْ فَذَلِّلْنِيْ، وَفِيْ أَعْيُنِ النَّاسِ فَعَظِّمْنِيْ، وَمِنْ سَيِّءِ الْأَخْلَاقِ فَجَنِّبْنِيْ۔ اَللّٰهُمَّ إِنَّكَ سَأَلْتَنَا مِنْ أَنْفُسِنَا مَا لَا نَمْلِكُهُ إِلَّا بِكَ، فَأَعْطِنَا مِنْهَا مَا يُرْضِيْكَ عَنَّا۔

﴿١٩٤﴾ اَللّٰهُمَّ إِنِّيْ أَسْأَلُكَ إِيْمَانًا دَائِمًا، وَّأَسْأَلُكَ قَلْبًا خَاشِعًا، وَّأَسْأَلُكَ عِلْمًا نَّافِعًا، وَّأَسْأَلُكَ يَقِيْنًا صَادِقًا، وَّأَسْأَلُكَ دِيْنًا قَيِّمًا، وَّأَسْأَلُكَ الْعَافِيَةَ مِنْ كُلِّ بَلِيَّةٍ، وَّأَسْأَلُكَ تَمَامَ الْعَافِيَةِ، وَأَسْأَلُكَ دَوَامَ الْعَافِيَةِ، وَأَسْأَلُكَ الشُّكْرَ عَلَى الْعَافِيَةِ، وَأَسْأَلُكَ الْغِنٰى عَنِ النَّاسِ۔

﴿١٩٥﴾ اَللّٰهُمَّ إِنِّيْ أَسْتَغْفِرُكَ لِمَا تُبْتُ إِلَيْكَ مِنْهُ ثُمَّ عُدْتُّ فِيْهِ، وَأَسْتَغْفِرُكَ لِمَا أَعْطَيْتُكَ مِنْ نَّفْسِيْ ثُمَّ لَمْ أُوْفِ لَكَ بِهٖ،

Arḥamar-rāḥimīn(a). Ilayka Rabbī fa ḥabbibnī, wa fī nafsī laka Rabbī fa dhallilnī, wa fī aʿyunin-nāsi fa ʿaẓẓimnī, wa min sayyi'il-'akhlāqi fa jannibnī. Allāhumma innaka sa'altanā min anfusinā mā lā namlikuhū illā bik(a), fa aʿṭinā minhā mā yurḍīka ʿannā.

194. Allāhumma innī as'aluka īmānan dā'ima(n), wa as'aluka qalban khāshiʿa(n), wa as'aluka ʿilman nāfiʿa(n), wa as'aluka yaqīnan ṣādiqa(n), wa as'aluka dīnan qayyima(n), wa as'alukal-ʿāfiyata min kulli baliyya(tin), wa as'aluka tamāmal-ʿāfiya(ti), wa as'aluka dawāmal-ʿāfiya(ti), wa as'alukash-shukra ʿalal-ʿāfiya(ti), wa as'alukal-ghinā ʿanin-nās(i).

195. Allāhumma innī astaghfiruka limā tubtu ilayka minhu thumma ʿudttu fīh(i), wa astaghfiruka limā aʿṭaytuka min nafsī

fulfill. I beg forgiveness for Your gifts from which I drew strength only to use it in your disobedience. I beg forgiveness for all those good actions that I intended for Your sake only but later mixed other motives in them. O Allah, do not humiliate me as You do have full knowledge of me and do not punish me as You do have all power over me.

(196) O Allah, Lord of the seven heavens and of the Great Throne (ʿArsh), be sufficient for me in all matters of concern in whatever way and place You will.

(197) Allah is sufficient for me for my religion. Allah is sufficient for my worldly matters. Allah is sufficient for everything that concerns me. Allah is sufficient to take care of anyone who causes aggression against me. Allah is sufficient for me against anyone who is jealous of me. Allah is sufficient for me against anybody who holds evil intentions against me. Allah is sufficient for me at the time of death. Allah is sufficient for me during the questioning (by angels) in the grave. Allah is sufficient for me when my actions are weighed in the

---

(196) [Composite: ʿAlī ibn Abī Ṭālib. *Kanz al-ʿUmmāl* #3433]
According to a ḥadīth, whoever says this duʿā', Allah will drive away his worries.

(197) [Buraydah al-Aslamī. *Kashf al-Khafā'* #1134]
According to a ḥadīth whoever says this duʿā' after the Fajr ṣalāt, he will find Allah will suffice for his needs.

وَأَسْتَغْفِرُكَ لِلنِّعَمِ الَّتِيْ أَنْعَمْتَ بِهَا عَلَيَّ فَتَقَوَّيْتُ بِهَا عَلٰى مَعَاصِيْكَ، وَأَسْتَغْفِرُكَ لِكُلِّ خَيْرٍ أَرَدْتُّ بِهٖ وَجْهَكَ فَخَالَطَنِيْ فِيْهِ مَا لَيْسَ لَكَ. اَللّٰهُمَّ لَا تُخْزِنِيْ فَإِنَّكَ بِيْ عَالِمٌ، وَّلَا تُعَذِّبْنِيْ فَإِنَّكَ عَلَيَّ قَادِرٌ۔

﴿١٩٦﴾ اَللّٰهُمَّ رَبَّ السَّمٰوٰتِ السَّبْعِ وَرَبَّ الْعَرْشِ الْعَظِيْمِ، اكْفِنِيْ كُلَّ مُهِمٍّ مِّنْ حَيْثُ شِئْتَ وَمِنْ أَيْنَ شِئْتَ۔

﴿١٩٧﴾ حَسْبِيَ اللهُ لِدِيْنِيْ، حَسْبِيَ اللهُ لِدُنْيَايَ، حَسْبِيَ اللهُ لِمَا أَهَمَّنِيْ، حَسْبِيَ اللهُ لِمَنْ بَغٰى عَلَيَّ، حَسْبِيَ اللهُ لِمَنْ حَسَدَنِيْ، حَسْبِيَ اللهُ لِمَنْ كَادَنِيْ بِسُوْءٍ، حَسْبِيَ اللهُ عِنْدَ الْمَوْتِ، حَسْبِيَ اللهُ عِنْدَ الْمَسْأَلَةِ فِي الْقَبْرِ، حَسْبِيَ اللهُ عِنْدَ

thumma lam ūfi laka bih(ī), wa astaghfiruka lin-niʿamil-latī anʿamta bihā ʿalayya fa taqawwaytu bihā ʿalā maʿāṣīk(a), wa astaghfiruka likulli khayrin aradttu bihī wajhaka fa khālaṭanī fīhi mā laysa lak(a). Allāhumma lā tukhzinī fa innaka bī ʿālim(un), wa lā tuʿadh-dhibnī fa innaka ʿalayya qādir.

196. Allāhumma Rabbas-samāwātis-sabʿi wa Rabbal-ʿarshil-ʿaẓīm(i), ik-finī kulla muhimmim min ḥaythu shi'ta wa min ayna shi't(a).

197. ḤasbiyAllāhu lidīnī, ḥasbiyAllāhu lidunyāy(a), ḥasbiyAllāhu limā ahammanī, ḥasbiyAllāhu limam baghā ʿalayy(a), ḥasbiyAllāhu liman ḥasadanī, ḥasbiyAllāhu liman kādanī bisū'(in), ḥasbiyAllāhu ʿindal-mawt(i), ḥasbiyAllāhu ʿindal-mas'alati

balance on the Day of Judgment. Allah is sufficient for me when I have to pass over the Ṣirāṭ Bridge. Allah is enough for me as there is no god besides Him; on Him have I relied and to Him do I turn.

(198) O Allah, I seek from You the reward of the grateful, the reception of the close ones, the company of the prophets, the belief of the truthful, the humbleness of the fearful, and the devotion of the true believers—all my life so that You give me death in this state, O the Most Merciful of those who show mercy.

(199) O Allah, I beseech You by virtue of the blessings You have abundantly poured on me, the good tests that You have subjected me to, and the favors You have bestowed on me, to admit me in Paradise by Your grace, favor, and mercy.

(200) O Allah, I beg of You an everlasting faith, upright guidance, and beneficial knowledge.

---

(198) [Abū Hurayrah. *Kanz al-ʿUmmāl* #4945]

(199) [ʿAbdullāh ibn Masʿūd. *Kanz al-ʿUmmāl* #3784]

(200) [Anas ibn Mālik. *Kanz al-ʿUmmāl* #3789]

الْمِيْزَانِ، حَسْبِيَ اللهُ عِنْدَ الصِّرَاطِ، حَسْبِيَ اللهُ لَا إِلٰهَ إِلَّا هُوَ، عَلَيْهِ تَوَكَّلْتُ وَإِلَيْهِ أُنِيْبُ۔

﴿١٩٨﴾ اَللّٰهُمَّ إِنِّيْ أَسْأَلُكَ ثَوَابَ الشَّاكِرِيْنَ، وَنُزُلَ الْمُقَرَّبِيْنَ، وَمُرَافَقَةَ النَّبِيِّيْنَ، وَيَقِيْنَ الصِّدِّيْقِيْنَ، وَذِلَّةَ الْمُتَّقِيْنَ، وَإِخْبَاتَ الْمُوْقِنِيْنَ، حَتّٰى تَوَفَّانِيْ عَلٰى ذٰلِكَ يَا أَرْحَمَ الرَّاحِمِيْنَ۔

﴿١٩٩﴾ اَللّٰهُمَّ إِنِّيْ أَسْأَلُكَ بِنِعْمَتِكَ السَّابِغَةِ عَلَيَّ، وَبَلَائِكَ الْحَسَنِ الَّذِيْ ابْتَلَيْتَنِيْ بِهٖ، وَفَضْلِكَ الَّذِيْ أَفْضَلْتَ عَلَيَّ، أَنْ تُدْخِلَنِيَ الْجَنَّةَ بِمَنِّكَ وَفَضْلِكَ وَرَحْمَتِكَ۔

﴿٢٠٠﴾ اَللّٰهُمَّ إِنِّيْ أَسْأَلُكَ إِيْمَانًا دَائِمًا، وَّهَدْيًا قَيِّمًا، وَّعِلْمًا نَّافِعًا۔

fil-qabr(i), ḥasbiyAllāhu ʿindal-mīzān(i), ḥasbiyAllāhu ʿindaṣ-ṣirāṭ(i), ḥasbiyAllāhu lā ilāha illā huw(a), ʿalayhi tawakkaltu wa ilayhi unīb.

198. Allāhumma innī as'aluka thawābash-shākirīn(a), wa nuzulal-muqarrabīn(a), wa murāfaqatan-nabiyyīn(a), wa yaqīnaṣ-ṣiddīqīn(a), wa dhillatal-muttaqīn(a), wa ikhbātal-mūqinīn(a), ḥattā tawaffānī ʿalā dhālika yā Arḥamar-rāḥimīn.

199. Allāhumma innī as'aluka biniʿmatikas-sābighati ʿalayy(a), wa balā'ikal-ḥasanil-ladhib-talaytanī bih(ī), wa faḍlikal-ladhī afḍalta ʿalayy(a), an tudkhilaniyal-Jannata bimannika wa faḍlika wa raḥmatik.

200. Allāhumma innī as'aluka īmānan dā'ima(n), wa hadyan qayyima(n), wa ʿilman nāfiʿa.

(201) O Allah, indebt me not to an immoral person whom I may have to pay back in this world and in the Hereafter.

(202) O Allah, forgive my sins, broaden my moral outlook, purify my income, make me content with Your provisions, and let not my heart turn to anything that You have withheld from me.

(203) O Allah, I seek Your protection from everything You have created and I make You my shelter against them. Grant me with You confidant status, closeness, and a beautiful retreat. Make me among those who are fearful of standing before You and of Your warnings and who look forward to meeting with You. Make me among those who turn to You in sincere repentance. I beseech You for deeds that will be accepted, knowledge that will lead to success, efforts that will be appreciated, and a business that will never fail.

---

(201) [Muʿādh ibn Jabal. *Kanz al-ʿUmmāl* #3810]

(202) [ʿAlī ibn Abī Ṭālib. *Kanz al-ʿUmmāl* #5061]

(203) [Composite: Anas ibn Mālik. *Kanz al-ʿUmmāl* #3850; Abū Hurayrah. *Kanz al-ʿUmmāl* #3855]
closeness and a beautiful retreat: Refers to the following verse from the Qur'ān: "And he enjoyed, indeed, precedence with Us, and the finest retreat" (*Ṣād*, 38:40).
fearful . . . look forward to meeting with You: A believer always lives between hope and fear.
business that will never fail: This refers to the Qur'anic verse, "Those who recite the Book of Allah, establish ṣalāt, and spend (in charity) out of what We have provided for them, secretly and openly, look forward to a business that will never fail" (*al-Fāṭir,* 35:29).

﴿٢٠١﴾ اَللّٰهُمَّ لَا تَجْعَلْ لِّفَاجِرٍ عِنْدِيْ نِعْمَةً أُكَافِيْهِ بِهَا فِي الدُّنْيَا وَالْاٰخِرَةِ۔

﴿٢٠٢﴾ اَللّٰهُمَّ اغْفِرْ لِيْ ذَنْبِيْ، وَوَسِّعْ لِيْ خُلُقِيْ، وَطَيِّبْ لِيْ كَسْبِيْ، وَقَنِّعْنِيْ بِمَا رَزَقْتَنِيْ، وَلَا تُذْهِبْ قَلْبِيْ إِلٰى شَيْءٍ صَرَّفْتَهٗ عَنِّيْ۔

﴿٢٠٣﴾ اَللّٰهُمَّ إِنِّيْ أَسْتَجِيْرُكَ مِنْ جَمِيْعِ كُلِّ شَيْءٍ خَلَقْتَ وَأَحْتَرِسُ بِكَ مِنْهُنَّ۔ وَاجْعَلْ لِّيْ عِنْدَكَ وَلِيْجَةً، وَّاجْعَلْ لِّيْ عِنْدَكَ زُلْفٰى وَحُسْنَ مَاٰبٍ، وَّاجْعَلْنِيْ مِمَّنْ يَّخَافُ مَقَامَكَ وَوَعِيْدَكَ وَيَرْجُوْ لِقَائَكَ، وَاجْعَلْنِيْ مِمَّنْ يَّتُوْبُ إِلَيْكَ تَوْبَةً نَّصُوْحًا، وَّأَسْأَلُكَ عَمَلًا مُّتَقَبَّلًا، وَّعِلْمًا نَّجِيْحًا، وَّسَعْيًا مَّشْكُوْرًا، وَّتِجَارَةً لَّنْ تَبُوْرَ۔

201. Allāhumma lā tajʿal lifājirin ʿindī niʿmatan ukāfīhi bihā fid-dunyā wal-ākhirah.

202. Allāhummagh-fir lī dhambī, wa wassiʿ lī khuluqī, wa ṭayyib lī kasbī, wa qanniʿnī bimā razaqtanī, wa lā tudh-hib qalbī ilā shay'in ṣarraftahū ʿannī.

203. Allāhumma innī astajīruka min jamīʿi kulli shay'in khalaqta wa aḥtarisu bika minhunn(a). Waj-ʿal lī ʿindaka walīja(tan), waj-ʿal lī ʿindaka zulfā wa ḥusna ma'āb(in), waj-ʿalnī mimman yakhāfu maqāmaka wa waʿīdaka wa yarjū liqā'ak(a), waj-ʿalnī mimman yatūbu ilayka tawbatan naṣūḥa(n), wa as'aluka ʿamalam mutaqabbala(n), wa ʿilman najīḥa(n), wa saʿyam mashkūra(n), wa tijāratan lan tabūr.

(204) O Allah, I beg You for release from the Fire. O Allah, help me in the pangs and agonies of death.

(205) O Allah, forgive me, have mercy on me, and join me with the Highest Companion.

(206) O Allah, I seek Your protection from that I should join any partner with You knowingly and I seek Your forgiveness if I have ever done so unknowingly. I seek Your protection that any kin should pray against me because of my failure to discharge my obligations toward him. O Allah, I seek Your protection from the evil of that which crawls on its stomach, and the evil of that which walks

---

(204) [Composite: Anas ibn Mālik. *Kanz al-ʿUmmāl* #4966; ʿĀ'ishah. *Kanz al-ʿUmmāl* #3629]

The pangs and agonies of death have different purposes. They may sometimes happen to disbelievers as punishment. They may happen to sinners as recompense for their sins. They may be a means of elevating the ranks of the pious. Also what a dying person feels and what other people observe may be two different things. Thus we cannot pass judgment on a person by observing his death.

(205) [ʿĀ'ishah. *Sunan at-Tirmidhī* #3418]

This was the duʿā' of the Prophet ﷺ on his deathbed. It is highly desirable that one should be making this duʿā' as death approaches.

(206) [Composite: Abū Bakr. *Majmaʿ az-Zawā'id* #17670; Zayd ibn Thābit. *Majmaʿ az-Zawā'id* #17059; ʿAbdullāh ibn ʿAbbās. *Kanz al-ʿUmmāl* #3790; Ibid. *Majmaʿ az-Zawā'id* #17429; Al-Barā'. *Kanz al-ʿUmmāl* #3817; ʿAbdullāh ibn ʿAmr ibn al-ʿĀṣ. *Kanz al-ʿUmmāl* #3786]

اَللّٰهُمَّ إِنِّيْ أَعُوْذُ بِكَ مِنْ أَنْ أُشْرِكَ بِكَ شَيْئًا وَّأَنَا أَعْلَمُهُ، وَأَسْتَغْفِرُكَ لِمَا لَا أَعْلَمُ

Shirk (associating partners with Allah) is the greatest sin. Its most blatant form is declaring and worshipping more than one deity; its subtle forms are many. They consist in the belief—and the action in the belief—that some other person also shares an attribute of Allah ﷻ. The Prophet ﷺ explained that it is *shirk* to say that →

﴿٢٠٤﴾ اَللّٰهُمَّ إِنِّيْ أَسْأَلُكَ فِكَاكَ رَقَبَتِيْ مِنَ النَّارِ۔ اَللّٰهُمَّ أَعِنِّيْ عَلٰى غَمَرَاتِ الْمَوْتِ وَسَكَرَاتِ الْمَوْتِ۔

﴿٢٠٥﴾ اَللّٰهُمَّ اغْفِرْ لِيْ وَارْحَمْنِيْ وَأَلْحِقْنِيْ بِالرَّفِيْقِ الْأَعْلٰى۔

﴿٢٠٦﴾ اَللّٰهُمَّ إِنِّيْ أَعُوْذُ بِكَ مِنْ أَنْ أُشْرِكَ بِكَ شَيْئًا وَّأَنَا أَعْلَمُهُ، وَأَسْتَغْفِرُكَ لِمَا لَا أَعْلَمُ۔ وَأَعُوْذُ بِكَ أَنْ تَدْعُوَ عَلَيَّ رَحِمٌ قَطَعْتُهَا۔ اَللّٰهُمَّ إِنِّيْ أَعُوْذُ بِكَ مِنْ شَرِّ مَنْ يَّمْشِيْ عَلٰى

204. Allāhumma innī as'aluka fikāka raqabatī minan-nār(i). Allāhumma aʿinnī ʿalā ghamarātil-mawti wa sakarātil-mawt.

205. Allāhummagh-fir lī war-ḥamnī wa alḥiqnī bir-rafīqil-'aʿlā.

204. Allāhumma innī aʿūdhu bika min an ushrika bika shay'an wa ana aʿlamuh(ū), wa astaghfiruka limā lā aʿlam(u). Wa aʿūdhu bika an tadʿuwa ʿalayya raḥimun qaṭaʿtuhā. Allāhumma innī aʿūdhu bika min sharri man yamshī ʿalā baṭnih(ī), wa min sharri man

---

Allah and so and so gave me this thing. Or to say that if it were not for so and so, then so and so would have killed me. It is these forms that are less detectable than the "creeping of the ants."

According to a ḥadīth, saying this duʿā' three times a day will drive away all forms of *shirk* from one's life. Needless to say, this making of the duʿā' must be with full understanding and with a strong desire to stay free of *shirk*.

on two legs, and the evil of that which walks on four legs. O Allah, I seek Your protection from a wife who will make me old ahead of the old age. I seek Your protection from the child who will bring evil consequences to me. I seek Your protection from the wealth that will turn into punishment for me. O Allah, I seek Your protection from harboring any doubts about the Truth after attaining firm conviction. I seek Your protection against the cursed Shayṭān. I seek Your protection from the harm of the Day of Judgment. O Allah I seek Your protection from a sudden death, snake bite, beasts, drowning, burning, falling on anything, and from being killed with a fleeing troop.

---

that any kin should pray against me: Establishing family ties is a highly emphasized act of virtue in Islam and severing them is a major sin that can destroy a person. Our obligation is to discharge the rights of other family members on us even when they do not reciprocate. This duʿā' shows the extreme concern that a believer has regarding this obligation.
sudden death: We seek protection from sudden calamities and sudden death. However, if one does encounter that then we should seek comfort from other traditions that promise martyrdom for a person facing such death. This is similar to the case of sickness. We never seek it and always ask for good health. However when we do fall sick, we seek comfort from the aḥādith that tell us that it becomes a means of forgiveness of one's sins.

بَطْنِهٖ، وَمِنْ شَرِّ مَنْ يَّمْشِيْ عَلٰى رِجْلَيْنِ، وَمِنْ شَرِّ مَنْ يَّمْشِيْ عَلٰى أَرْبَعٍ۔ اَللّٰهُمَّ إِنِّيْ أَعُوْذُ بِكَ مِنْ إِمْرَأَةٍ تُشَيِّبُنِيْ قَبْلَ الْمَشِيْبِ، وَأَعُوْذُ بِكَ مِنْ وَّلَدٍ يَّكُوْنُ عَلَيَّ وَبَالًا، وَّأَعُوْذُ بِكَ مِنْ مَّالٍ يَّكُوْنُ عَلَيَّ عَذَابًا۔ اَللّٰهُمَّ إِنِّيْ أَعُوْذُ بِكَ مِنَ الشَّكِّ فِي الْحَقِّ بَعْدَ الْيَقِيْنِ، وَأَعُوْذُ بِكَ مِنَ الشَّيْطَانِ الرَّجِيْمِ، وَأَعُوْذُ بِكَ مِنْ شَرِّ يَوْمِ الدِّيْنِ۔ اَللّٰهُمَّ إِنِّيْ أَعُوْذُ بِكَ مِنْ مَّوْتِ الْفُجَاءَةِ، وَمِنْ لَّدْغِ الْحَيَّةِ، وَمِنَ السَّبُعِ، وَمِنَ الْغَرَقِ، وَمِنَ الْحَرَقِ، وَمِنْ أَنْ أَخِرَّ عَلٰى شَيْءٍ، وَّمِنَ الْقَتْلِ عِنْدَ فِرَارِ الزَّحْفِ۔

yamshī ʿalā rijlayn(i), wa min sharri man yamshī ʿalā arbaʿ(in). Allāhumma innī aʿūdhu bika min imraʾatin tushayyibunī qablal-mashīb(i), wa aʿūdhu bika min waladin yakūnu ʿalayya wabāl-a(n), wa aʿūdhu bika mim mālin yakūnu ʿalayya ʿadhāba(n). Allāhumma innī aʿūdhu bika minash-shakki fil-ḥaqqi baʿdal-yaqīn(i), wa aʿūdhu bika minash-shayṭānir-rajīm(i), wa aʿūdhu bika min sharri Yawmid-dīn(i). Allāhumma innī aʿūdhu bika mim mawtil-fujāʾa(ti), wa min ladghil-ḥayya(ti), wa minas-sabuʿ(i), wa minal-gharaq(i), wa minal-ḥaraq(i), wa min an akhirra ʿalā shayʾ(in), wa minal-qatli ʿinda firāriz-zaḥf.

Concluding Duʿā'

اَللّٰهُمَّ اغْفِرْ ذُنُوْبَنَا، وَاسْتُرْ عُيُوْبَنَا، وَاشْرَحْ صُدُوْرَنَا، وَاحْفَظْ قُلُوْبَنَا، وَنَوِّرْ قُلُوْبَنَا، وَيَسِّرْ أُمُوْرَنَا، وَحَصِّلْ مُرَادَنَا، وَتَمِّمْ تَقْصِيْرَنَا، اَللّٰهُمَّ نَجِّنَا مِمَّا نَخَافُ، يَا حَفِيَّ الْأَلْطَافِ۔

Allāhummagh-fir dhunūbanā, was-tur ʿuyūbanā, wash-raḥ ṣudūranā, waḥ-faẓ qulūbanā, wa nawwir qulūbanā, wa yassir umūranā, wa ḥaṣṣil murādanā, wa tammim taqṣīranā. Allāhumma najjinā mimmā nakhāf(u), yā Ḥafiyyal-'alṭāf.

O Allah, forgive our sins, cover our faults, put our minds at rest, protect and enlighten our hearts, facilitate our tasks, let us achieve our goals, make up for our shortcomings, and protect us from whatever we are afraid of. O the One Who is always on the lookout to extend His Kindness!

[This concluding duʿā' was added by Maulwī Muḥammad Shafī Bijnaurī, a disciple of Mawlānā Ashraf ʿAlī Thānawī and an original publisher of the *Munājāt*. Its source is unknown; it has been retained for its obvious beauty and comprehensiveness.]

APPENDIX

REFERENCES

Brief references to duʿā' sources have been provided in the commentary sections. This appendix provides detailed references for each duʿā' in Arabic. The first forty duʿā's are from the Qur'ān. The great majority of the remaining duʿā's are from Ḥadīth books, as referenced here. For a few duʿā's the reference provided is for al-Ḥizb al-Aʿẓam, the collection of duʿā's by Mullā ʿAlī al-Qārī that was the main source for Munājāt. They could not be traced to original Ḥadīth books.

(١) البقرة: ٢٠١
(٢) البقرة: ٢٥٠
(٣) البقرة: ٢٨٦
(٤) آل عمران: ٨
(٥) آل عمران: ١٦
(٦) آل عمران: ١٩١
(٧) آل عمران: ١٩٢
(٨) آل عمران: ١٩٣
(٩) آل عمران: ١٩٤
(١٠) الأعراف: ٢٣
(١١) الأعراف: ١٢٦
(١٢) الأعراف: ١٥٥
(١٣) يونس: ٨٥-٨٦
(١٤) يوسف: ١٠١
(١٥) إبراهيم: ٤٠
(١٦) إبراهيم: ٤١
(١٧) الإسراء: ٢٤
(١٨) الإسراء: ٨٠
(١٩) الكهف: ١٠
(٢٠) طه: ٢٥-٢٨
(٢١) طه: ١١٤
(٢٢) الأنبياء: ٨٣
(٢٣) الأنبياء: ٨٩
(٢٤) المؤمنون: ٢٩
(٢٥) المؤمنون: ٩٧-٩٨
(٢٦) المؤمنون: ١٠٩
(٢٧) الفرقان: ٦٥
(٢٨) الفرقان: ٧٤
(٢٩) النمل: ١٩
(٣٠) القصص: ٢٤
(٣١) العنكبوت: ٣٠
(٣٢) غافر: ٧
(٣٣) غافر: ٨-٩
(٣٤) الأحقاف: ١٥
(٣٥) القمر: ١٠
(٣٦) الحشر: ١٠
(٣٧) الممتحنة: ٤
(٣٨) الممتحنة: ٥
(٣٩) التحريم: ٨
(٤٠) نوح: ٢٨

(٤١) عائشة – صحيح البخاري: كتاب الدعوات (باب الاستعاذة من أرذل العمر ومن فتنة الدنيا وفتنة النار) رقم ٥٨٩٨

(٤٢) زيد بن أرقم – صحيح مسلم: كتاب الذكر والدعاء والتوبة والاستغفار (باب التعوذ من شر ما عمل ومن شر ما لم يعمل) رقم ٤٨٩٩

(٤٣) أبو أمامة الباهلي – سنن الترمذي: أبواب الدعوات عن رسول الله ﷺ، رقم ٣٤٤٣

(٤٤) عبد الله بن مسعود – المستدرك للحاكم: المجلد الأول، كتاب: الدعاء، والتكبير، والتهليل، والتسبيح، والذكر، رقم ١٥٧/ ١٩٥٧

(٤٥) جابر بن عبد الله – كنز العمال: المجلد الثاني، كتاب الأذكار من قسم الأقوال (الإكمال من الفصل السادس في جوامع الأدعية) رقم ٣٧٨٧

(٤٦) عثمان بن أبي العاص وامرأة من قريش – مسند الإمام أحمد: مسند الشاميين (حديث عثمان بن أبي العاص عن النبي ﷺ) رقم ١٧٢٢٩

(٤٧) أبو موسى الأشعري – صحيح البخاري: كتاب الدعوات (باب قول النبي ﷺ «اللهم اغفر لي ما قدمت وما أخرت») رقم ٥٩٢٠

(٤٨) أبو موسى الأشعري – صحيح مسلم: كتاب الذكر والدعاء والتوبة والاستغفار (باب التعوذ من شر ما عمل ومن شر ما لم يعمل) رقم ٤٨٩٦
(٤٩) عبد الله بن عمرو بن العاص – صحيح مسلم: كتاب القدر (باب تصريف اللّه تعالى القلوب كيف شاء) رقم ٤٧٩٨
(٥٠) علي بن أبي طالب – صحيح مسلم: كتاب الذكر والدعاء والتوبة والاستغفار (باب التعوذ من شر ما عمل ومن شر ما لم يعمل) رقم ٤٩٠٤
(٥١) عبد الله بن مسعود – صحيح مسلم: كتاب الذكر والدعاء والتوبة والاستغفار (باب التعوذ من شر ما عمل ومن شر ما لم يعمل) رقم ٤٨٩٨
(٥٢) أبو هريرة – صحيح مسلم: كتاب الذكر والدعاء والتوبة والاستغفار (باب التعوذ من شر ما عمل ومن شر ما لم يعمل) رقم ٤٨٩٧
(٥٣) طارق الأشجعي – صحيح مسلم: كتاب الذكر والدعاء والتوبة والاستغفار (باب فضل التهليل والتسبيح والدعاء) رقم ٤٨٦٥
(٥٤) مركب: (١) أنس بن مالك – المستدرك للحاكم: المجلد الأول، كتاب: الدعاء، والتكبير، والتهليل، والتسبيح، والذكر، رقم ١٤٤/ ١٩٤٤ — (٢) عائشة – صحيح البخاري: كتاب الدعوات (باب الاستعاذة من أرذل العمر ومن فتنة الدنيا وفتنة النار) رقم ٥٨٩٨ — (٣) عائشة – صحيح البخاري: كتاب صفة الصلاة (باب الدعاء قبل السلام) رقم ٧٨٩ — (٤) أنس بن مالك – صحيح البخاري: كتاب الجهاد والسير (باب من غزا بصبي للخدمة) رقم ٢٦٧٩ — (٥) سعد بن أبي وقاص – صحيح البخاري: كتاب الجهاد والسير (باب ما يتعوذ من الجبن) رقم ٢٦١٠ — (٦) زيد بن أرقم – صحيح مسلم: كتاب الذكر والدعاء والتوبة والاستغفار (باب التعوذ من شر ما عمل ومن شر ما لم يعمل) رقم ٤٨٩٩
(٥٥) عبد الله بن عباس – سنن الترمذي: أبواب الدعوات عن رسول الله ﷺ، رقم ٣٤٧٤
(٥٦) أبو أمامة الباهلي – سنن ابن ماجه: المجلد الثاني، كتاب الدعاء (باب دعاء رسول الله ﷺ) رقم ٣٨٢٦
(٥٧) عبد الله بن مسعود – سنن أبي داود: كتاب الصلاة (باب التشهد) رقم ٨٢٥
(٥٨) (١) شداد بن أوس – سنن الترمذي: أبواب الدعوات عن رسول الله ﷺ، رقم ٣٣٢٩ — (٢) شداد بن أوس – المستدرك للحاكم: المجلد الأول، كتاب: الدعاء، والتكبير، والتهليل، والتسبيح، والذكر، رقم ٧٢/ ١٨٧٢
(٥٩) عبد الله ابن عمر – المستدرك للحاكم: المجلد الأول، كتاب: الدعاء، والتكبير، والتهليل، والتسبيح، والذكر، رقم ١٣٤/ ١٩٣٤
(٦٠) (١) عبد الله ابن عمر – رياض الصالحين: كتاب آداب النوم والإضطجاع (باب آداب المجلس والجليس) رقم ٨٣٤ — (٢) عبد الله ابن عمر – سنن الترمذي: أبواب الدعوات عن رسول الله ﷺ، رقم ٣٤٣٤
(٦١) عمر بن الخطاب – سنن الترمذي: أبواب تفسير القرآن (باب ومن سورة المؤمنون) رقم ٣٠٩٧
(٦٢) عمران بن حصين – سنن الترمذي: أبواب الدعوات عن رسول الله ﷺ، رقم ٣٤٠٥
(٦٣) عمران بن حصين – مسند الإمام أحمد: أول مسند البصريين (حديث عمران بن حصين عن النبي ﷺ) رقم ١٩١٤١
(٦٤) أبو هريرة – كنز العمال: المجلد الثاني، كتاب الأذكار من قسم الأقوال (الفصل الثاني في آداب الدعاء) رقم ٣٢٠١
(٦٥) (١) معاذ بن جبل – سنن الترمذي: أبواب تفسير القرآن (باب ومن سورة ص) رقم ٣١٥٩

— (٢) ثوبان بن بجدد - المستدرك للحاكم: المجلد الأول، كتاب: الدعاء، والتكبير، والتهليل، والتسبيح، والذكر، رقم ١٣٢/ ١٩٣٢
(٦٦) أبو الدرداء - سنن الترمذي: أبواب الدعوات عن رسول الله ﷺ، رقم ٣٤١٢
(٦٧) عبد الله بن يزيد الخطمي الأنصاري - سنن الترمذي: أبواب الدعوات عن رسول الله ﷺ، رقم ٣٤١٣
(٦٨) أنس بن مالك - سنن الترمذي: أبواب القدر (باب ما جاء أن القلوب بين أصبعي الرحمن) رقم ٢٠٦٦
(٦٩) (١) عبد الله بن مسعود - كنز العمال: المجلد الثاني، كتاب الأذكار من قسم الأفعال (الأدعية المطلقة) رقم ٥٠٨٨ — (٢) عبد الله بن مسعود - المستدرك للحاكم: المجلد الأول، كتاب: الدعاء، والتكبير، والتهليل، والتسبيح، والذكر، رقم ١٢٨/ ١٩٢٨
(٧٠) أبو هريرة - المستدرك للحاكم: المجلد الأول، كتاب: الدعاء، والتكبير، والتهليل، والتسبيح، والذكر، رقم ١١٩/ ١٩١٩
(٧١) أنس بن مالك - المستدرك للحاكم: المجلد الأول، كتاب: الدعاء، والتكبير، والتهليل، والتسبيح، والذكر، رقم ٧٩/ ١٨٧٩
(٧٢) عمار بن ياسر - سنن النسائي: المجلد الثالث، كتاب السهو (باب الدعاء بعد الذكر) رقم ١٢٨٩
(٧٣) عائشة - سنن ابن ماجه: المجلد الثاني، كتاب الدعاء (باب الجوامع من الدعاء) رقم ٣٨٣٦
(٧٤) (١) عائشة - سنن ابن ماجه: المجلد الثاني، كتاب الدعاء (باب الجوامع من الدعاء) رقم ٣٨٣٦ — (٢) عائشة - المستدرك للحاكم: المجلد الأول، كتاب: الدعاء، والتكبير، والتهليل، والتسبيح، والذكر، رقم ١١٤/ ١٩١٤
(٧٥) بسر بن أرطأة - مسند الإمام أحمد: مسند الشاميين (حديث بسر بن أرطاة رضي الله تعالى عنه) رقم ١٦٩٧٠
(٧٦) مركب: (١) عبد الله بن مسعود - كنز العمال: المجلد الثاني، كتاب الأذكار من قسم الأقوال (الفصل السادس في جوامع الأدعية) رقم ٣٦٧٩ — (٢) عمر بن الخطاب - كنز العمال: المجلد الثاني، كتاب الأذكار من قسم الأفعال (الأدعية المطلقة) رقم ٥٠٣٥
(٧٧) أنس بن مالك - مجمع الزوائد للحافظ الهيثمي: المجلد العاشر، كتاب الأدعية (أبواب في الصلاة على النبي ﷺ ونحو ذلك: باب فيما يستفتح به الدعاء من حسن الثناء على الله سبحانه والصلاة على النبي محمد ﷺ) رقم ١٧٢٦٦
(٧٨) (١) أبو هريرة - كنز العمال: المجلد الثاني، كتاب الأذكار من قسم الأقوال (الفصل السادس في جوامع الأدعية) رقم ٣٧٠٠ — (٢) معاذ بن جبل - سنن أبي داود: كتاب الصلاة (باب في الاستغفار) رقم ١٣٠١
(٧٩) عبد الله بن عباس - المستدرك للحاكم: المجلد الأول، كتاب: الدعاء، والتكبير، والتهليل، والتسبيح، والذكر، رقم ٧٨/ ١٨٧٨
(٨٠) عبد الله ابن عمر - المستدرك للحاكم: المجلد الأول، كتاب: الدعاء، والتكبير، والتهليل، والتسبيح، والذكر، رقم ١٨٦/ ١٩٨٦
(٨١) (١) بريدة الأسلمي - المستدرك للحاكم: المجلد الأول، كتاب: الدعاء، والتكبير، والتهليل، والتسبيح، والذكر، رقم ١٣١/ ١٩٣١ — (٢) بريدة الأسلمي - الجامع الصغير: المجلد الثالث، تتمة باب حرف الألف، رقم ٢٨٨٢
(٨٢) (١) أم سلمة - كنز العمال: المجلد الثاني، كتاب الأذكار من قسم الأقوال (الإكمال من الفصل السادس في جوامع الأدعية) رقم ٣٨٢٠ — (٢) أم سلمة - المستدرك للحاكم: المجلد الأول، كتاب:

الدعاء، والتكبير، والتهليل، والتسبيح، والذكر، رقم ١١١/ ١٩١١

(٨٣) عائشة – المستدرك للحاكم: المجلد الأول، كتاب: الدعاء، والتكبير، والتهليل، والتسبيح، والذكر، رقم ١٨٧/ ١٩٨٧

(٨٤) مركب: (١) أنس بن مالك – مجمع الزوائد للحافظ الهيثمي: المجلد العاشر، كتاب الأدعية (أبواب في الصلاة على النبي ﷺ ونحو ذلك: باب فيما يستفتح به الدعاء من حسن الثناء على الله سبحانه والصلاة على النبي محمد ﷺ) رقم ١٧٢٦٧ — (٢) أبو صرمة – مسند الإمام أحمد: مسند المكيين (حديث أبي صرمة رضي الله تعالى عنه) رقم ١٥١٩٤

(٨٥) مركب: (١) عمر بن الخطاب – سنن النسائي: كتاب الاستعاذة (الاستعاذة من سوء العمر) رقم ٥٤٠٢ — (٢) عبد الله بن عباس – صحيح مسلم: كتاب الذكر والدعاء والتوبة والاستغفار (باب التعوذ من شر ما عمل ومن شر ما لم يعمل) رقم ٤٨٩٤ — (٣) أبو هريرة – صحيح البخاري: كتاب الدعوات (باب التعوذ من جهد البلاء) رقم ٥٨٧١ — (٤) عائشة – صحيح مسلم: كتاب الذكر والدعاء والتوبة والاستغفار (باب التعوذ من شر ما عمل ومن شر ما لم يعمل) رقم ٤٨٩١ — (٥) عبد الله ابن عمر – صحيح مسلم: كتاب الرقاق (باب أكثر أهل الجنة الفقراء وأكثر أهل النار النساء وبيان الفتنة بالنساء) رقم ٤٩٢٢ — (٦) شكل بن حميد – سنن الترمذي: أبواب الدعوات عن رسول الله ﷺ، رقم ٣٤١٤ — (٧) أبو هريرة – كنز العمال: المجلد الثاني، كتاب الأذكار من قسم الأقوال (الفصل السادس في جوامع الأدعية) رقم ٣٦٨٨ — (٨) أبو اليسر – سنن أبي داود: كتاب الصلاة (باب في الاستعاذة) رقم ١٣٢٨

(٨٦) بريدة الأسلمي – كنز العمال: المجلد الثاني، كتاب الأذكار من قسم الأقوال (الفصل السادس في جوامع الأدعية) رقم ٣٦٧٥

(٨٧) مركب: سمرة بن جندب وأبي بن كعب – مجمع الزوائد للحافظ الهيثمي: المجلد العاشر، كتاب الأدعية (باب الأدعية المأثورة عن رسول الله ﷺ التي دعا بها وعلمها) رقم ١٧٤٢٥ أ ١٧٣٥٩

(٨٨) مركب: (١) عبد الله بن مسعود – مسند الإمام أحمد: مسند المكثرين من الصحابة (مسند عبد الله بن مسعود رضي الله تعالى عنه) رقم ٣٦٣٢ — (٢) أم سلمة – مسند الإمام أحمد: باقي مسند الأنصار (حديث أم سلمة زوج النبي ﷺ) رقم ٢٥٣٦٤

(٨٩) أبو هريرة – كنز العمال: المجلد الثاني، كتاب الأذكار من قسم الأقوال (الإكمال من الفصل الثاني في آداب الدعاء) رقم ٣٢٨٦

(٩٠) عبد الله بن مسعود – سنن الترمذي: أبواب الدعوات عن رسول الله ﷺ، رقم ٣٣١٢

(٩١) أبو مالك الأشعري – سنن أبي داود: كتاب الأدب (باب ما يقول إذا أصبح) رقم ٤٤٢١

(٩٢) عبد الله ابن عمر – سنن أبي داود: كتاب الأدب (باب ما يقول إذا أصبح) رقم ٤٤١٢

(٩٣) أنس بن مالك – المستدرك للحاكم: المجلد الأول، كتاب: الدعاء، والتكبير، والتهليل، والتسبيح، والذكر، رقم ٢٠٠/ ٢٠٠٠

(٩٤) أبو أمامة الباهلي – معجم الطبراني الكبير: باب الصاد (صدي بن العجلان: فضال بن جبير عن أبي أمامة) رقم ٨/٢٦٥

(٩٥) عبد الرحمٰن ابن أبزى – مصنف ابن أبي شيبة: المجلد السادس، كتاب الدعاء (باب ما يستحب أن يدعو به إذا أصبح) رقم ٢٩٢٦٨

(٩٦) (١) أبو الأزهر الأنماري – سنن أبي داود: كتاب الأدب (باب ما يقال عند النوم) رقم ٤٣٩٥ — (٢) أبو الأزهر الأنماري – المستدرك للحاكم: المجلد الأول، كتاب: الدعاء، والتكبير، والتهليل، والتسبيح، والذكر، رقم ١٨٢/ ١٩٨٢

(٩٧) حفصة – سنن أبي داود: كتاب الأدب (باب ما يقال عند النوم) رقم ٤٣٨٨

(٩٨) خالد بن الوليد – مجمع الزوائد للحافظ الهيثمي: المجلد العاشر، كتاب الأذكار (باب ما يقول إذا أرق أو فزع) رقم ١٧٠٦٣
(٩٩) عائشة – كنز العمال: المجلد الثامن، كتاب الصلاة من قسم الأفعال (ذيل التهجد) رقم ٢٣٤١٧
(١٠٠) أبو هريرة – كنز العمال: المجلد الثاني، كتاب الأذكار من قسم الأقوال (الفصل السادس في جوامع الأدعية) رقم ٣٦٣٣
(١٠١) عمر بن الخطاب – سنن الترمذي: أبواب الطهارة (باب فيما يقال بعد الوضوء) رقم ٥٠
(١٠٢) مركب: (١) عائشة – سنن النسائي: كتاب الاستعاذة (الاستعاذة من ضيق المقام يوم القيامة) رقم ٥٤٤٠ — (٢) عائشة – صحيح مسلم: كتاب صلاة المسافرين وقصرها (باب الدعاء في صلاة الليل وقيامه) رقم ١٢٨٩
(١٠٣) (١) عبد الله بن عباس – صحيح البخاري: كتاب الدعوات (باب الدعاء إذا انتبه بالليل) رقم ٥٨٤١ — (٢) عبد الله بن عباس – صحيح مسلم: كتاب صلاة المسافرين وقصرها (باب الدعاء في صلاة الليل وقيامه) رقم ١٢٧٩
(١٠٤) أبو حميد – مسند الإمام أحمد: مسند المكيين (حديث أبي أسيد الساعدي رضي الله تعالى عنه) رقم ١٥٤٧٧ — (٢) الحزب الأعظم: يوم الأحد، رقم ١٠
(١٠٥) أبو هريرة – سنن ابن ماجه: كتاب المساجد والجماعات (باب الدعاء عند دخول المسجد) رقم ٧٦٥
(١٠٦) أبو حميد – صحيح مسلم: كتاب صلاة المسافرين وقصرها (باب ما يقول إذا دخل المسجد) رقم ١١٦٥
(١٠٧) (١) أبو أيوب الأنصاري – المستدرك للحاكم: المجلد الثالث، كتاب معرفة الصحابة رضي الله تعالى عنهم (ذكر مناقب أبي أيوب الأنصاري رضي الله تعالى عنه) رقم ١٥٤٠/ ٥٩٤٢ — (٢) أبو أمامة الباهلي – معجم الطبراني الكبير: باب الصاد (صدي بن العجلان: مطرح بن يزيد أبو المهلب عن عبيد الله بن زحر)
(١٠٨) أم سلمة – معجم الطبراني الكبير: ذكر أزواج رسول الله ﷺ (أم سلمة :سفينة مولى أم سلمة عن أم سلمة)
(١٠٩) عبد الله بن مسعود – معجم الطبراني الكبير: باب الظاء (عبد الله بن مسعود الهذلي)
(١١٠) مصنف ابن أبي شيبة: المجلد السادس، كتاب الدعاء (الرجل يخاف السلطان ما يدعو؟) رقم ٢٩١٧١
(١١١) علي بن أبي طالب – سنن الترمذي: أبواب الدعوات عن رسول الله ﷺ، رقم ٣٤٨٦
(١١٢) مركب: عبد الله بن عباس وعبد الله بن جعفر – كنز العمال: المجلد الثاني، كتاب الأذكار من قسم الأقوال (الفصل السادس في جوامع الأدعية) رقم ٣٦١٤/٣٦١٣
(١١٣) عبد الله بن مسعود – المستدرك للحاكم: المجلد الأول، كتاب: الدعاء، والتكبير، والتهليل، والتسبيح، والذكر، رقم ١٥٧/ ١٩٥٧
(١١٤) (١) عبد الله ابن عمر – كنز العمال: المجلد الثاني، كتاب الأذكار من قسم الأقوال (الفصل السادس في جوامع الأدعية) رقم ٣٦٥٧ — (٢) عبد الله ابن عمر – مجمع الزوائد للحافظ الهيثمي: المجلد العاشر، كتاب الأدعية (باب الأدعية المأثورة عن رسول الله ﷺ التي دعا بها وعلمها) رقم ١٧٤١٠
(١١٥) علي بن أبي طالب – سنن الترمذي: أبواب الدعوات عن رسول الله ﷺ، رقم ٣٤٤٢
(١١٦) مركب: (١) قطبة بن مالك – كنز العمال: المجلد الثاني، كتاب الأذكار من قسم الأقوال (الفصل السادس في جوامع الأدعية) رقم ٣٦٧١ — (٢) أبو أمامة الباهلي – سنن الترمذي: أبواب

الدعوات عن رسول الله ﷺ، رقم ٣٤٤٣ — (٣) أبو هريرة - المستدرك للحاكم: المجلد الأول، كتاب: الدعاء، والتكبير، والتهليل، والتسبيح، والذكر، رقم ١٥١/ ١٩٥١ — (٤) عبد الله بن عمرو بن العاص - سنن النسائي: كتاب الاستعاذة (الاستعاذة من غلبة الدين) رقم ٥٣٨٠ — (٥) أبو هريرة - سنن النسائي: كتاب الاستعاذة (الاستعاذة من الجوع) رقم ٥٣٧٣ — (٦) ابن أبي مليكة - صحيح البخاري: كتاب الرقاق (باب في الحوض) رقم ٦١٠٤ — (٧) زيد بن ثابت - صحيح مسلم: كتاب الجنة، وصفة نعيمها وأهلها (باب عرض مقعد الميت من الجنة أو النار عليه وإثبات عذاب القبر والتعوذ منه) رقم ٥١١٢ — (٨) عقبة بن عامر - معجم الطبراني الكبير: باب الظاء (عقبة بن عامر الجهني: علي بن رباح عن عقبة بن عامر)

(١١٧) علي بن أبي طالب - سنن الترمذي: أبواب الدعوات عن رسول الله ﷺ، رقم ٣٤٤٢

(١١٨) علي بن أبي طالب - كنز العمال: المجلد الثاني، كتاب الأذكار من قسم الأقوال (الفصل السادس في جوامع الأدعية) رقم ٣٦٣٧

(١١٩) مركب: (١) أبو هريرة - سنن الترمذي: أبواب الدعوات عن رسول الله ﷺ، رقم ٣٥٣٠ — (٢) جابر بن عبد الله - كنز العمال: المجلد الثاني، كتاب الأذكار من قسم الأقوال (الفصل السادس في جوامع الأدعية) رقم ٣٦٤٤

(١٢٠) الهيثم بن مالك الطائي - كنز العمال: المجلد الثاني، كتاب الأذكار من قسم الأقوال (الفصل السادس في جوامع الأدعية) رقم ٣٦٤٨

(١٢١) عبد الله بن عمرو بن العاص - كنز العمال: المجلد الثاني، كتاب الأذكار من قسم الأقوال (الفصل السادس في جوامع الأدعية) رقم ٣٦٥٠

(١٢٢) مركب: كعب بن عجرة وأبو هريرة - كنز العمال: المجلد الثاني، كتاب الأذكار من قسم الأقوال (الفصل السادس في جوامع الأدعية) رقم ٣٦٥٣/ ٣٦٥٤

(١٢٣) علي بن أبي طالب - كنز العمال: المجلد الثاني، كتاب الأذكار من قسم الأقوال (الفصل السادس في جوامع الأدعية) رقم ٣٦٥٥

(١٢٤) أبو هريرة - مجمع الزوائد للحافظ الهيثمي: المجلد العاشر، كتاب الأدعية (باب الأدعية المأثورة عن رسول الله ﷺ التي دعا بها وعلمها) رقم ١٧٣٩٣

(١٢٥) مركب: أبو هريرة وأبو سعيد الخدري - كنز العمال: المجلد الثاني، كتاب الأذكار من قسم الأقوال (الفصل السادس في جوامع الأدعية) رقم ٣٦٥٨/ ٣٦٥٩

(١٢٦) أم معبد الخزاعية - كنز العمال: المجلد الثاني، كتاب الأذكار من قسم الأقوال (الفصل السادس في جوامع الأدعية) رقم ٣٦٦٠

(١٢٧) عبد الله ابن عمر - كنز العمال: المجلد الثاني، كتاب الأذكار من قسم الأقوال (الفصل السادس في جوامع الأدعية) رقم ٣٦٦١

(١٢٨) عبد الله ابن عمر - كنز العمال: المجلد الثاني، كتاب الأذكار من قسم الأقوال (الفصل السادس في جوامع الأدعية) رقم ٣٦٦٢

(١٢٩) عائشة - المستدرك للحاكم: المجلد الأول، كتاب: الدعاء، والتكبير، والتهليل، والتسبيح، والذكر، رقم ٩٨/ ١٨٩٨

(١٣٠) أنس بن مالك - ابن السني: باب ما يقول إذا أصبح، رقم ٣٩

(١٣١) أبو سعيد الخدري - مجمع الزوائد للحافظ الهيثمي: المجلد العاشر، كتاب الأذكار (باب ما يقول إذا أصبح وإذا أمسى) رقم ١٦٩٩٨

(١٣٢) أبو بكر الصديق - سنن الترمذي: أبواب الدعوات عن رسول الله ﷺ، رقم ٣٤٣٨

(١٣٣) عبد الله ابن عمر - كنز العمال: المجلد الرابع، كتاب البيوع من قسم الأقوال (آداب متفرقة من الإكمال) رقم ٩٣٢٣

(١٣٤) أنس بن مالك – صحيح البخاري: كتاب الجهاد والسير (باب البيعة في الحرب أن لا يفروا) رقم ٢٧٤١
(١٣٥) أنس بن مالك – سنن الترمذي: أبواب الزهد (باب ما جاء أن فقراء المهاجرين يدخلون الجنة قبل أغنيائهم) رقم ٢٢٧٥
(١٣٦) عائشة – سنن ابن ماجه: المجلد الثاني، كتاب الدعاء (باب الاستغفار) رقم ٣٨١٠
(١٣٧) (١) عبد الله بن عباس – سنن الترمذي: أبواب الدعوات عن رسول الله ﷺ، رقم ٣٣٤١ — (٢) عبد الله بن عباس – معجم الطبراني الكبير: باب الظاء (أحاديث عبد الله بن العباس بن عبد المطلب بن هاشم بن عبد مناف: علي بن عبد الله بن عباس عن أبيه) رقم ١٠/ ٢٨٤
(١٣٨–١٤٤) (١) عبد الله بن عباس – كنز العمال: المجلد الثاني، كتاب الأذكار من قسم الأقوال (الفصل السادس في جوامع الأدعية) رقم ٣٦٠٨ — (٢) عبد الله بن عباس – كنز العمال: المجلد الثاني، كتاب الأذكار من قسم الأفعال (الأدعية بعد الصلاة) رقم ٤٩٨٨
(١٤٤) عبد الله ابن عمر – مجمع الزوائد للحافظ الهيثمي: المجلد العاشر، كتاب الأدعية (باب الأدعية المأثورة عن رسول الله ﷺ التي دعا بها وعلمها) رقم ١٧٤٠٩
(١٤٥) (١) صهيب الرومي – كنز العمال: المجلد الثاني، كتاب الأذكار من قسم الأقوال (الفصل السادس في جوامع الأدعية) رقم ٣٦٧٦ — (٢) صهيب الرومي – كنز العمال: المجلد الثاني، كتاب الأذكار من قسم الأقوال (الإكمال من الفصل السادس في جوامع الأدعية) رقم ٣٧٤٠
(١٤٦) عبد الله ابن عمر – صحيح مسلم: كتاب الذكر والدعاء والتوبة والاستغفار (باب ما يقول عند النوم وأخذ المضجع) رقم ٤٨٨٧
(١٤٧) عبد الله ابن عمر – كنز العمال: المجلد الثاني، كتاب الأذكار من قسم الأقوال (الفصل السادس في جوامع الأدعية) رقم ٣٦٦٣
(١٤٨) أبو هريرة – كنز العمال: المجلد الثاني، كتاب الأذكار من قسم الأقوال (الفصل السادس في جوامع الأدعية) رقم ٣٦٨٦
(١٤٩) أبو هريرة – صحيح مسلم: كتاب البر والصلة والآداب (باب من لعنه النبي ﷺ أو سبه أو دعا عليه وليس هو أهلا لذلك كان له زكاة وأجرا ورحمة) رقم ٤٧٠٧
(١٥٠) مركب: (١) أنس بن مالك – سنن أبي داود: كتاب الصلاة (باب في الاستعاذة) رقم ١٣٢٩ — (٢) أبو هريرة – سنن أبي داود: كتاب الصلاة (باب في الاستعاذة) رقم ١٣٢٢ — (٣) شداد بن أوس – سنن الترمذي: أبواب الدعوات عن رسول الله ﷺ، رقم ٣٣٢٩ — (٤) أبو هريرة – سنن الترمذي: أبواب الدعوات عن رسول الله ﷺ، رقم ٣٥٢٣ — (٥) عائشة – سنن ابن ماجه: المجلد الثاني، كتاب الدعاء (باب الجوامع من الدعاء) رقم ٣٨٣٦ — (٦) علي بن أبي طالب – سنن أبي داود: كتاب الأدب (باب ما يقال عند النوم) رقم ٤٣٩٣ — (٧) أبو مالك الأشعري – سنن أبي داود: كتاب الأدب (باب ما يقول إذا أصبح) رقم ٤٤٢١ — (٨) عبد الله بن عمرو بن العاص – سنن الترمذي: أبواب الدعوات عن رسول الله ﷺ، رقم ٣٤٥٢ — (٩) زيد بن ثابت – مسند الإمام أحمد: مسند الأنصار (حديث زيد بن ثابت عن النبي ﷺ) رقم ٢٠٦٧٨ — (١٠) عائشة – سنن النسائي: كتاب قيام الليل وتطوع النهار (باب ذكر ما يستفتح به القيام) رقم ١٥٩٩
(١٥١) (١) علي بن أبي طالب – كنز العمال: المجلد التاسع، كتاب الطهارة من قسم الأفعال (أذكار الوضوء) رقم ٢٦٦٩٠ — (٢) الحزب الأعظم: يوم الأربعاء، رقم ١٣
(١٥٢) علي بن أبي طالب – كنز العمال: المجلد التاسع، كتاب الطهارة من قسم الأفعال (أذكار الوضوء) رقم ٢٦٩٩٣
(١٥٣) علي بن أبي طالب – كنز العمال: المجلد التاسع، كتاب الطهارة من قسم الأفعال (أذكار الوضوء) رقم ٢٦٦٩٢

(١٥٤) (١) علي بن أبي طالب - كنز العمال: المجلد التاسع، كتاب الطهارة من قسم الأفعال (أذكار الوضوء) رقم ٢٦٦٩٠ — (٢) الحزب الأعظم

(١٥٥) علي بن أبي طالب - كنز العمال: المجلد التاسع، كتاب الطهارة من قسم الأفعال (أذكار الوضوء) رقم ٢٦٦٩٢

(١٥٦) معاوية بن أبي سفيان - ابن السني: ١٩. باب ما يقول إذا قال المؤذن: حي على الصلاة حي على الفلاح، رقم ٩٢

(١٥٧) أنس بن مالك - ابن السني: ٢٢. باب كيف مسألة الوسيلة، رقم ١٠٠

(١٥٨) سعد بن أبي وقاص - المستدرك للحاكم: المجلد الأول، كتاب الصلاة (من كتاب الإمامة وصلاة الجماعة) رقم ٧٥/ ٧٤٨

(١٥٩) سمرة بن جندب - مجمع الزوائد للحافظ الهيثمي: المجلد الثاني، كتاب الصلاة (باب ما يستفتح به الصلاة) رقم ٢٦١٥

(١٦٠) (١) عمر بن الخطاب - الأذكار النووية: كتاب ما يقوله إذا دخل في الصلاة (باب القنوت في الصبح) رقم ١٣١ — (٢) الحزب الأعظم: يوم الأربعاء، رقم ١٧-١٩

(١٦١) عبد الله بن مسعود - مجمع الزوائد للحافظ الهيثمي: المجلد الثاني، كتاب الصلاة (باب التشهد والجلوس والإشارة بالإصبع فيه) رقم ٢٨٦٢

(١٦٢) أبو سعيد الخدري - كنز العمال: المجلد الثامن، كتاب الصلاة من قسم الأفعال (ذيل أدب الصلاة) رقم ٢٢٥٥١

(١٦٣) (١) أنس بن مالك - كنز العمال: المجلد السابع، كتاب الشمائل من قسم الأقوال (الصلاة) رقم ١٧٩١٥ — (٢) الحزب الأعظم: يوم الأربعاء، رقم ٢١-٢٢

(١٦٤) أنس بن مالك - ابن السني: ٣٠. باب ما يقول في دبر صلاة الصبح، رقم ١٣٨

(١٦٥) أبو سعيد الخدري - كنز العمال: المجلد الثاني، كتاب الأذكار من قسم الأفعال (الأدعية بعد الصلاة) رقم ٤٩٧٧

(١٦٦) أبو أمامة الباهلي - كنز العمال: المجلد الثاني، كتاب الأذكار من قسم الأقوال (الأدعية بعد الصلاة من الإكمال) رقم ٣٤٧٩

(١٦٧) عبد الله بن عباس - ابن السني: ٣٠. باب ما يقول في دبر صلاة الصبح، رقم ١٣٣

(١٦٨) عبد الله ابن عمر - مسند الإمام أحمد: مسند المكثرين من الصحابة (مسند عبد الله بن عمر ين الخطاب رضي الله تعالى عنهما) رقم ٥١٠٠

(١٦٩) (١) عبد الله بن عباس - كنز العمال: المجلد السابع، كتاب الصلاة من قسم الأقوال (الأكمال) رقم ٢١٥٤٩ — (٢) عبد الله بن عباس - مجمع الزوائد للحافظ الهيثمي: المجلد الثاني، كتاب الصلاة (باب صلاة التسبيح) رقم ٣٦٧٩

(١٧٠) عبد الله بن مسعود - مجمع الزوائد للحافظ الهيثمي: المجلد الثاني، كتاب الصلاة (أبواب العيدين: باب الدعاء يوم العيد) رقم ٣٢٢٦

(١٧١) مركب: (١) أبو أمامة الباهلي - كنز العمال: المجلد الأول، كتاب الأذكار من قسم الأقوال (الفصل الثالث في آداب التلاوة) رقم ٢٧٨٤ — (٢) فضائل القرآن لأبي منصور المظفر

(١٧٢) الحزب الأعظم: يوم الأربعاء، رقم ٣٤

(١٧٣) عبد الله بن مسعود - الفردوس الأخبار للديلمي: المجلد الأول، ذكر الأدعية التي دعا بها النبي ﷺ في أوقات شتى، رقم ١٨١٢

(١٧٤) مركب: (١) عائشة - صحيح مسلم: كتاب الصلاة (باب ما يقال في الركوع والسجود) رقم ٧٥١ — (٢) أم سلمة - سنن الترمذي: أبواب الدعوات عن رسول الله ﷺ، رقم ٣٣٤٩ — (٣) عبد الله بن جعفر - كنز العمال: المجلد الثاني، كتاب الأذكار من قسم الأقوال (الفصل

السادس في جوامع الأدعية) رقم ٣٦١٣ — (٤) عبد الله ابن عمر - كنز العمال: المجلد الثاني، كتاب الأذكار من قسم الأقوال (الفصل السادس في جوامع الأدعية) رقم ٣٦٧٨ — (٥) عائشة بنت قدامة - كنز العمال: المجلد الثاني، كتاب الأذكار من قسم الأقوال (الفصل السادس في جوامع الأدعية) رقم ٣٦٤٩
(١٧٥) مركب: (١) أبو بكر الصديق - تخريج أحاديث الإحياء: المجلد الأول، كتاب الأذكار والدعوات (الباب الثالث في أدعية مأثورة) — (٢) الحزب الأعظم: يوم الأربعاء، رقم ٤٥ — (٣) عبد الله بن عباس - كنز العمال: المجلد الخامس عشر، كتاب المعيشة والعادات من قسم الأقوال (الأكمال من الفصل الأول في النوم وآدابه وأذكاره) رقم ٤١٣٢٦
(١٧٦) مركب: (١) عائشة - كنز العمال: المجلد الثاني، كتاب الأذكار من قسم الأقوال (الفصل السادس في جوامع الأدعية) رقم ٣٦٩٨ — (٢) عمر بن الخطاب وعلي بن أبي طالب - الفردوس الأخبار للديلمي، رقم ١٢٩٠
(١٧٧) (١) علي بن أبي طالب - كنز العمال: المجلد الثاني، كتاب الأذكار من قسم الأقوال (الأكمال أدعية الهم والكرب والحزن من الفصل الخامس) رقم ٣٤٤١ — (٢) علي بن الحسين - كنز العمال: المجلد الثاني، كتاب الأذكار من قسم الأفعال (أدعية الهم والخوف) رقم ٥٠١٤
(١٧٨) علي بن أبي طالب - كنز العمال: المجلد الثاني، كتاب الأذكار من قسم الأقوال (الأكمال أدعية الهم والكرب والحزن من الفصل الخامس) رقم ٣٤٤١
(١٧٩) مركب: (١) جابر بن عبد الله - كنز العمال: المجلد الثاني، كتاب الأذكار من قسم الأفعال (الأدعية المطلقة) رقم ٥١١٠ — (٢) الحزب الأعظم: يوم الأربعاء، رقم ٤٠ — (٣) علي بن أبي طالب - كنز العمال: المجلد الثاني، كتاب الأذكار من قسم الأفعال (الأدعية المطلقة) رقم ٥٠٥٥
(١٨٠) عمر بن الخطاب - سنن الترمذي: أبواب الدعوات عن رسول الله ﷺ، رقم ٣٥١٠
(١٨١) مركب: (١) وفد عبد القيس - مسند الإمام أحمد: مسند الشاميين (حديث وفد عبد القيس عن النبي ﷺ) رقم ١٧١٦٣ — (٢) أبو أمامة الباهلي - معجم الطبراني الكبير: باب الصاد (صدي بن العجلان : سليمان بن حبيب المحاربي قاضي عمر بن عبد العزيز عن أبي أمامة صدي بن عجلان)
(١٨٢) مركب: (١) علي بن أبي طالب - كنز العمال: المجلد الثاني، كتاب الأذكار من قسم الأقوال (الإكمال من الفصل السادس في جوامع الأدعية) رقم ٣٨٥٧ — (٢) أنس بن مالك - مجمع الزوائد للحافظ الهيثمي: المجلد العاشر، كتاب الأدعية (باب الأدعية المأثورة عن رسول الله ﷺ التي دعا بها وعلمها) رقم ١٧٣٨٣ — (٣) الحزب الأعظم: يوم الخميس، رقم ١٧-١٩
(١٨٣) مركب: (١) الحزب الأعظم: يوم الخميس، رقم ٢٠ — (٢) عبد الله بن عباس - كنز العمال: المجلد الثاني، كتاب الأذكار من قسم الأقوال (الإكمال من الفصل السادس في جوامع الأدعية) رقم ٣٨٠١
(١٨٤) أنس بن مالك - كنز العمال: المجلد الثاني، كتاب الأذكار من قسم الأفعال (الأدعية المطلقة) رقم ٥١٠٦
(١٨٥) الحزب الأعظم: يوم الخميس، رقم ٣٠
(١٨٦) أبو بكر الصديق - كنز العمال: المجلد الثاني، كتاب الأذكار من قسم الأفعال (الأدعية المطلقة) رقم ٥٠٣٤
(١٨٧) أبو سعيد الخدري - الفردوس الأخبار للديلمي
(١٨٨) أنس بن مالك - كنز العمال: المجلد الثاني، كتاب الأذكار من قسم الأفعال (الأدعية المطلقة) رقم ٥١٠٠
(١٨٩) عبد الله ابن عمر - كنز العمال: المجلد الثاني، كتاب الأذكار من قسم الأقوال (الإكمال من الفصل السادس في جوامع الأدعية) رقم ٣٧٩٧

(١٩٠) مركب: (١) سعيد المقبري (مرسلا) - كنز العمال: المجلد الثاني، كتاب الأذكار من قسم الأقوال (الفصل السادس في جوامع الأدعية) رقم ٣٦٦٦ — (٢) أبو أمامة الباهلي - ابن السني: ٣٧. باب ما يقول إذا قام على باب المسجد، رقم ١٥٥ — (٣) سعد بن أبي وقاص - كنز العمال: المجلد الثاني، كتاب الأذكار من قسم الأقوال (الفصل السادس في جوامع الأدعية) رقم ٣٦٨٧ — (٤) سمرة بن جندب - مجمع الزوائد للحافظ الهيثمي: المجلد الثاني، كتاب الصلاة (باب ما يستفتح به الصلاة) رقم ٢٦١٥ — (٥) أنس بن مالك - ابن السني: ٣٠. باب ما يقول في دبر صلاة الصبح، رقم ١٢٠ — (٦) أبو هريرة - كنز العمال: المجلد الثاني، كتاب الأذكار من قسم الأقوال (الإكمال من الفصل السادس في جوامع الأدعية) رقم ٣٧٧٥ — (٧) الحزب الأعظم: يوم الأربعاء، رقم ٢٣ — (٨) الحزب الأعظم: يوم الخميس، رقم ٣

(١٩١) الحزب الأعظم: يوم الخميس، رقم ١

(١٩٢) مركب: (١) الحزب الأعظم: يوم الخميس، رقم ٢ — (٢) أنس بن مالك - كنز العمال: المجلد الثاني، كتاب الأذكار من قسم الأفعال (الأدعية المطلقة) رقم ٥١٠٣ — (٣) حذيفة بن اليمان - مجمع الزوائد للحافظ الهيثمي: المجلد العاشر، كتاب الأدعية (باب الأدعية المأثورة عن رسول الله ﷺ التي دعا بها وعلمها) رقم ١٧٣٩٦

(١٩٣) مركب: (١) جابر بن عبد الله - الفردوس الأخبار للديلمي: المجلد الأول، ذكرالأدعية التي دعا بها النبي ﷺ في أوقات شتى، رقم ١٨٠٥ — (٢) جابر بن عبد الله - كنز العمال: المجلد الثاني، كتاب الأذكار من قسم الأفعال (الأدعية المطلقة) رقم ٥١١١ — (٣) عبد الله بن مسعود - كنز العمال: المجلد الثاني، كتاب الأذكار من قسم الأفعال (الأدعية المطلقة) رقم ٥٠٨٧ — (٤) أبو هريرة - الجامع الصغير: المجلد الثاني، تتمة باب حرف الألف، رقم ١٤٥٩

(١٩٤) علي بن أبي طالب - كنز العمال: المجلد الثاني، كتاب الأذكار من قسم الأفعال (الأدعية المطلقة) رقم ٥٠٥٥

(١٩٥) عبد الله ابن عمر - كنز العمال: المجلد الثاني، كتاب الأذكار من قسم الأفعال (الأدعية المطلقة) رقم ٥١٢٦

(١٩٦) علي بن أبي طالب - كنز العمال: المجلد الثاني، كتاب الأذكار من قسم الأقوال (الأكمال أدعية الهم والكرب والحزن من الفصل الخامس) رقم ٣٤٣٣

(١٩٧) بريدة الأسلمي - كشف الخفاء: المجلد الثاني، حرف الحاء المهملة، رقم ١١٣٤

(١٩٨) أبو هريرة - كنز العمال: المجلد الثاني، كتاب الأذكار من قسم الأفعال (أماكن الإجابة) رقم ٤٩٤٥

(١٩٩) عبد الله بن مسعود - كنز العمال: المجلد الثاني، كتاب الأذكار من قسم الأقوال (الإكمال من الفصل السادس في جوامع الأدعية) رقم ٣٧٨٤

(٢٠٠) أنس بن مالك - كنز العمال: المجلد الثاني، كتاب الأذكار من قسم الأقوال (الإكمال من الفصل السادس في جوامع الأدعية) رقم ٣٧٨٩

(٢٠١) معاذ بن جبل - كنز العمال: المجلد الثاني، كتاب الأذكار من قسم الأقوال (الإكمال من الفصل السادس في جوامع الأدعية) رقم ٣٨١٠

(٢٠٢) علي بن أبي طالب - كنز العمال: المجلد الثاني، كتاب الأذكار من قسم الأفعال (الأدعية المطلقة) رقم ٥٠٦١

(٢٠٣) مركب: (١) أنس بن مالك - كنز العمال: المجلد الثاني، كتاب الأذكار من قسم الأقوال (الإكمال من الفصل السادس في جوامع الأدعية) رقم ٣٨٥٠ — (٢) أبو هريرة - كنز العمال: المجلد الثاني، كتاب الأذكار من قسم الأقوال (الإكمال من الفصل السادس في جوامع الأدعية) رقم ٣٨٥٥

(٢٠٤) مركب: (١) أنس بن مالك - كنز العمال: المجلد الثاني، كتاب الأذكار من قسم الأفعال (الأدعية بعد الصلاة) رقم ٤٩٦٦ — (٢) عائشة - كنز العمال: المجلد الثاني، كتاب الأذكار من قسم الأقوال (الفصل السادس في جوامع الأدعية) رقم ٣٦٢٩

(٢٠٥) عائشة - سنن الترمذي: أبواب الدعوات عن رسول الله ﷺ (باب ما جاء في عقد التسبيح باليد) رقم ٣٤١٨

(٢٠٦) مركب: (١) أبو بكر الصديق - مجمع الزوائد للحافظ الهيثمي: المجلد العاشر، كتاب الزهد (أبواب في الرياء ونحوه: باب ما يقول إذا خاف شيئاً من ذلك) رقم ١٧٦٧٠ — (٢) زيد بن ثابت - مجمع الزوائد للحافظ الهيثمي: المجلد العاشر، كتاب الأذكار (باب ما يقول إذا آوى إلى فراشه وإذا انتبه.) رقم ١٧٠٥٩ — (٣) عبد الله بن عباس - كنز العمال: المجلد الثاني، كتاب الأذكار من قسم الأقوال (الإكمال من الفصل السادس في جوامع الأدعية) رقم ٣٧٩٠ — (٤) عبد الله بن عباس - مجمع الزوائد للحافظ الهيثمي: المجلد العاشر، كتاب الأدعية (باب دعاء داود صلى الله عليه وسلم) رقم ١٧٤٢٩ — (٥) البراء - كنز العمال: المجلد الثاني، كتاب الأذكار من قسم الأقوال (الإكمال من الفصل السادس في جوامع الأدعية) رقم ٣٨١٧ — (٦) عبد الله بن عمرو بن العاص - كنز العمال: المجلد الثاني، كتاب الأذكار من قسم الأقوال (الإكمال من الفصل السادس في جوامع الأدعية) رقم ٣٧٨٦